Shop Talk and War Stories

Shop Talk and War Stories

American Journalists Examine Their Profession

Jan Winburn
The Baltimore Sun

BEDFORD / ST. MARTIN'S
Boston ♦ New York

For Bedford / St. Martin's

Developmental Editor: Alice Mack
Production Editor: Bernard Onken
Production Supervisor: Jennifer Wetzel
Marketing Manager: Richard Cadman
Art Director: Lucy Krikorian
Text Design: Claire Seng-Niemoeller
Copy Editor: Pat Phelan
Cover Design: Lucy Krikorian
Cover Photo: Robert Nickelsberg / Getty Images
Composition: Macmillan India Limited, Bangalore, India
Printing and Binding: Haddon Craftsmen, Inc.,
an R.R. Donnelley & Sons Company

President: Joan E. Feinberg
Editorial Director: Denise B. Wydra
Publisher for History and Communication: Patricia Rossi
Director of Marketing: Karen R. Melton
Director of Editing, Design, and Production: Marcia Cohen
Managing Editor: Erica T. Appel

Library of Congress Control Number: 2002110179

Manufactured in the United States of America.

8 7 6 5 4
f e d c b

For information, write: Bedford / St. Martin's, 75 Arlington Street, Boston, MA 02116 (617-399-4000)

ISBN: 0-312-40105-1

Acknowledgments

Acknowledgments and copyrights are continued at the back of the book on pages 272–274, which constitute an extension of the copyright page.

Preface

When journalists talk about their work, they do so with a degree of passion and insight often absent from standard textbooks. This collection of first-person readings seeks to bridge that gap by introducing the voices of forty-one working professionals who describe not only how journalism is practiced but how it is lived.

The readings are drawn from a range of sources: speeches, professional journals, trade magazines, online publications, advice columns, and memoirs. They are teeming with practical advice and inspirational stories from print, broadcast, and online journalists. Among the contributors are legendary editors and reporters whose names have become synonymous with prize-winning work, as well as journalists whose names are less familiar but who practice their craft expertly under the pressure of daily deadlines.

In these pages students will find:

Practical advice on the essential skills of reporting, writing, and interviewing. Claudia Dreifus of *The New York Times* addresses the importance of pre-interview preparation. Bob Woodward and Carl Bernstein, *The Washington Post*'s famous investigative team, demonstrate techniques for winning over uncooperative sources. Award-winning feature writer Ken Fuson of *The Des Moines Register* offers entertaining and thought-provoking insights into the advice of the profession's best coaches.

Thoughtful observations on all types of coverage. Reporters who cover a "beat," editors who manage investigative projects, a writer who practices literary journalism, a specialist who uses computer databases—these voices reflect the many dimensions of a single craft.

A discussion of journalism ethics and community issues. Because journalists must meet standards beyond fair and accurate reporting, *Shop Talk and War Stories* includes personal reflections from professionals who have grappled with serious ethical issues and considered their responsibility to the communities they cover. These chapters include the observations of (Portland) *Oregonian* editor Sandra Mims Rowe about how the terrorist attacks of September 11, 2001, helped journalism rediscover its sense of purpose.

A preview of journalism's new frontier. In the age of the image and the Web link, today's journalism student must be prepared to face the challenges of a multimedia workplace. Broadcasters Robert Krulwich, Jeff Greenfield, and Jim Wooten discuss memorable TV storytelling, live coverage of presidential elections, and the searing experience of witnessing civil war and genocide. Students get a first-hand account of the innovative nexus of the Internet frontier and traditional newspaper reporting from Mark Bowden, author of *Black Hawk Down* and prize-winning reporter for *The Philadelphia Inquirer.* And editor Dan Okrent raises the challenge and specter of "the death of print."

Shop Talk and War Stories is a valuable supplemental text whose readings were carefully chosen and arranged to complement standard textbooks. To a student's understanding of journalism it will add an intimate, illuminating portrait of the profession drawn by some of the best in the business.

ACKNOWLEDGMENTS

My thanks to the reporters and editors who gave me permission to share their insights in this book. They are not only accomplished journalists but generous teachers.

I thank my editors at Bedford/St. Martin's — Michael Bagnulo, Patricia Rossi, and Alice Mack — for their enthusiasm, dedication, and guidance.

I owe much to my colleagues at *The Baltimore Sun*; they instruct and inspire me every day. I am grateful to my friends at The Poynter Institute, who awakened and nurtured my desire and ability to teach and who have found ways to support and challenge me.

And finally, I want to thank Gary Dorsey, who is his dual roles as spouse and fellow journalist has brought joy to my life and my work.

Jan Winburn

Contents

Shop Talk and War Stories

Chapter 1

BEGINNINGS

First impressions are the most indelible. Even prize winning journalists with storied careers often recall the lessons they learned during their first days as cub reporters.

This chapter offers the early insights of four journalists whose experiences range from news and feature writing to broadcast reporting to editing the country's most revered newspaper. Rick Bragg remembers learning how important it is to remain humble. Anna Quindlen emphasizes the need to bring humanity, empathy, and sincerity to every assignment. Garrick Utley describes his television debut under the steady hand of a mentor. And Joseph Lelyveld, at the end of a career that took him to the pinnacle of the profession as executive editor of *The New York Times,* urges young journalists to follow not scripted career paths but their deepest passions.

Together, the advice of these writers forms a valuable primer for any journalist at the advent of his or her career.

RICK BRAGG

Rick Bragg won the Pulitzer Prize for feature writing in 1996, but he acquired his skill for storytelling long before that. As a boy growing up in the foothills of the Appalachian Mountains in northeastern Alabama, he sat rapt on the front porches of relatives as they spun yarns full of drama and surprise. Consequently, Bragg knew "how to tell a story long before I ever sat down to write one." His journalistic journey is itself a remarkable story. He grew up poor and never finished college, but he worked his way to the staff of *The New York Times* and received an invitation to study at Harvard University as a fellow in the prestigious Nieman Foundation for Journalism.

In this selection from his 1997 best-selling memoir, *All Over But the Shoutin'*, Bragg describes his leap from the small pond of *The Birmingham News* to the nationally recognized *St. Petersburg Times*. Bragg would eventually make a big splash at the Florida paper (and be wooed away), but here he relates his humble beginnings and conveys two important lessons: Never consider an assignment beneath you, and respect the dignity of the people you write about.

Chicken Killers and True Heartbreak

The St. Pete *Times* was not a big newspaper in circulation—though it was twice as big as any paper I had ever worked for—but it was big in reputation. It was, consistently, year after year, one of the top ten newspapers in America. I would normally have been a little scared of it, of proving myself there. But the editor who hired me, Paul Tash, told me that it takes all manner and texture of people to make a good newspaper, and he would be glad to say he was hiring a reporter from Possum Trot, Alabama. Randy Henderson, my editor at *The Birmingham News,* had told me that, too. As long as there was at least one such person in every newspaper I went to, I knew I would be fine.

But it was the interview down there that sold me. The managing editor, Mike Foley, had a bust of Elvis in his office. I thought I might fit in, in a place like that. From some floors in the building, you could even see the bay.

On a chilly, rainy afternoon in March, I said good-bye to my momma with two hundred dollars in an envelope. I made sure she knew how to find me in case of an emergency, and told her to call me collect. I told her that Florida is just a quick plane ride away, that I could be home in a few hours if she ever needed me. That might sound silly to people who vacation in Europe and ride planes every week. To my momma, who had never been more than three hundred miles away from home in her life, who had never been anywhere close to an airplane except for the crop duster that swooped down over our house to get to the cotton fields, Tampa Bay was a million miles away. She cooked me some stew beef with potatoes and onions, which is my favorite, and tried not to cry. Before I left she gave me an envelope with a card in it, and told me not to open it until that night. It had a ten-dollar bill in it.

I said good-bye to my girlfriend with some roses and a promise to keep in touch that we both knew was more civility than anything else, and headed south. I got into St. Petersburg about four-thirty, too late to get a hotel room. I went straight to the beach at Clearwater and watched the sun come up, which was stupid because I had forgotten which side the water was on. It only sets over the water, genius, I said to myself, as it rose over my shoulder.

It was an odd place, in many ways. Pinellas County was paved from Tampa Bay to the beaches, pretty much, with all manner of people living elbow to elbow in little pastel tract houses, rambling brick ranchers and bayside mansions. To find the reasons why people ever came here in the first place, you had to live on the edge of it, by that beautiful water, or drive inland, through the sugar cane, to the heart of it. I rented a small apartment near the bay that was perhaps the most peaceful place I had ever lived. At night, when the water in the little inlet I lived on was smooth as glass, you could sit on the ground and watch the mullet jump, and egrets and other wading birds would take pieces of peeled orange out of your hands. I heard the other reporters complain about how slow it was and dull it was, how life was just one big Early Bird Dinner Special, but I loved it. The editors hurt my feelings sometimes, by sending me to do stories that I thought were frivolous, but it was hard to be miserable living by the beach.

The highlight of my time there, at least in the first few months, was the story of Mopsy the chicken. The little bayside town of Dunedin, north of Clearwater, had been the target of a serial killer. It seemed that a bobcat was, night after night, slaughtering the chickens of the retirees. The editor walked up to me, straight-faced, and told me that there had been a bobcat attack the night before but the chicken had miraculously survived, clawed but still clucking. The chicken's name, he told me, was Mopsy. I said something to the effect that he had to be kidding. Two minutes later, I was motoring to the quiet and peaceful city of Dunedin. I was twenty-nine years old. I had won a whole wallful of journalism awards and risked my life in bad neighborhoods and prisons and hurricanes. I was going to interview a goddamn chicken.

The chicken had indeed had all the feathers raked off its ass, but when I approached it, it went squawking off across the yard. I supposed they would have to get it some counseling. I interviewed its owners instead, drove to a little parking lot by the water, sat in the car for a half-hour and rubbed my eyes. At home, Mopsy would be covered in gravy about now.

I went back to the newspaper office determined to get even. I would write the most overwritten crap of my life, I decided, something so purple and lurid that the editors would feel bad about sending me on the story. I began it this way:

"Mopsy has looked into the face of death, and it is whiskered."

It ran in the paper that way. All the editors told me what a good job I did, and not too long after that I got a promotion that would, I believed, take me away from stories about butt-gnawed chickens for the rest of my natural life.

The moral, I suppose, was this: Do not, on purpose, write a bunch of overwritten crap if it looks so much like the overwritten crap you usually write that the editors think you have merely reached new heights in your craft.

They promoted me to the state desk covering southwest Florida, including the Everglades, which had an almost magical appeal to me, a boy from the foothills. . . .

The newspaper gave me time and opportunity to tell stories about everything from poachers in the beautiful, mysterious Everglades to the bizarre case of a woman who had been beaten and brain-damaged by an attacker seventeen years in the past, but it only became a murder case when she finally died from a seizure brought on by her injuries. I wrote about criminals who stalked the elderly, about the last Florida panthers on earth, dying slowly in the Everglades. I wrote about mercury poisoning in the swamps and wetlands, and interviewed a man who married his own daughter and swore, "I didn't know." (He also told me that once, when he worked at a bar in Vegas, he used a nail to punch a hole in the belt of Elvis's jumpsuit, to give the King a little more room to shake it.) But mostly, I was a serious journalist. . . .

I have said a few times that I try to lend dignity and feeling to the people I write about, but that is untrue. All you do is uncover the dignity, the feeling, that is already there. I learned to do that there.

In the spring of 1990, we learned that a woman in St. Petersburg had given birth to twins, joined at the chest, what people usually call Siamese twins. My editors sent me to try and convince the family to write about it. I made the mother a simple promise. I would portray her children as two distinct personalities, as little babies with a complicated medical condition, nothing more. I said I would treat the story, their story, with dignity. I kept my promises.

I spent months on what would be a tragic tale. I followed them from their birth, wrapped in each other's arms, and through their surgeries, and finally followed their young mother and father through two funerals.

It was as heartbreaking a thing, on a purely personal level, as I had ever done. I will always remember the day I saw them in the nursery's intensive care unit, the first time I had ever seen so many lives so near to death. To me, it seemed that anything, a faint breeze, a whisper, a loud sound, anything, could take them away. And in the middle of all those tiny, delicate, premature babies were the twins. I wanted to make perfect the way I described that place, those babies, and make other people see what I saw and feel what I felt. Almost all the time, you just paint a picture with the words and let people make up their own minds and emotions, but this time I wanted to force them to feel.

"Nurses on the late shift called the twins Miracle Babies," I wrote, "but there never seem to be enough miracles to go around. Most babies in the neonatal intensive care unit at All Children's Hospital are born too soon, incomplete. Some last for a while and then slip away, like beads off a broken string."

We are taught in this business to leave our emotions out of a story, to view things with pure and perfect objectivity, but that was impossible on this story. I learned that objectivity is pure crap, if the pain is so strong it bleeds onto the yellowed newsprint years, or even decades, later.

The momma and daddy and one of the grandmas thanked me for it, sometime later, and I didn't know what to say.

ANNA QUINDLEN

Sometimes a young journalist is toughened by experience. Sometimes it's the other way around: She starts out tough and is softened by what she learns.

When *New York Times* reporter Anna Quindlen began her career in the 1970s, she was determined to be taken seriously by her older, mostly male colleagues so she drank Scotch shots and vowed to keep her "feelings" out of her stories. She had a knack for writing about people—features that were at the time labeled "human-interest" stories—and at first she tried to abide by the rules of news reporting that demanded she remain remote from her subjects, objective and skeptical.

But the Pulitzer-winning writer, columnist, and now bestselling novelist soon learned it was other qualities that made her good at what she did. In this piece, written in 1986 for the *Times*'s weekly Hers column, Quindlen talks about those qualities: compassion for one's subject, a willingness to listen, the effort to comprehend. Human-interest reporting, she discovered, requires reporters to be themselves: in other words, to be fully human.

Hearts and Minds

For most of my adult life, I have been an emotional hit-and-run driver, that is, a reporter. I made people like me, trust me, open their hearts and their minds to me and cry and bleed onto the pages of my neat little notebooks, and then I went back to a safe place and I made a story out of it. I am good at what I do, and so often the people who read those stories cried, too. When they were done they turned the page and when I was done I went on to another person, another story, went from the cop's wife whose husband had never come home to the impoverished 80-year-old Holocaust survivor to the family with the missing child. I stepped in and out of their lives as easily as I did a pair of shoes in the morning, and when I was done I wrote my piece and I went home, to the husband who had not been killed, the bank account that was full, the child safe in his high chair. Sometimes I carried within me, for a day or a week or sometimes even longer, the resonances of their pain. But they were left with the pain itself. It was not always as bad as I've made it sound. Sometimes I covered people who wanted to be covered and wrote about things that were not arrows to the heart: pothole programs, town meetings, the cost of living, the G.N.P. But I was good at something called human interest reporting, just at the time that human interest reporting became the vogue, and so I have spent a good deal of time in the home of vulnerable strangers, setting up a short-term relationship, making them one-shot friends.

While they were lowering their defenses, I was maintaining my objectivity, which made it possible for me, in a kind of shorthand reminiscent of the "if u cn rd ths" ads on the subway, to put down in my notebook observations like "strokes [baby's] head and starts to cry" or "removes picture of parents from drawer and tells how they were killed by SS."

I am proud of what I do, and I am ashamed of it, too. I am reasonably sensitive and not too ruthless and so I have sometimes saved people from their own revelations and sometimes helped them by giving them the feeling that they were talking to someone who thought they were unique. I have never really understood why they talked to me.

I am in one of the few businesses in which a service is provided, not to the people we deal with directly, but only to the faceless thousands who read about them. Sometimes reporters call our house to talk to my husband, who has tried some newsworthy cases, and I do not miss the irony of the fact that I find them more or less a nuisance, depending on whether they call in the middle of dinner and how officious they are about the absolute necessity of their task.

Some people I have interviewed told me they thought they could help others know they were not alone, and I suspect they were right, and some people said they thought publicity might help them, and they were right, too. Occasionally I would write a story about someone in a bad spot and I would get checks for them in the mail, and I'd pass them along and think, "Well, that's good." But that wasn't why I did the stories. I did them for me.

I still do, although not on a regular basis. I still write stories and some of them are pithy explorations of unspeakable pain. I did a magazine piece not long ago about breast cancer and I sat one night in a conference room listening to eight women talk about the feeling of taking off their blouses and seeing the zipper of the scar, and I sat there, my two perfectly good breasts slowly swelling with milk for the baby at home, and felt like the worst sort of voyeur, a Peeping Tom of the emotions. Afterward some of them came to me and said how glad they were that I was writing about them, so that others would understand, and I tried to take solace from that. But all I felt was disgust at myself.

It was a good piece. It helped people understand what it is like to live with breast cancer.

I know there are good reasons to do what I do. The more we understand worlds outside our own orbit, the better off we will be. I know there are people who do not believe reporters feel any of these things, that we file our feelings with the clippings, that both are soon dried out beyond saving. That's not true. The problem is that some time ago we invented a kind of new journalism and then tried to play it with old journalism rules. We came to a rape victim with the same feelings about objectivity and distance that we had brought to a press conference, and that was not fair—not so much to the rape victim, but to ourselves.

Some years ago I did a story about Stan and Julie Patz. Their names are probably familiar; their son, Etan, age 6, disappeared in 1979, and they have opened their door to reporter after reporter because anything might bring him home.

I interviewed Julie several years after he had gone, and at some point during our conversation, my eyes filled and tears began. I thought I felt her pain—now that I have children of my own, I realized I hadn't a clue to what her pain was—but I was also angry at myself for being, after years of practice and journalism review articles, so unprofessional. I thought that what was the right response for a human being was the wrong response for a reporter.

Years have passed, and Julie's son is still missing. In the meantime, I have had two of my own. For a while I looked for Etan's face in every playground and schoolyard, but then I stopped. I am ashamed of that. I am proud of the story I wrote. I had the story, and Julie had the life. I still think of her sometimes, and of her pain. Now that I work as a reporter less, I am capable of bringing my emotions to it more.

Perhaps there are no unwritten rules that say you are not to feel these things. Perhaps I made them up out of my own insecurities and stereotypes, the way I insisted on drinking Scotch shots when I first got into the newspaper business so that everyone would know I was serious stuff, not just some kid. Some of this is changing for the better, I think. The day the space shuttle exploded, at the end of the evening news, it looked to me as if Dan Rather was trembling on the verge of tears when he signed off. For a moment I was able to forget the cameras hovering over the faces of Christa McAuliffe's parents as they looked up to see their eldest child blown to bits, and to forget that if

I were still in the newspaper business I might have been there too, scribbling, "Mother lays head on father's shoulder." It appeared that Rather's emotions and his profession were merging, and it made me feel a little better about myself. But the part of me that still looks at every disaster as a story wondered for just a moment if his contact lenses were bothering him, or the light was in his eyes.

GARRICK UTLEY

Garrick Utley is a familiar face to viewers of serious television journalism. Before joining CNN in 1997, he spent thirty years covering international affairs for NBC News and three years as chief foreign correspondent for ABC News. He has reported from more than seventy countries and was assigned to NBC's Saigon bureau during the Vietnam War. His reporting on Soviet-American relations won him the Overseas Press Club's Edward R. Murrow Award in 1984. He also received the George Foster Peabody Award for his work on the program "Vietnam: Ten Years Later."

In this selection from his 2000 memoir, *You Should Have Been Here Yesterday,* Utley recalls his first assignment, at age twenty-three, as an NBC Radio stringer in Brussels. It was 1963. Television news was at a pivotal crossroads, and Utley was eager to make the leap to the relatively young medium. Guided by NBC News correspondent John Chancellor, Utley faced the lens of the camera for the first time.

Initiation

I arrived by train, which, then as now, is the best way to travel in Europe. I traveled light, which is the best way to travel anywhere. In one hand I carried a suitcase, in the other a portable typewriter, and in the inside pocket of an ill-fitting sport jacket, a letter. The suitcase held the meager wardrobe of a twenty-three-year-old American. The letter, carefully folded in my pocket, was the chance I had hoped for: an offer from NBC News correspondent John Chancellor, a journalist of exceptional class and experience. He was inviting me to be his office assistant, coffee maker, bill payer, and NBC Radio stringer in Brussels. The pay was $62.50 a week, which, I was informed, was nonnegotiable. Still, I asked myself, what was money when I had a foot in the network door?

Only there was no door; there was not even an office. Chancellor had arrived in Brussels a week before and had not yet found a suitable bureau. So we enjoyed the pleasures of an interim office—a table at an outdoor cafe, where each morning we met over coffee and croissants to read the newspapers and plan the day. I was soon relishing the style as well as the substance of journalism and was learning how both were about to change dramatically. NBC's evening newscast, the *Huntley-Brinkley Report,* and the *CBS Evening News with Walter Cronkite* were expanding from fifteen minutes to a half hour. Chancellor had been sent to Europe to provide the longer reports that the new program would demand. He explained that I was getting in on the ground floor of a new era in television news. A thirty-minute program each weekday evening promised more than twice the time to cover the news and offered new ways to present it. There would be as many as five film reports a night, each running two and a half minutes to five minutes. The possibilities seemed limitless. Television news was growing up.

By early September 1963, the half-hour network news was on NBC and CBS. We had rented office space, and I found myself alone in it most of the time as Chancellor traveled across Europe in search of stories. There was a message in that activity, although I did not fully understand it at the time. The longer half-hour format demanded that the correspondent travel to the location of the news event. This was better journalism, and it was also better television. Viewers wanted to see the reporter on the scene. Moreover, a three- or four-minute report had to be produced as well as reported. The correspondent as storyteller had to provide a narrative line—the requisite beginning, middle, and end to each report. These were new concepts in television news. Fortunately for me, in 1963, many radio journalists were still unable or unwilling to make the leap to the new medium, which provided an opportunity for a newcomer eager to learn how to work with pictures and sound as well as words. As I minded the NBC office in Brussels, offering occasional radio reports or submitting story ideas for television coverage, I wondered how long I would have to wait for my chance.

About six months, as it turned out. New York requested a brief report for NBC's *Huntley-Brinkley Report*. Length: forty-five seconds, on camera. Subject: the sale of chemical plants to the Soviet Union by Western European companies at a time when American firms were not allowed to compete for sales to the Communists. It was not exactly a burning issue of the day, so I realized that I was facing an audition. I hurriedly gathered more information on chemical plants than I thought any viewer would want to know, looked for a location with a suitable European background for my television debut, then stayed up until two A.M. writing a script.

The next morning I awoke with a case of opening-day jitters. I was starting at the very top of the profession on the *Huntley-Brinkley*

Report, the most-watched news program in the United States. If I failed, if the corporate mandarins back in New York turned their invisible thumbs down, I could only work my way down the professional ladder. I read the script again and was disappointed in what I found to be a report of marginal importance and certainly of no general interest. Still, I understood that what the faceless producers and executives in New York were looking for was simply whether a would-be correspondent in Brussels, whose face they did not know, would be "acceptable for television," to use the network language of the time. I looked nervously out the window on a gray March morning and hoped that rain would not interfere with the filming. As I dressed, I repeated the advice and admonition offered by John Chancellor: "Keep your sentences short, and your voice low." The plan was for a film crew from the NBC News bureau in London to arrive that afternoon. They would film my on-camera "standup" and ship it on the overnight cargo flight to New York for broadcast the next evening.

The cameraman and his sound assistant arrived on time in Brussels, but unfortunately the camera and the rest of their equipment landed in Paris. For travelers lost luggage is an inconvenience, but for television news crews it brings work to a dead stop. An airline employee with a practiced, professional smile assured us the camera would be on the next plane from Paris. It was not. Then on the next flight, we were again assured. It was not. A call from our Paris office promised that it would be on the last flight arriving at 10:30 P.M., which would allow barely an hour to film before the departure of the midnight cargo flight. This dilemma at least left us time for a leisurely dinner. One of Belgium's virtues is its cooking. You can get a good meal anywhere, including the Brussels airport, which is about as demanding a test as exists. The cameraman, Chris Callery, his assistant, and I slipped into a corner table of the restaurant. My eyes, guided by my meager salary, searched for the budget special, the usual grilled steak with french fries. Chris, though, went right to the top of the menu, found fresh oysters, and ordered eighteen of them. "That will make up for the bother of all this waiting," he said with great relish. I was impressed. Television people obviously knew how to live well, at least on assignment and with an expense account.

We worked our way slowly through dinner as Chris told stories of wars he had covered in the Congo, South Yemen, and Cyprus. "Compared to that," I said, "it must be boring to film one short report by a novice reporter." "Not at all," he replied. "A few months ago they sent me from London to South America, and the only thing I shot was one lousy on-camera standup with a correspondent. They want me to go—I go." He called it being a "fireman," but a fireman, I could see, who traveled the world first-class while eating oysters on the run.

Suddenly the stories stopped. Chris's healthy, tanned face had turned a sickly, pasty hue. Without a word he rose from his chair and walked rapidly to the men's room with as much dignity as he could muster. The oysters had struck. We now had no cameraman.

John Chancellor arrived to oversee my debut as the camera equipment finally turned up on the last flight. We maneuvered it through the customs bureaucracy and set it up, along with the lights, in a small passenger lounge across the hall from a conveniently located men's room. There would be no atmospheric European background, just a beige curtain in the room and a fake potted fern in front of it. We had no choice. Outside, the Sabena cargo plane was being prepared for its departure. We had half an hour, at the most, to film a good "take."

I stood in front of a television camera for the first time and rehearsed reading my script. I looked up and saw the camera lens. No longer was it a simple device for capturing a picture. Now it was an intimidating, impersonal object with all the warmth and reassurance of a rifle barrel aimed between my eyes. It was an alien creature that took but did not give back. Every television broadcaster has to face it—the lens—the only visual channel to reach the audience. You have to make it your friend or at the very least your tool. There is no way around it, only through it.

"Imagine you are speaking to a friend in Chicago," Chancellor suggested, sensing my unease. "Don't think of the millions of viewers watching. Think of one person." It didn't help. I saw only the cold, dark lens, and I heard awkward phrases spilling from my mouth that bore no resemblance to the crafted words in my script.

"Let's try it," Chancellor said, undeterred, as he crossed the hall to Chris's sanctuary, stuck his head in the door of the men's room, and shouted, "You're on!" Chris came out, still wan of face, focused the camera, and we tried the first take. No good. The sentences were short and declarative, but that was because my eyes were glued to the script. The camera was filming the top of my head.

And so it continued, much to the amusement of a small crowd that had gathered to watch the ordeal. Between each take Chris would retire to the men's room and return after a few minutes. Takes two, three, and four were better, but not good enough for Chancellor, who was watching my performance and his watch with equal intensity.

Take five was acceptable, but we needed one more to be sure that there were two good versions for the film editors in New York to choose from. Take nine did it. The soundman unloaded the film and ran with it to the waiting plane. Chris Callery turned off the lights and disappeared again across the hall. Chancellor and I found a bar nearby. We sat down on stools and each ordered a cognac. I felt glum.

Chancellor, though, was encouraged and offered some memorable advice for a beginner in television. "Forget what happened around you. Forget the bad takes. The audience will never see them," he said. "The only thing that counts on television is what ends up on the screen. I think you've made it."

JOSEPH LELYVELD

Joseph Lelyveld began working at *The New York Times* as a copyboy in 1962, and retired almost forty years later as executive editor. During his long and illustrious career, he was a foreign correspondent in London, New Delhi, Hong Kong, and Johannesburg. (His book *Move Your Shadow,* based on his reporting in South Africa, won the Pulitzer Prize in 1986.) And in the mid-1970s, he covered Washington—"I've always described it as my most foreign assignment," he says. Lelyveld, however, spent more time outside the capital than in it, staying away from "the pack." He advises young journalists to do just that in this excerpt from a commencement speech delivered at Columbia University in May 2001, just four months before his retirement. He also offers this tip for anyone new to the profession: Let curiosity—"deeply felt impulses"—be your guide.

A Life Not Infrequently Thrilling

. . . [L]et me tell you how I got into journalism in the first place. Basically I fell into it, having discovered that I had too short an attention span for any respectable profession or form of scholarship. Besides, already a graduate-school dropout, I needed a way to continue my student deferment from the draft, which existed even in those pre–Vietnam era days. At first, journalism school for me was a quick-fix answer to that distinctly unworthy need rather than a way to advance some clear aspiration. Very vaguely, I wanted to be a writer of some kind; preferably, the paid kind. But I'd no idea then where journalism could lead—and that, it soon turned out, was the beauty part, that was what would make journalism as a life not infrequently thrilling. I didn't want a destination, I discovered. I had the infantile wish for instant gratification, which, when you think about it, may be the foundation of daily journalism. I wanted to plunge into something interesting right away.

So it happened that when my class graduated in that long ago spring, I was already on my way to Asia, a journey I'd fallen into with the same sudden impulsiveness that had led me to Columbia. Early in the school year, following an evening of drinks with a journalist of an older generation whom I'd fastened onto as a mentor, I had filled in an application for a fellowship to Burma—a country about which I knew next to nothing except that this journalist had just been there and made it sound intriguing in a Kiplingesque, road-to-Mandalay, land-of-pagodas, cloak-and-dagger kind of way. Filling in that application was like buying a lottery ticket—a ticket on which the long-shot payoff was a year in a country about as far away from here as it was possible to go on the face of the globe, so far away that the fare for flying there across the Pacific and East Asia turned out to be the same as the fare for flying there across the Atlantic and Europe. The judges of the contest failed to discern that my application was based on absolutely nothing besides my desire to go far, far away. And so my child bride and I were able to translate that fellowship into two round-the-world air tickets, with about a dozen pages and thirty-six stops each, [and] a year of low-class, high-adventure travel, from which I emerged ready to face the Army at last and with what was finally a single, clear ambition: I wanted to get back to Asia as the correspondent for *The New York Times* in India.

It didn't happen all at once. When I got out of the Army, I showed up at the *Times* to claim my future on the strength of some articles I'd written from Burma as a stringer on a monthly retainer of exactly zero dollars. "We liked your articles from Burma," the first editor I encountered said, "and I'm pleased to tell you we have an opening on the nightside for a copyboy."

The next *Times* editor I met laughed in my face and rightly so. He'd just heard my comeback to that dazzling offer: "I'm twenty-four years old already," I'd said, "and I'm not getting any younger."

Fast forward. Nearly three years pass, and I'm called to the *Times* foreign desk. "So you want to be a foreign correspondent," the foreign editor began. "Where would you like to go?"

"Asia," I said.

"We have a man in Asia," said the foreign editor, a painfully shy mandarin with a Columbia pedigree named Manny Freedman. "How would you like to go to Africa?" My heart sank. "South Africa," he elaborated. My heart was in my shoes, but I managed to mumble, "I'd love it," or something to that effect. And, strangely enough, I did love it, but that's another story.

Don't worry. This is not going to be the story of my life: more like what the Germans call a *bildungsroman*, the story of how I came of age, although I'm not sure I ever did—I just got older in a business that allows you to sustain the illusion that you're young and raring to go well past your prime. In any case, I feel obliged as a commencement speaker to try to extract a message from my fond ramblings. What could it possibly be?

Well, try this: I found through sheer dumb luck that journalism, and specifically newspapering, suited a deep need I seemed to have not to know what was going to happen next in my life. I found that I thrived on surprise and that there were people who might pay me to cultivate that instinct, to go out in the world and discover surprises that could then be packaged as news. I found a line of work in which you could have a career without being a careerist.

If you can forgive me for being so self-referential and self-indulgent, let me try to illustrate the point by returning again to my first year out of journalism school. I didn't do much in what wasn't yet the tragic, military-ridden land that Burma later became except hang out and wander—hang out in tea shops and the Rangoon night bazaar with Burmese students and newspaper types and travel in the hinterland on second-class rail coaches and buses converted from World War II lorries. But somehow that exotic but aimless experience—in ways I couldn't have possibly anticipated—became the foundation of a newspaper career. For starters, it made me a plausible candidate in the eyes of *Times* editors to be a foreign correspondent when I had only a year and a half of real reporting experience under my belt.

Not only that, my wayward year in Burma also had everything to do with the kind of correspondent I eventually became. I traveled hard on dirt roads in a poor country before I ever had a wallet-full of embossed credit cards entitling me to fly on jets or stay in the best hotels. I didn't meet cabinet ministers or ambassadors but made lasting friendships with a bunch of young Asians and learned to see the world through their eyes, shedding some of my own culture-bound, Cold-War-era assumptions in order to gain that meeting of minds. I wouldn't have said so till many years later, but my sense of how you find out what's really going on, how you report stories, began to be shaped in those tea shops and bazaars: You hang out, and you listen hard.

My later career choices remained more impulsive than calculated—impossible sometimes to explain, even to myself. They were driven, I can now see, by a desire to repeat the amazing good fortune and sense of discovery I had on that first aimless venture in Asia after Columbia.

At the various junctures in my life, as I swung back and forth between foreign and domestic assignments, I would say that I was looking to expand my writing opportunities. I also had a strange and probably vainglorious notion for a newspaperman, that I was trying to build a coherent body of work: that poor countries, not developed countries, were part of my bailiwick; that race was one of my subjects and some other things weren't, except when they were too good, too hot, to ignore. My coherent body of work, I now suspect, was actually more of a patchwork, but my editors somehow endured and even capitalized on my restlessness. And somehow that restlessness, the fact that I kept running away to dabble in new subjects, like new majors in college, eventually made me a not-illogical person to be an editor: I had been all over the map and the paper. The thought of such an immobilizing fate never grazed my consciousness before I was forty, and I ran back to writing after my first editing stint. But then I somehow got stuck, discovering at a late date that I had a passion to help preserve and advance the paper to which I'd devoted half my life.

If anything is relevant in all this to your lives in another century, it's that all real experience is finally valuable in our business, an asset that accrues interest and keeps paying off in surprising ways. Real experience is different from a line on a resumé. It's about making a connection with something that matters in the world, not just for your own sake but for the sake of readers, viewers, users—whatever you call them—the consumers, not the perpetrators, of journalism. And those consumers—a point that's easily overlooked in the scramble for what's called market share—also happen to be citizens.

I had to become an editor before I finally made that simple connection, before I truly grasped the elementary notion that journalism can be—should be—has to be—seen as, basically, a life of service. As a reporter, I got away with my self-centered search for fulfillment for a quarter of a century. As an editor, I find myself repeating the same lines from a kind of Poor Joe's Almanac, and one of them goes like this: "Newspapers don't exist for the fulfillment of journalists. They exist for readers." I spout it when a proposal for a project seems too grandiose, when an anecdotal lead spins out of control, or when a story seems flabby and long. Of course, I know better than anyone that the joke's on me, on the self-centered reporter I once was. Well, God bless self-centered reporters seeking fulfillment—so long, that is, as they're also seeking stories that matter, that make some difference, small or large.

Stories that really matter in the world may or may not be stories that move ratings or sell papers. You don't report on missile shields, Kosovo, energy technology, lobbying in Trenton, or the drug war in Peru in order to build circulation. But if you build trust, your readers will understand that these stories matter to their lives. And if you tell them well, they will be read—tell them really well, and they'll make a lasting impression. Stories that matter are stories that cry out to be told or, less dramatically, that it's our duty to tell because, just like a house, a democracy that isn't ventilated gets moldy.

The focus groups beloved by some managers bent on what's likely to be termed "product enhancement" can't tell you what those stories are. And they're dangerous when they tell you what they're not, what subjects to steer clear of because of presumed reader ennui. As a journalist, whether reporting or assigning reporters, your focus has to be outside, not inside, your newsroom. You've got to study up and get out into the world. And if you want to do more than repackage what's already known, you're probably going to have to get away from the media pack and the media pack's agenda. As I was saying, you've got to hang out and listen hard.

It's the paradox of our so-called information age, I contend, that for all its multitude of talking heads and multimedia infinitude of information sources, there's less actual reporting going on than there used to be. To cite the obvious, no one has yet found a viable economic model to support independent reporting on the Internet. The networks have retreated from the world and slashed their actual coverage costs. The newsweeklies still cover the world but on sharply reduced budgets when it comes to foreign affairs, which now have only a token presence in their domestic editions. It's not a whole lot better with newspapers.

There's less reporting going on in some places, and more that merely seems to be reporting going on in others. If as originally scheduled, Timothy McVeigh had been executed this morning, you would have thought that all the reporters and mobile broadcasting vans in the world were in Terre Haute, Indiana, to beam back stand-uppers from outside the wall of the federal penitentiary. Yes, we can still do saturation coverage on a big execution, just as newspapers raced to do when Bruno Hauptmann was electrocuted in the Lindbergh kidnapping case in the thirties. But does such wallowing, however many megabytes it consumes, increase the sum of human knowledge by more than a few bytes? So far as I can see, in the so-called information age, as it's experienced on cable TV at such moments, saturation coverage usually means the constant stirring of the same meager set of facts into a pudding of groundless or all too obvious speculation. It's a business, it's a phenomenon, but is it journalism? Some of you will have to decide.

There was a time, along about the start of the Gulf War, when I wondered whether newspapers could survive this phenomenon, whether anyone would want to read us after seeing the war on the tube hour after hour after nerve-racking hour. Then, I started to notice, they weren't seeing the war—the war was somewhere else. They were seeing briefings and listening to lots of urgent reports that had to be recast or pulled back later in the day because they didn't check out. They were listening mostly to talk, gushing conventional wisdom; in the process, they were experiencing all the confusion and false starts that a good reporter has to work through in order to file an informed, coherent dispatch. We've endured these media firestorms again and again this last decade—from the Gulf War to the garbled on-the-hoof attempts to digest the Starr Report or the Supreme Court decision in *Bush v. Gore* . . . in front of the cameras—and now when young journalists ask me whether it makes sense to go to work in a possibly dying industry at their age, I find I believe more than ever in what we do, that I've no qualms about trying to lure them our way. A few years ago it was sort of avant-garde, sort of fashionable to say that editors were elitist agenda setters whose service could be dispensed with in the Internet age. They were unnecessary filters. Now I think it can be argued that they've never been needed more to sort out the chaff—and the chads. . . .

My prophecy—I said I might attempt one—is that newspapers will survive if they deserve to survive. And they—and other means of getting the story out—will deserve to survive if they offer something more nourishing than junk food for the mind, something that gives citizens a common framework for understanding what's really going on. But I didn't mean to end on what might be construed as a corporate note. I mean to end by urging you to fight the good fight where you won't inevitably lose, and go where your heart takes you so long as it's close to a story or stories you—and the people you mean to serve—ought to care about.

The poet Auden once exhorted a graduating Harvard class to "take short views." I think that's particularly apropos for journalists starting out. If it's not immediately apparent what that means, I'd venture that short views are the opposite of long views. They're deeply felt impulses rather than prudent life plans. They should usually be honored because, like my impulsive Asian odyssey in my first year out of here, they can change your life in ways you never imagined.

Chapter 2

REPORTING

A good reporter's notebook contains twice as much material as the writer can use. Some editors call this over-reporting. Smart ones know it as building "authority."

A reporter can never know too much. However, because deadline constraints often cut into reporting time, a journalist benefits from good organizational skills. To write a good story under deadline, it is essential to know where to go for information and how to organize your reporting and writing.

In this chapter, four journalists examine some of the less appreciated facets of reporting. Steve Woodward uses an in-depth story written on deadline to illuminate the way solid reporting and clear thinking can help a reporter write well under pressure. Jay Mathews addresses journalism's pressing need for accuracy and examines newspaper conventions that discourage careful fact-checking. Geneva Overholser examines the pitfalls of anonymous sources. Jeff Klinkenberg identifies *where* as the most under-reported *w* in American journalism and gives his prescription for reporting on place.

STEVE WOODWARD

Steve Woodward founded and managed business publications for American City Business Journals, the nation's largest chain of weekly business newspapers. He has worked as a business editor and was among the first reporters in the nation to cover the collapsing Enron Corporation, a local story for his newspaper, *The Oregonian,* in Portland, where Enron owned the regional electric company. His articles on the failure of Enron's 401(k) retirement plan received a first-place National Headliner Award for business news coverage in 2002.

Woodward's successful coverage of the business world, however, is less the result of special knowledge than it is the application of good instincts, superb organizational skills, and dogged reporting. It is not surprising then that Woodward has written memorably about all manner of subjects—from suburban news, city hall, and science (for *The Kansas City Star*) to health care, technology, and the culture and subculture of the Northwest (for *The Oregonian*). Since joining the Portland paper in 1988, he has profiled corporate chieftains, New Age gurus, a homeless murder victim, and a one-armed, poetry-writing cabdriver.

In this selection, taken from *The Oregonian*'s August 1997 in-house newsletter, Woodward offers organizational, writing, and reporting tips that are useful for covering any subject.

Power Tools

Score one for fanatical organization.

There's simply no other way to approach an in-depth, behind-the-scenes analysis of the biggest business deal in Oregon history—especially if it involves a company you've never written about before and you've been given 36 hours to turn it around.

We've had easier assignments.

It was late Thursday afternoon on the week U.S. Bancorp announced it would merge with First Bank Systems Inc. of Minneapolis, Minn. Jacqui Banaszynski approached me about working with Alan Ota to produce an Al Sunday piece on how this nearly $9 billion deal came together.

My main problem was that Alan, the only reporter fully conversant with the deal, was up to his hairline chasing daily stories on the merger. Moreover, he had to fly to Los Angeles the very next morning to attend a long-scheduled wedding. So I would have to take the lead.

And I didn't even remember the name of U.S. Bancorp's CEO.

Deep in the throes of writing another Sunday piece on biotechnology, I did the only thing a sensible reporter could do: I stared at Jacqui blankly. I stammered in protest. I began to panic.

Then I took my own advice: Calm down and get organized.

Organization Tool No. 1

The deep breath. When you're short on time and long on chaos, the worst thing you can do is pick up the phone and start dialing. The best thing you can do is take a deep breath, clear your head and think.

In my case, the thinking went something like this: Who's the reader for this story? What IS the story? What's this deal all about? Who's First Bank System? For that matter, who's U.S. Bancorp? What's the real significance of this event? Who are the human beings involved, and why did they make the decisions they made?

As I answered each question for myself, I began to see the story outline evolve. This would be a great opportunity to teach lay readers about the human drama inherent in business. Readers would come to understand the deal by looking through the eyes of the people who made it happen. And they could learn a little something about how banks really work.

I put in a call to Mary Ruble, U.S. Bancorp's longtime spokeswoman and an acquaintance of the past 13 years. I asked her to begin clearing the way for me to interview the key individuals involved in the deal.

Meanwhile, I knew I had to educate myself about each bank before I could ask the kinds of informed questions that would give me the answers I needed. Thus I turned to . . .

Organization Tool No. 2

The three-ring binder. The last thing I wanted was a desktop cluttered with notebooks, papers and annual reports. Even a bulging file folder filled with background material would be minimally useful. I simply didn't have time to waste sifting through piles of paper to find the right piece of information.

So I set up a three-ring binder with dividers for U.S. Bancorp and for First Bank. Into the binder would go relevant financial data for each company, such as balance sheets and income statements, a complete list of company directors and phone numbers, a list of top executives; full text of recent press releases, a list of each company's major shareholders and a list of research analysts who follow each stock. In the front of the binder went copies of the merger announcement and news clips.

Getting the actual information was simple. I just called it up on . . .

Reporting Tool No. 1

The Bloomberg. Simply stated, this machine is the greatest invention in the history of business journalism. Yes, you can get stock prices on it. You can also get detailed information on officers, directors and shareholders, on past financial performance, on insider trading, on every press release a company has issued over the past few years, on—well, you get the idea. (If you're so inclined, you can even find information on karaoke bars that cater to Swedish businessmen in Singapore. Seriously.)

I supplemented the Bloomberg background information with more stuff gleaned from . . .

Reporting Tool No. 2

The World Wide Web. First stop was the Securities and Exchange Commission (www.sec.gov), where I downloaded the most recent annual 10-K reports, quarterly reports and proxy statements for both banks. Then I cruised to each bank's Web site to pick up mountains of corporate, product and historical information. In addition, the Web phone directories (particularly www.four11.com) came in handy for finding home phone numbers of some directors outside the Portland area.

Again, all the relevant paperwork went into the three-ring binder.

By the time my ring binder was full, Mary Ruble had called back with good and bad news. The bad news: Gerry Cameron, U.S. Bancorp's CEO, was tied up in meetings in New York all day and would not be available until he returned to Portland on Tuesday. The good news: Anders Giltvedt, the bank's corporate development chief and one of three people who carried the load on the merger negotiations, was available Friday afternoon. This would prove to be the key interview that provided the master framework for the story.

While waiting for my interview time to arrive, I read through the material in the ring binder and the downloaded reports, which I had saved in a separate computer subdirectory called USBANK.

Using my Bloomberg list, I systematically began leaving messages for outside directors (that is, non-employee directors) of both banks.

I reached only one, a director of First Bank whose assistant agreed only to fax me a statement on her enthusiasm for the deal.

Friday afternoon came. I spent nearly two hours in a U.S. Bancorp conference room with Giltvedt, letting him walk me through the entire merger process from beginning to end.

I got back to the office to check messages. No one had called back.

So again, using Bloomberg information, I cold-called a portfolio manager at Columbia Management Co., which is one of the biggest holders of U.S. Bancorp stock. He alerted me to . . .

Reporting Tool No. 3

The teleconference. Like, welcome to business in the '90s, man. Public companies often use this tool to communicate with stock analysts throughout the country whenever they have a major announcement. The beauty of the teleconference is that it's recorded and archived. All I needed was the main phone number and an access code, which my newfound portfolio manager buddy provided for me.

An hour and one sore ear later, I had numerous quotes from U.S. Bancorp's top two executives, as well as their own recounting of how the merger came together.

On Saturday morning, I got my first return phone call from a U.S. Bancorp director, Ben Whiteley, chairman of Standard Insurance Co. and a huggable bear of a nice guy. His recollection of events differed slightly from Giltvedt's, but the gist was the same. In addition, he dropped a gold nugget: The board had originally decided to stay independent, but several directors had second thoughts on their way home from the February board meeting. Those second thoughts turned the tide toward First Bank.

Whiteley also provided the story's kicker: "If you do it with your heart, you wouldn't do it." Even before he finished his sentence, I knew I had the closing words of the story.

At this point I had a good story, but not yet a great one. On Saturday afternoon, I finished a draft for Patrick Chu. We reached the same conclusion: The story would be several magnitudes better if we waited until Tuesday to talk directly to CEO Cameron and Vice Chairman Bob Sznewajs. I considered that to be . . .

Organization Tool No. 3

The 11th-hour reprieve. A deadline is a marvelous device for forcing a reporter to confront the essence of a story—and to get the damned thing written. But there's nothing quite like an 11th-hour reprieve to make it better.

That reprieve allowed me to access . . .

Reporting Tool No. 4

Alan K. Ota. Every team should have one. Alan is the Energizer Bunny of reporters—relentless, focused, tenacious, untiring and tough as nails. As soon as he returned from Los Angeles on Monday, he plunged into the behind-the-scenes story, even as he continued cranking out daily stories.

Alan worked the phones like a commission-only telemarketer with 10 kids and a mortgage the size of Albania. Dialing for dollars, I like to call it. He went down the list of directors, many of whom he knew from past contacts, and struck pay dirt. Joshua Green was happy to chat about the plane ride during which five directors voiced their misgivings about turning down a deal from First Bank. Alan asked about everything: Who said what to whom, what kind of plane was it, who sat in which seats?

Alan reached Dan Nelson, the former heir apparent to CEO Cameron. That's when he found out Nelson had taken early retirement from U.S. Bancorp mainly because of a long bout with hepatitis caused by eating tainted shrimp at a bankers convention in Hawaii. Wonderful detail.

Alan reached John Elorriaga, the larger-than-life retired CEO of U.S. Bancorp who had been Cameron's mentor. Elorriaga recounted a conversation in which Cameron lamented, "They're circling, John. They want to buy the bank. What do I do?"

You couldn't buy a quote like that if your life depended on it.

Alan also provided . . .

Reporting Tool No. 5

Trade journal articles. Nothing beats a banking industry magazine for covering the nitty-gritty of the business. Out of the trade journals poured interviews with the top executives of both banks, corporate strategy pieces and a wealth of background information available nowhere else.

As Alan took over the brunt of the reporting, I wrote through the story several times.

The goal of the final story was complex: to bring together analysis, explanation, emotion and drama in one seamless tale. Fortunately, I had made a critical decision early on—to begin writing the first draft even before the first interview. By the time the story went to press Tuesday evening, we had written through the entire story at least half a dozen times. By understanding how the action would unfold, we were able to use . . .

Writing Tool No. 1

Cliffhangers. Borrowing Charles Dickens' techniques of serial novel writing, we constructed a series of short "plays," each zeroing in on a specific event or subject. Each play ended with a minor cliffhanger, a short graf that left the resolution up in the air and lured the reader on to the next play.

> Cameron, however, issued a caveat to his board members: Once they started down this track, the train would be hard to stop. If they found that a merger looked too good to pass up . . . The directors understood. They gave Cameron the go-ahead.

A major challenge was to weave explanatory journalism into the narrative, without breaking the train of action. Fortunately, there's . . .

Writing Tool No. 2

Interior monologue Instead of letting the reporters' voices lecture the readers, we let the key players do the explaining themselves through a kind of implied interior monologue, or self-talk. And by letting the key players also ask their own questions, we led readers into the executives' thought processes.

Among the questions Cameron tried to answer:

How would employees fare under an acquisition? Like all major mergers, layoffs would be a given. The question for U.S. Bancorp was: How well would First Bank treat those who lost their jobs?

In addition to revealing the bankers' thoughts, we had to reveal their humanity — a trait too often lost when business people are portrayed as one-dimensional automatons in gray suits. This story, in particular, screamed for rich, three-dimensional treatment because of the emotional nature of the deal. That means reaching deep into the tool bag for . . .

Writing Tool No. 3

Emotional description. Not once did we physically describe any of the key players, other than to mention that Anders Giltvedt was

Norwegian. In Cameron's case, we sought to humanize him by using emotional description:

> He had joined the bank as a 17-year-old part-time apprentice, met his best friend there and fell in love with a clerk who would later become his wife.

Emotional description is universal. It connects the reader immediately with the people in the story and opens the reader to the possibility of seeing events through the eyes of the people involved. And fortunately, in Cameron's case, the Energizer Bunny had gathered those little eggs of wisdom in the course of doing a profile of the CEO last summer.

It was no mistake that the emotional description of Cameron went high in the story, even before we summarized the acquisition itself.

Diametrically opposite the story's emotional aspects was the cold, hard analysis of the deal. To keep the explication crisp and clear, we used

Writing Tool No. 4

Parallel structure. An entire section of the story became a verbal tennis match. The sentences bounced back and forth between U.S. Bancorp and First Bank as the story laid out the similarities and differences between the two.

> U.S. Bancorp excels at the "spread" business: taking in deposits and lending them out at a higher rate.
> First Bank, in contrast, is unsurpassed in the art of non-interest income: collecting fees for services.

Or this example of parallel structure within a single sentence (a model borrowed from Genesis):

> The price was good, the economy was good, the banking environment was good and the fit with First Bank was good.

Finally, the lede was crucial to setting the tone and pace of the story. We had to tell the reader this would be a high-stakes tale with tons of drama. It had to draw in readers who would normally skip a straightforward business story. The lede, in other words, had to carry a ton of freight. That meant dredging out . . .

Writing Tool No. 5

The Mysterious-Chronological-Low-Flesch-Index-"It-went-from" Lede. It's not flashy, but it works.

> It went from a secret meeting in a Portland hotel room to an $8.8 billion deal in four months flat.

The lede did lots of duty, both in what it said and in what it didn't say. It provided an image—a secret meeting in a Portland hotel room—that any reader could visualize immediately. The very use of the word "secret" told readers this would not be a straightforward business story. The word "deal," rather than "acquisition" or "transaction," kept the Flesch Index low and set a breezy tone. And the phrase "four months flat" implied a fast pace, both for the deal and for the story.

At the same time, the lede intentionally omitted the words "banking," "business," "industry," "spokesman" or any other eye-glazing, turn-off verbiage. The lede didn't even mention U.S. Bancorp or First Bank System Inc. We knew the headline, summary deck and cutline would do the heavy lifting for us on basic identifications.

But enough about the lede.

JAY MATHEWS

Jay Mathews knows about holding people accountable. As an education reporter and columnist for *The Washington Post,* he often challenges the conventional wisdom of American education. His book *Class Struggle: What's Wrong (and Right) With America's Best Public High Schools* took the first detailed look at the dynamics of elite public high schools and revealed how schools denied many students a chance to take their most demanding courses. An excerpt of the book was featured in *Newsweek,* and the *American School Board Journal* named it one of the most notable education books of 1998. Mathews's column, Class Struggle, which examines local and national education issues, often debunks the widely accepted tenets of education—like the notion that today's students benefit from "grade inflation." He won the National Education Reporting Award in 1984 for a series on job retraining for automobile workers.

He is the author of four books, among them *Escalante: The Best Teacher in America,* published in 1988. It grew from a six-year study of Garfield High School and the Advanced Placement calculus teacher, Jaime Escalante, celebrated in the film *Stand and Deliver*. Mathews's book *Harvard Schmarvard* will be published in 2003.

In this 1992 essay for *The New Republic,* Mathews challenged the newspaper taboo of showing stories to sources. Why shouldn't journalists, he argues, hold themselves to the same tests of openness and accuracy that they demand in others?

Just Checking

The New York Times has beaten me to several stories and so, I admit, I love to see them screw up. A recent twenty-nine-paragraph, front-page correction was a case in point. A National Academy of Sciences panel had not, as the *Times* had originally reported, called for a moratorium on DNA fingerprinting. It would be childish of me to wallow in such a perverse pleasure any more than I already have if there were not a lesson for both readers and reporters, made no less relevant by the *Times*'s swift and professional confession of error.

How many times have you seen something written about yourself, or a subject you knew well, and winced at some small flaw? We journalists know we rarely get it exactly right. We run corrections, but anyone who has worked as a reporter or editor knows how narrowly the correctable mistake is defined and how many errors never get corrected. The real problem is not so much mega-booboos like the *Times* story, which tend to get noticed and fixed, but the innumerable little errors. Spreading from newspaper to television to magazine and back again, they are magnified by repetition into bigger ones, and nibble away at press credibility. The Chinese government has shamelessly exploited an initial false report, still believed in the West, that students were massacred in Tiananmen Square (as opposed to other parts of the city) to discredit coverage of the crack-down. Many people still think that Eugene McCarthy won the most votes in the 1968 New Hampshire primary and that even slight exposure to asbestos will kill you.

As far back as anyone I know can remember, it has been a firm if unwritten rule of newspaper work that no source sees a story before it is published. That would be tantamount, the rule said, to giving the source permission to write the story, or at least to make great mischief if the story offended in some way. I can't remember how I learned this ancient prohibition. By the time I reached *The Washington Post* twenty years ago, I knew it was the worst kind of deviant behavior, akin to wearing a Nixon-Agnew button to work. Seven years ago I began to break that rule. Since then I have encountered a few others doing the same. I wish there were more.

I've always been somewhat prissy about what I write. As a young reporter I would run my stories through my head before I went to sleep, wondering if I had gotten a nuance right, explained a development clearly. I double-checked facts, but occasionally an error would wiggle through my safety net. There didn't seem to be anything more I could do about it until the day I decided to risk a violation of the taboo. I did it to protect an old friend. He'd helped me arrange interviews at an Indian tribal office in Montana where he was both a tribal member and a staff economist. It was a very political story, and an error, I thought, could do him harm. I swore him to secrecy and read him the story. He caught one minor mistake, a misstatement of the amount paid for a local dam. I made the correction, sent in the story, and then thought about it. He had not asked me to change my view of what happened. No quotes were altered. I slept well that night. I decided to try it again.

Dr. Leonard Bailey corrected my description of one of the arteries he had fixed to a baboon's heart implanted in a sick human infant. A Pasadena police lieutenant told me I had misidentified the helicopter used in the city's little war against medfly spraying. Each time I would warn that I was checking only for factual accuracy, not approval. If they told me something was wrong, I would double-check before I made the change.

The reactions surprised me. Prickly publicists who usually complained about failure to use their bosses' middle initials began to offer bits of information critical of their employers. Scientists who had snorted at the thought of getting anything right in a newspaper began calling with story ideas. People being skewered cursed the tormentors I was quoting but never demanded a retraction.

None of the bogeymen materialized. No one complained to my editors about the slant of a story. No one tried to persuade my sources to deny unfavorable quotes. People occasionally tried to change their own quotes but would back off when I explained that was not possible. No one attempted to blow my few exclusives, though I was careful to save my reading of such stories for the very last moment.

I have encountered only one instance of misbehavior by someone who got an early look. A California politician's chief aide was so pleased that *The Washington Post* had presented his boss in a favorable light that he leaked this fact to several Los Angeles television stations before the story was published. I scooped myself by a few hours, but no permanent harm was done.

In 1985 I wrote an article in the *Washington Journalism Review* defending my working habits, mostly as an act of self-protection. I wanted my editors to know what I was doing and at the same time get their blessing into print. The reaction to my confession from this limited audience was mixed, to say the least. An editor of the *San Jose Mercury News* posted it on his bulletin board with an approving note. A journalism professor wrote to say if I couldn't stand the heat, I should try another occupation. One of my favorite *Washington Post* editors, the late Howard Simons, told me I was committing a heresy. A few other reporters, I learned, were doing the same, with the tacit approval of their editors. I eventually concluded that the taboo was just one more hoary anachronism, the product of old fears and unexamined assumptions.

I do not think newspapers should require reporters to show stories to sources. That would risk lawsuits on those few occasions when it is not possible to reach a source. What I suggest instead are a few limited, casual experiments, and I know a good place to start. There is one kind of news story—the obituary—where errors can cause real emotional pain. The only time most people ever have direct contact with a journalist is when they are interviewed for an obituary on their father or mother in the local paper. A mistake, even a small one, feels like someone scratched the coffin with a rusty nail.

Why shouldn't editors encourage obit writers to show such stories to relatives before publication? No one is going to leak the story to the competition. No one is going to try to take political advantage. Time is rarely an issue. It would be the simplest thing to fax a draft to a son or daughter to check for factual errors. If that worked, who knows what might happen next?

As reporters we are accustomed to exposing automakers who slap together cars and depend on recalls to make everything right. We have excoriated prosecutors who locked up innocents and then, discovering their error, set them free with a bare apology. Many of my colleagues think that front-page corrections are preferable to leaping into the unknown, but I don't. It's time we applied the principles of openness and accuracy we monitor in others to the practices we engage in ourselves.

GENEVA OVERHOLSER

In every job she has held in journalism—as a newspaper editor, ombudsman, columnist, and professor—Geneva Overholser has helped the profession take a hard look at itself.

Under her editorship, *The Des Moines Register* won the Pulitzer Prize for public service in 1991 for reporting on the rape of an Iowa woman whom the newspaper named, with the victim's consent. This represented a departure from the routine practice in newsrooms of shielding sexual assault victims by withholding their names. Overholser had argued that the policy actually stigmatized the women rather than protecting them.

Overholser's experience includes editorial writing for *The New York Times* and working as ombudsman for *The Washington Post.* She served nine years on the Pulitzer Prize board and holds an endowed chair at the University of Missouri School of Journalism. As a syndicated columnist and a regular contributor to the *Columbia Journalism Review*, she continues to play a strong role in examining the media.

In this selection from her syndicated columns, Overholser examines the press's use of anonymous sources. When information is provided by law-enforcement officials, she says, the media is sometimes too easily persuaded to attribute the material to anonymous "authorities" instead of insisting the information be provided on the record. Even with a trusted source, she points out, journalists must not abandon their responsibility to examine motive and agenda before granting anonymity.

What We've Got Here Is a Failure to Be Skeptical

We media types pride ourselves on our skepticism; it safeguards our independence from other powers. Yet something about law-enforcement officials makes us go all weak-kneed with gullibility. As *The Boston Globe* recently reminded us, the results can be pretty awful.

You've probably heard of the late January [2001] murders of two Dartmouth College professors, Half and Susanne Zantop. New Hampshire authorities kept their investigation quiet. Everyone seemed at a loss for motives, much less suspects. Then the *Globe,* in a big front-page story on Feb. 16, seemed to have found the key.

"Love Affair Eyed in N.H. Killings: Husband Involved with Unidentified Woman, Officials Say," read the headline. "Investigators believe the killings of Dartmouth College professors Half and Susanne Zantop were crimes of passion, most likely resulting from an adulterous love affair involving Half Zantop, according to authorities close to the case," read the opening paragraph.

It was quite a story. It was based entirely on anonymous law-enforcement sources. And it was wrong. The Hanover, N.H., police chief said later, "We have no shred of evidence regarding this adulterous affair." On Feb. 19, two teenage boys from a neighboring town were arrested in the case. And on Feb. 21, *Globe* editor Matt Storin wrote a front-page note to readers. "The sources now concede that the extramarital affair theory is not correct," he said.

Even in the awful aftermath, the *Globe* seems to feel that, if only we knew who the sources were, we'd understand. "We put our trust in three law-enforcement officials who we had every reason to believe had intimate, up-to-date knowledge of the investigation," Storin wrote.

Another *Globe* editor, who oversaw the story, said: "We had solid sources developed by two of our best and most experienced reporters who were giving us information which we had every reason to believe was true and correct. And these sources are authoritative. We're not talking about campus cops who just fell off the turnip truck."

"Authoritative" packs a walloping punch for journalists. And who is more "authoritative" than the "authorities" themselves? When law-enforcement officials speak, we grow unaccustomedly credulous—and all too willing to cover them with anonymity.

The results can be bad—for individuals, for the press's image, for the nation. Witness the way Ken Starr and colleagues played much of the Washington press corps during the Monica Lewinsky scandal. As a study conducted by the Committee of Concerned Journalists said, the coverage "at certain points showed a penchant to reflect the suspicions of prosecutors and investigators out of balance with the denials of the accused. . . . There are cautions . . . about whether the news media in an increasingly instantaneous and competitive media environment are always maintaining adequate skepticism."

When the media provide the big megaphone to anonymous law-enforcement officials, the agendas driving those officials are often overlooked. Take the Richard Jewell case. Jewell, you'll recall, was pegged as the "prime suspect" in the Olympic Park bombing in Atlanta in 1996—until 88 days later when "authorities" officially declared him no longer a "target."

The world's attention was already focused on Atlanta when the bomb hit. Fear spread through the huge crowds. Only 10 days earlier, TWA Flight 800 had exploded off Long Island. Was this a new reign of terrorism in America? Pressure on authorities to show they had the case under control was extraordinary. They couldn't do it without the media.

Just as anonymity fuels these stories, anonymity makes it hard to clean up the damage they do. After the crash of EgyptAir Flight 990 in late 1999, stories cited anonymous authorities declaring that the co-pilot had said, "I made my decision now." The quote, they said, came from the plane's voice recorder. The next day, a named official—Jim Hall, head of the National Transportation Safety Board—said the recorder had no such quote.

Power jockeying between the NTSB and the FBI appears to lie behind this confusion. But media corrections of the original story only leave you wondering. When you've pledged anonymity to your sources, there's little you can say when you find that they've led you astray.

Press readiness to go along with authorities eager to manipulate us through anonymous leaks sometimes seems to turn out just swell. Take the Unabomber case, a steady stream of leakage from anonymous "federal officials."

Whatever the outcome, though, principles are trampled along the way. One is the presumption of innocence. Another is the notion that the media are independent from all other powers. When it comes to law enforcement, especially, it ain't necessarily so.

JEFF KLINKENBERG

One admirer calls Jeff Klinkenberg the Thoreau, Audubon, Russell Baker, and Edward Hoagland of Florida—"an open-eyed but innocent and gentle chronicler of Florida's amazing pleasures." The prize-winning columnist for the *St. Petersburg Times* writes vividly and lyrically about his native state. He is the author of *Real Florida* and *Dispatches from the Land of Flowers*. In this selection, taken from a newspaper's in-house publication, Klinkenberg presents a primer for reporters who could stand to awaken their sense of place.

Reporting the Fifth W: Where

"The face of the water, in time, became a wonderful book—a book that was a dead language to the uneducated passenger, but which told its mind to me without reserve, delivering its most cherished secrets as if it uttered them with a voice. And it was not a book to be read once and thrown aside, for it had a new story to tell each day."

—Mark Twain
Life on the Mississippi

Consider the Five W's: Who is character. What is plot. When is chronology. Why is motive. Where is place, the boundaries of the story.

Journalists are pretty good at getting the first four into their work. But "Where" is the least explored and the most poorly executed W in American journalism.

"Ideas of place give us the rudiments of narration: a story, its teller, and a setting," writes Princeton's William Howarth, the editor of *The John McPhee Reader*. "Without some 'sense of place' and its all-important locators, we could not describe, relate, read or write."

Oh, yeah? A lot of us in the news business give it a try. Why do so many of us write so ineffectively about place? My guess is time and inclination.

Time: As deadline approaches, many of us spend dwindling minutes thinking only in terms of plot and motive and possibly character.

Inclination: We grow up thinking place is unimportant. Many of us have an undeveloped sense of place in our own lives—we're unfamiliar with our own backyards—and we don't know what things are or how they relate. We live in cookie-cutter cities, with the same old shops, same old entertainment. Some of us may believe "Television will show this. So I won't even bother."

Meanwhile, the best writing weaves place into narrative and creates literature. Think of Mark Twain on the Mississippi, Cormac McCarthy on Mexico, Peter Matthiessen on the Everglades—the land in their work becomes another character.

How Can We All Do It Better?

1. Be there. Sounds obvious, but how many times do we end up doing our reporting over the telephone? Sometimes a reporter has time for nothing else, but sometimes the reporter is lazy. Stories filled with disembodied "talking head" experts from government and law seldom are memorable. Specific details, about people and place, gathered by a reporter on the scene, are rewards a writer can sprinkle through a story to hold readers.

Francis X. Clines, who wrote "About New York" for *The New York Times,* sometimes came to the office without an idea for a column. But he always said that if he could go somewhere—if he left the office—he knew he'd be OK.

2. Arrive early and stay late. Give yourself time to let "place" soak in. Many good writers like to spend a few extra minutes reporting, looking for interesting detail, and avoid struggling later. If you have to, get out of the office on your own time. Show your editor what a reporter who spends time on the scene can do.

I wrote a series of essays about the Everglades in 1992. I practically grew up fishing and canoeing there, and became melancholy on the day my reporting was finished. I didn't want to leave. But a six-hour drive, and some hard writing, lay ahead. I made one last swing through a little-explored section of the park, Long Pine, looking for a last detail or something magical. I saw no Florida panther, but I found my ending—the metaphor I needed to explain the wonder of a wilderness set so very close to a civilization closing in for the kill.

> It's time to go home. A cold front is barreling down the state. The wind picks up and the sky turns gray. It will rain soon. I load the bicycle into the truck and drive the road through the hurricane-broken pines. In the tall grass next to the road something big moves. I catch it out of the corner of my eye and return for a better look.
>
> The Eastern diamondback rattlesnake, as long as I am tall, is coiled and nervous. It's wild, beautiful, deadly. I crack open my

> door to see what will happen. What happens is the snake rattles ominously. I rev the engine. The snake rattles again. The Indians who once called this land home considered the rattlesnake the Lord of the Woods, the protector of the plant nation.
>
> I have goose bumps in the presence of the Lord.

3. A good question to ask is: "What's that?" Find an expert who can identify key landmarks for you, from buildings to trees and animals, to sounds.

Gene Miller, who won two Pulitzers, was part of a Knight-Ridder team sent to Ohio to investigate the Kent State shootings in 1970. A bell tolled on campus. He found the person in the music department who could tell what note the bell was tolling. It was a small detail in a story full of details that helped capture the irony of a pastoral campus shaken by a bloodbath.

I read a dry story recently about a neighborhood dispute. A man had built a tree house for his grandchildren. The neighborhood association called the tree house an eyesore. I wish the reporter had asked, "What kind of a tree is the house in?," visited the house and described the neighborhood from that high perch. What kind of neighborhood, and what kind of neighbors, oppose tree houses?

"What kind of palm is that? Was that fish that just jumped a mullet? That bird on your seawall? Could it be a great blue heron? What's the difference between a heron and an egret? What do I smell?" They're always good questions.

4. Become an expert about the community you cover. Find out as much as you can about living things, human, animal and plant. First thing I do when traveling is learn relevant natural and human history. I visit museums and buy books. I'm always working on my botany. I never travel without a bird guide, and sometimes I listen to tape recordings of bird calls on my truck radio while driving. When I was a boy, I fished when I should have been studying. The glorious results of a misspent youth have paid off handsomely a number of times.

5. Develop your eye. As Thoreau wrote in an 1851 journal, "The question is not what you look at, but what you see." What's special about this place? Thoreau again: "All things in this world must be seen with the morning dew on them, must be seen with youthful, early opened, hopeful eyes." As an exercise, walk into your back yard, look around, close your eyes and recall specific details of what you've just seen.

6. Look for telling details. Writing about the Everglades, I might be tempted to drop into my story a list of a dozen rare plant species and show the overwhelming diversity. Yet a writer may want to concentrate on a single, telling detail. If it's the oppressive heat, hammer it, not once but several times. Into the narrative, in different places, weave in the humidity, the dripping sweat, the need to constantly drink, the short tempers. Make the reader feel it. In the summer, in the Everglades, it is possible to breathe in mosquitoes. Hammer it!

7. Let place become a character in your story. In weather stories, flood, drought or hurricane winds, place is everything. Ditto for the environment. Don't know why, but environmental writers sometimes are the least likely to infuse their stories with place. They like to sentence readers to breakfast with talking-head politicians, scientists and statistic-spouting lobbyists. Place is an afterthought in stories that beg for description and even wonder.

8. Never, ever let a story subject come to your office for an interview if you can help it. Interview your subject in his natural habitat. Years ago, the author of a sea turtle book came to St. Petersburg to promote his latest. We sat in my office and gabbed. "Let's go get a beer," he said, and we headed toward the nearest tavern. A turtle, shockingly dead and stinking, lay in the parking lot of Mastry's Bar and Grill, a half mile from the nearest water. "It's the turtle hex," shouted my turtle expert, who went on to explain his superstitions. I was ecstatic: I had my lead. The day after my story published, I began to believe in the turtle hex myself. On the way home from the office, my van caught fire and burned to the ground.

9. Take a field trip with your story subject. Among other things, place can provoke new information, funny stories and great dialogue. The way people talk and what they talk about is influenced by their surroundings. They may whisper in church, shout on the basketball court, talk nonsense after a couple of tall boys at Mastry's. Or they may start chatting about something remarkable they've just seen, something important. Open your notebook or turn on your tape recorder.

Totch Brown, 73, grew up when the Everglades was wild frontier. He took me on a long, slow boat ride to show me his favorite parts. We arrived at an island in the national park known as "The Watson Place." Watson was a notorious man, possibly a murderer. Peter Matthiessen even wrote about him in a novel called *Killing Mister Watson*. One day the nervous residents of the nearest town, Chokoloskee, killed Watson. Totch's mother was a witness. Standing among the mosquitoes and the mangroves on Watson's deserted sun-baked key, Totch told a family story that painted a word-picture portrait of one hard land:

"It happened in 1910," Totch says. "Three bodies come a-floatin' down the river. The people in Chokoloskee, they knew Watson done it. So one day they hear him comin'—you could hear his boat motor a long way off—and they get ready. They say, 'Watson, the killin' has got to stop. Give up your arms.' Watson says wait a minute—he didn't kill those people, but he knows who done it. He says he'll bring the killer in.

"A while later, Watson comes back to Chokoloskee. The men in town are waitin' for him on the dock. Watson, he's got a hat with a hole in it in one hand, and his shotgun in the other, when he steps on the dock. Watson says, 'He wouldn't come. I had to kill him.' The men say, 'Watson, that ain't good enough. Give up your arms.'

"Well, he pretends like he's throwin' his shotgun down, but then swings it up on the people on the dock and pulls the triggers for both barrels. The gun pops—shells was made of paper back then and they had got all wet. So Watson reaches for his .38. A man shoots a hole in him. Then everybody else opens up. They say there was 38 bullets in him when it was over.

"My mother seen it from the beach that day. She was 17."

10. Ask people about their "sacred" places. For me, the Florida Keys is more than a picturesque string of sub-tropical islands. It's where I spent the happiest days of my youth, fishing, with my brother and my dad. My system of values springs from those special moments, at that special place.

The people you interview also have sacred places. Find them. They're vaults where we store ideas.

"Where did you grow up?," "What did you enjoy doing when you were a child?" and "Where did you do it?" can open emotional doors. Ask that doting grandfather: "Did you have a tree house when you were a boy?" When you interview somebody in their home, ask for a tour. Every picture, every book, every piece of furniture, can tell a story. In a widow's house, perhaps it is the shrine she has constructed to her late husband.

Chip Scanlan, a former *St. Petersburg Times* reporter, was interviewing a woman whose husband died from lung cancer. Chip asked if he could look around the house. The widow showed him their bedroom, their bed. Chip got the quote to end his moving story.

"It feels like one big nightmare," she says. "Maybe I will wake up, and he will be in bed with me. But I know it's not going to be so. Would you believe it? I take his after-shave lotion and spray it on his pillow just so I can smell him. Just the smell of it makes me feel like he's with me."

Totch Brown, my old Everglades wild man, spent his life netting mullet, poaching alligators and smuggling marijuana, an indiscretion that landed him in prison in old age. Late in the afternoon I drove him home. He lived in the tiny, charming community of Chokoloskee. Totch didn't see his hometown through my big-city eyes:

"I used to see people sittin' on their porches after supper, tellin' the old stories to the young people," Totch laments, looking out the truck window. "Now nobody's on their porches."

As we pull into his driveway, I am thinking about the changes an old Everglades wild man like Totch Brown has seen during his lifetime.

"Now, after supper, everybody runs for the TV," he thunders. "The other night, I saw people screwin' on TV! People let their kids watch that garbage! TV, it's a terrible thing."

The moneylenders were in Totch's temple, his sacred place. It was the end of my story.

Chapter 3

INTERVIEWING

It is intimate business, the art of the interview. It begins by learning how to *really* listen. Many reporters are astonished to hear, while reviewing a taped interview, how often they interrupt their subject, how quickly they fill in awkward silences, or how much time they spend talking themselves.

This is not to say that a good interviewer simply lobs questions and records answers. As you will see in this chapter, whether composing a Q and A for a magazine or prodding a reluctant source for an investigative piece, a reporter must invest equally in preparation and improvisation.

Jack Hart reminds us of the importance of researching the subject exhaustively by interviewing friends and relatives and by examining clips, books, and tapes. Claudia Dreifus and the Watergate team of Bob Woodward and Carl Bernstein emphasize less tangible aspects of interviewing—like how to loosen up a subject or when to abandon prepared questions for more spontaneous queries.

All of these writers rely on instinct, sensitivity, and a bit of luck. They are, above all, skilled listeners known for their unusual success at the art of the interview.

JACK HART

Thirty years of teaching writing, writing about writing, and editing writers has taught Jack Hart that most writing problems are interviewing problems. As he says in this article, drawn from the December 1993 in-house newsletter at *The Oregonian,* where he is managing editor and writing coach, "You can't write it if you don't have it."

Getting the interview, preparing, asking the right questions, and knowing when to let silence work its magic—all are part of the mysterious art of the interview. But Hart, who is the editor of two Pulitzer Prize–winning stories and whose column The Writer's Workshop was long a feature in *Editor & Publisher* magazine, aims to demystify this important process.

The Art of the Interview

You can't write it if you don't have it.

Which is a fundamental truth that writing gurus too often overlook. . . . Good reporting is the heart of all good writing.

And because newspaper journalists gather most of their information by talking to people, reporting is mostly interviewing. It follows, then, that writing problems are often interviewing problems.

- Does the writing lack emotion? Maybe the writer's interviewing style put sources on the defensive, causing them to bottle up their feelings behind a facade of empty, officious pronouncements.
- Does the writing lack detail? Maybe the writer asked the kind of questions that produced abstractions instead of vivid specifics.
- Does the writing lack the great anecdotes that light up the work of fine feature writers? Maybe the writer needed to put more into the conversation so that the source would put more into hers.

Clearly, writing and interviewing go hand in hand. As John Brady, author of *The Craft of Interviewing,* notes, "Many editors consider the best interviewers to be, inescapably, the best writers."

So we'd be wise to heed the journalism professors, behavioral scientists, criminologists and others who study interviewing. They've examined how the best journalists, cops, social workers, psychologists, lawyers and other professionals dig out information with skillful questioning. What they've discovered is surprisingly consistent, and it suggests that there is indeed an art to the interview.

An art that, it seems, lies somewhere far removed from the stereotype most of us learned as cubs.

The Myth of the Journalistic Interview

Ken Metzler, the University of Oregon professor who pioneered journalism-school instruction in interviewing, says most of us grew up with a warped sense of what an interview should be. Our false ideal for the journalistic interview grew out of the clamoring crowd of shouting reporters typical of old movies, the Mike Wallace ambush interview or the *Meet the Press* celebrity grilling, all confrontational interviews that may make great theater but produce little real information.

The *Meet the Press* model is illuminating. Metzler notes that the show's guest sits on one side of the set behind a counter that is, in effect, a little fort. Three or four reporters sit on the other side of the set behind their own fort. The moderator opens hostilities, and then guest and journalists lob bombs back and forth between their respective battlements until the moderator declares a cease-fire.

Most of us quickly learn that such show-biz interviews are wildly inappropriate for virtually all newspaper purposes. But not many of us realize how deeply the stereotype colors our perceptions or how different a successful interview should be.

The Interview As an Exchange

The best interviews generate more information than either the source or the interviewer could produce separately. The interview sparks synergy, the burst of energy created when combining elements produces a whole greater than the sum of the parts.

That's the dimension Metzler was trying to tap when he titled his book *Creative Interviewing*. And it's integral to his very definition of what makes an interview: "A two-person conversational exchange of information on behalf of an audience to produce a level of intelligence neither person could produce alone."

That suggests that successful journalistic interviewers put as much into their interviews as they take away from them. They reveal something of themselves. They let their sources know where they are going and how they hope to get there. They try to enlist sources in a common cause, even when those same sources are defensive or antagonistic.

What Metzler seems to be suggesting is that the difference between good interviewers and bad ones is largely a matter of attitude. The good ones have overcome the Mike Wallace stereotype. They see their interview subjects as partners in a joint effort. They are less concerned with expressing their own opinions than they are with truly seeing the world from the subject's point of view.

They are, in other words, absolutely non-judgmental. Metzler notes that Carl Rogers defined a successful communication as one in which Party B persuades Party A to say what he really thinks and feels, regardless of what Party B believes. A good interviewer, says Metzler, comes to the interview to listen and understand, not to accuse and judge.

That doesn't mean a good interviewer has to be a sucker. Savvy journalistic interviewers are politely skeptical, even though they don't communicate that skepticism to the subject. And neither are they the cynical scam artists that Janet Malcolm described when she said that every journalist is "a kind of confidence man, preying on people's vanity, ignorance or loneliness, gaining their trust and betraying them without remorse." But an effective journalistic interviewer does have to put his own anger, righteousness and personal values aside, at least for a time.

Listen to the telephone interviews you hear taking place around you in [your] own newsroom. The best writers sound calm, reassuring and genuinely interested. They never turn into shouters who berate sources, demand information or threaten consequences. It is only the hacks who push their weight around.

Opening the Door

Most professional journalists are remarkably effective at getting to the sources they need. In one sense, that's not surprising. As A. J. Liebling pointed out, "There is almost no circumstance under which an American doesn't like to be interviewed. We are an articulate people, pleased by attention, covetous of being singled out."

Still, some sources are reluctant. Maybe they've been burned by past interviewers. Maybe their colleagues look down on publicity hounds. Maybe they're just busy.

Whatever the objection to an interview, most of us know a few tricks for getting past it. John Brady asked several master interviewers to reveal theirs:

- Carl Bernstein, one half of the Woodstein Watergate duo, says he and Bob Woodward often approached reluctant sources by offering an opportunity to set the record straight. "You tell them that if you've been in error, they're in a position to show you where you went wrong. We didn't think we were in error very often, but it's an effective introduction."

- Author Philip Marvin has his own version of the same technique. "Never ask to 'interview' a busy person," he says. "Rather, ask for an appointment to get his 'constructive criticism' of the background information you've already gathered."
- Alex Haley figured the best way to get an interview with a VIP was to charm the secretary. He sent flowers and ladled on the flattery. He said he'd even date a secretary to get good inside information or land a big interview.

But most of us aren't trying to land one of the big Alex Haley–style *Playboy* interviews that justify that kind of time and effort. We just want to get somebody to talk . . . in a hurry. And the toughest assignments involve getting a response from somebody who's accused of something.

In that situation, Nat Hentoff recommends a tried-and-true technique familiar to most veteran newspaper interviewers. "My usual procedure," says Hentoff, "is to tell him that since he will be in the story anyway, for the sake of accuracy, I would much prefer to get his statement firsthand."

Building Rapport

We trust those most who are most like us. And we talk most freely with those we trust. So successful interviewers usually work hard to find something in common with the interview subject. "The object," John Gunther once said, "is to get the subject relaxed, to make him really talk instead of just answer questions."

A little bit of common ground can bridge a chasm of personal differences. It's hard to imagine two more diametrically opposed personalities than those of Richard Nixon and Hunter Thompson. Yet Nixon once summoned—actually singled out and sent for—the doctor of gonzo for a private 90-minute conversation during a drive to the airport. The reason? Both men were fanatic NFL fans, and Nixon desperately wanted to talk football.

Savvy interviewers say they usually scout the interview subject's background to find points of commonality. When they walk into an office or home, they look for souvenirs or knickknacks that betray personal interests. Then they seize on those openings to establish some relationship.

An over-the-mantle shotgun opens a conversation on bird hunting. A movie poster kicks things off with some talk about a favorite film.

Of course, some real research in advance of the interview can pay even richer dividends. We do lots of minor, hurry-up interviews that must, of necessity, be pretty much off-the-cuff. But no truly accomplished journeyman would risk a major interview without at least checking the clips. And most will do considerably more digging. John Brady says, "Experienced writers agree that for every minute spent in an interview, at least 10 minutes should be spent in preparation."

The risks of ignorance are great. Brady reports that when Vivien Leigh arrived in Atlanta to celebrate a re-release of *Gone with the Wind,* a reporter asked her what part she played in the movie. She told him that "she did not care to be interviewed by such an ignoramus."

And when a reporter asked Bernard De Voto for an interview, the famed Harvard professor, historian and editor immediately agreed. Then the reporter said, "I'm sorry. I really didn't have time to look this up. Just exactly who are you, Mr. De Voto?"

"Young man," De Voto replied, "if you don't have time to look it up in *Who's Who* or your own library and find out, then I don't have time for you."

De Voto gave good advice. *Who's Who* is a minimum bit of background. The regional and specialized biographical dictionaries, such as *Who's Who in the West* and *American Men of Science*, are even more detailed.

Research can go a lot deeper, of course. And it should for a really big interview. A review of the periodical indices such as the *Readers' Guide to Periodical Literature* or an on-line search will turn up most of what's been written about anyone. Public records can yield valuable background, especially for investigative reporting. The point is to use knowledge as a lever that will open up the source. Cornelius Ryan, the novelist who wrote *The Longest Day*, said one of the basic rules of reporting was that you should "never interview anyone without knowing 60 percent of the answers."

Conducting the Conversation

All that preparation goes for naught if it doesn't translate into a candid, revealing interview. The experts agree on several factors that seem likely to help:

• Have a plan for the overall shape of the interview. After warming up the subject with some small talk, ask "can-openers"—the softball questions that get the subject relaxed and talking. Educational and career history questions fit the bill. So do questions about family lore or hobbies or well-known accomplishments.

Do the real work during mid-interview. And save the real zinger, your Columbo question, for the very end. In fact, you may want to try the true Columbo technique—poke your head back in the door and ask the Columbo question as you are leaving. "Oh, I almost forgot. There's just one more thing. . . ."

• Plan your interviews in logical order. Build to the big one so that you don't have to go back to a prime source for repeated questions as you uncover further information. Most sources will be happy to oblige if you call back once to iron out some details right before publication. That kind of a call will help convince them of your concern for accuracy—especially if you clear the way by asking permission for a call-back as you end the main interview.

But badgering a source with repeated calls is no way to build rapport or pry loose information, especially if the calls are accusatory. Not only will it create a hostile source, but it also exposes the reporter's own bad planning.

• Rough out general topic areas you want to cover, but don't write out complete questions. A reporter who reads her questions creates a stilted, excessively formal environment that isn't likely to produce much information. Besides, specific questions rule out a flexible conversation that easily adapts to productive twists and turns.

• Remember that specifics produce specifics. Abstract questions, conversely, produce abstract answers. Don't ask the new CEO how she felt about getting the job. Ask her what she was doing when she found out about it, whom she told first and what she said when she told that person.

• Offer cues and memory jogs. Most of us have only a fuzzy recollection of most things. But we can remember a lot more if we have a specific event to hang things on. "You had just returned to Chicago when the war broke out. How did you hear about it? What was the first thing you did?"

• Zero in on meaningful moments. Metzler points out that some of the most productive conversation in a personality interview takes the source back to key points in the subject's life. Look for crossroads, he advises, by asking the source about a time when his life could have gone in different directions. "I understand you had two choices for grad school. What made you decide to choose Minnesota?" And, Metzler further advises, look for epiphanies. "Did you suddenly realize that you weren't cut out for the priesthood?"

• Let the source know what you're up to. Clearly explaining your purpose will help the source relax and will keep him on track. If you want somebody's interpretation of an event, tell her so. If you want descriptive detail to help you set scenes, explain that, too. Explain what you're NOT interested in, as well. That will help head off one of the chief interviewing problems—the discursive source who wants to talk about everything but the subject at hand.

• Know the difference between interviewing for information and interviewing for story. If you're out to write a narrative, you'll have to press your source for the kind of descriptive detail that brings it to life. "Think about walking down the ramp and onto the dock. What did the boat look like? Was the sun shining? What was the light like? Were there any gulls? What was behind the boat? Who else was standing on the dock?"

The better educated the source, the more you'll have to press. Education teaches us to abstract generalities from our experience. So well-educated sources leave out the vivid details that bring a scene to life. That's one reason Phil Stanford says that blue-collar sources make the best interviews. They often produce highly detailed descriptions of an event, rather than reporting their own conclusions or filtering out all the specifics that they think are unimportant.

• Tell stories to get stories. Good anecdotes almost always come out of a relaxed conversation in which the interviewer spins a yarn and the source replies in kind. The best anecdotes illustrate a major theme in the finished story. So a skillful interviewer will tell stories related to some key concept. "I hear Sally's an incredibly hard worker. Her mother says she used to study under the covers with a flashlight. Does she bring her work along when she spends time with you?"

Telling stories on yourself may open up the source even more. Not only does telling a story tend to produce a story. But revealing something private about yourself also helps make a source feel safe enough to do likewise.

The famous yarn about Truman Capote and Marlon Brando illustrates both points. Capote interviewed Brando for a *New Yorker* profile, and Brando was uncharacteristically candid. He even talked about his mother's alcoholism. A friend asked why he'd been so loose-lipped. "Well," said Brando, "the little bastard spent half the night telling me about his problems. I figured the least I could do is tell him one of mine."

• Think about more than words. A high percentage of reporters' notebooks contain nothing but quotations. But the notebooks of the best newspaper writers are filled with much more. They scribble about details that catch their eyes, movements and gestures by the interview source and their own thoughts about the meaning of what the source is saying.

Metzler advises his students to follow the SCAM formula. As the interview progresses, the interviewer will remind himself to think about (1) setting, (2) character, (3) action, (4) meaning. Cynthia Gorney, the *Washington Post* writer who won an ASNE writing award with, among other stories, a profile of Theodore Geisel, clearly follows something like the SCAM approach. Her profile of Geisel, better known as Dr. Seuss, created meaning by probing a key element of Geisel's character—his obsessive perfectionism—to explain his success. It revealed different aspects of that character with an action line that led readers on a tour of Geisel's La Jolla home. And it helped drive the larger point home with details such as the observation that Geisel prominently displayed his father's 1902 rifle target, drilled in the bull, "to remind me of perfection."

• Watch for nonverbal cues. Diamond wholesalers supposedly watch a client's eyes when he examines a stone. If they dilate, the client likes what he sees, and the price will be higher.

That may be apocryphal, but the fact remains that we constantly send an array of nonverbal signals. Sensitive interviewers will pay attention to body posture, gesture, and muscle tension. And many good interviewers can recognize the distinctive change in voice quality that reveals when a source is lying.

• Watch out for what the social scientists call "contagion bias"—the tendency to telegraph your own feelings unconsciously.

Interview experts like to recall the story of Clever Hans, the famed turn-of-the-century German horse. The farmer who owned the animal would ask him the sum of two plus two. The horse would strike the ground four times with a hoof. Six divided by three? The horse would strike the ground twice.

The experts were baffled until they separated the horse from his owner by a screen, whereupon the horse suddenly lost his ability. It seems that the farmer visibly relaxed when the horse counted his way to the correct number. The horse saw the subtle cue and quit counting.

Human beings are even more suggestible. One experimenter showed a film of an auto crash and asked members of the audience to estimate its speed. Their average estimates varied from 31 mph to 41 mph depending on whether he asked if the cars "contacted," "hit" or "smashed."

• Work at listening. Average speech proceeds at 125 words a minute. Thought clips along at 500 words a minute. That means you can do a lot of mental drifting while your interview subject answers the last question. The best interviewers use that mental space as an opportunity to think about what the interviewee is saying, what it means and where the interview should turn next.

They also listen aggressively in ways that stimulate the source. They lean forward. They look into the source's eyes. They grunt and nod at appropriate times. They look so intensely interested that the source feels obligated to produce material that justifies all the attention.

What it all boils down to, in the end, is old-fashioned courtesy. Honest, interested, respectful interviewers score the biggest prizes almost every time. Hard-boiled, macho journalists who pride themselves on their cynical, tough-minded questions end up with more doors slammed in their faces than good stories. And cagey manipulators sometimes outsmart themselves.

John Brady tells the story of Harry Romanoff, of the old *Chicago Herald-Examiner,* who, according to a colleague, could "play the phone like Heifetz playing the violin."

Romy, as he was known, was famous for impersonating VIPs to pry information out of reluctant sources. After a South Side shooting, he called the switchboard at St. Bernard's Hospital, where some wounded cops had been taken. "This is the police commissioner," he said. "Connect me with one of my men there." He was patched through to the sixth floor, where a quiet voice said, "Yes?"

"This is the police commissioner," Romy repeated. "What's going on out there?"

The man at the other end gave him a detailed report. Romy was so impressed that he asked, "Who is this, anyway?"

"This is Police Commissioner Fitzmorris, Romy," said the quiet voice. "I knew you'd be calling."

CLAUDIA DREIFUS

She is the master of the Q and A, what she calls "that unique subspecialty of journalism." Dan Rather says being interviewed by her "is like playing tennis with Steffi Graf; do your best, and you'll learn a lot; anything less, and she'll pave the court with you."

Claudia Dreifus has made a career out of talking to some of the most intriguing people the world has to offer. She has interviewed cultural icons, world leaders, political dissidents, and cutting-edge scientists. Her savvy reporting and unquenchable curiosity make a Dreifus interview a revelation.

From 1981 through 1992, Dreifus was one of the regular *Playboy* interviewers. Her work has also appeared in *Ms., The Progressive, Modern Maturity,* and *The Nation*. Since 1993, her interviews have appeared regularly in *The New York Times*.

In this selection, drawn from the introduction to her 1997 book *Interview,* Dreifus addresses the magical elements of a successful interview—which she likens to an improvisational play—as well as mundane but important matters like the use of the tape recorder.

Preparation, Chemistry, and the Interview As an Act of Seduction

Some years ago, I happened to be sitting next to Ringo Starr — perhaps the wittiest and least appreciated of the Beatles—and we found ourselves chatting about his percussionist's craft. Starr believed himself to be one of the best drummers in all the rock and roll universe. Yet few pop historians agreed with him.

"It was always thought that I was in the background with those 'funny fills,' as the press used to call them," he complained sweetly. "Well, those 'funny fills' are my art! No one can play them like I do. A fill is when a drummer goes dud-dud-dud-dud, when you're filling in the gaps. I had this weird style of playing them, and it confused a lot of people. . . . Do you understand what I'm talking about?"

"Interviewing is something like drumming," I told Starr. "You stay in the background and people think you haven't done much."

"Id-jets," he returned, in perfect Liverpudlian.

More than a decade later, I found myself sharing a speeding New York taxi with a journalist of enormous reputation and accomplishment, an elegant woman in her eighties who'd witnessed firsthand some of the major events of this century. I had just begun publishing Q and A–style interviews for *The New York Times Magazine* and my work was eliciting a lot of comment.

"You know, Claudia, people wonder what it is that you actually do at the *Times,*" this legend commented, as our taxi lurched from one lane into another. "Just the other day, someone asked me, 'What's so special about asking questions and printing the answers? Anyone can do it.' "

"Oh, can they?" I asked frostily, adding: "There's a craft to those questions and answers."

"Of course there is," she allowed, not convincingly.

"Id-jet," I thought to myself.

There's something about interviewing—it may be the visual simplicity of the work, those deceptively uncomplicated Q's and A's—that results in the form being the abused and underappreciated stepchild of American journalism. Yet, for those of us who earn our daily bread as print interviewers—Studs Terkel, Lawrence Grobel, Robert Scheer, Oriana Fallaci—the interview is an elegant form, a showcase for ideas, personality and language—clean, unobtrusive, minimalist. And such fun.

"Good interviews read a little like great dramas," asserts John Wood, articles editor at *Modern Maturity,* which prints a lengthy Q and A with a different history-maker in every issue. "They have a beginning, a middle, and an end—and catharsis. In a good interview, subject and journalist are antagonists, and then come together, and it's all spontaneous."

The interviewer, in fact, creates a mini-play. The use of playwriting techniques is key to producing a readable product. Every exchange should be motivated, one line of questioning should lead to another logically, the story has to have internal integrity. In other words, there has to be a narrative to all these questions and answers. The ending ideally should have some connection to the lead. A reader hopefully should feel they've been on a journey that made sense.

I always tell myself: kid, you're writing a two-character play, and you're the minor one. The interview-subject is, of course, the lead. The interviewer is the supporting player who moves the story forward with an intelligent line of questioning. The interviewer can also be seen as the voice of the reader, making those ultra-logical queries a reader might make, were he/she in the room.

G. Barry Golson, who for twelve years as executive editor was the guiding force behind the *Playboy* Interview (and who now edits *Yahoo! Internet Life!!!*), agrees, and adds, "Instead of theater's many contributors, the Q and A depends on two people: the subject, of course, and the interviewer, who must be journalist, researcher, interrogator, actor, diplomat, playwright, editor. I always found it harder to hire good interviewers than good writers." . . .

Perhaps because it is such an intimate business, interviewing requires curiosity, empathy, a touch of charisma, and something that the Germans call *menshlichkeit*—humaneness.

But the great interviewers are also seducers. I remember Q and A–ing the Italian interviewer, Oriana Fallaci, and feeling that her skill was probably less in her well-advertised confrontations with subjects, and more in her charm—which was considerable, and burned like a Klieg on anyone in her presence.

Oriana Fallaci once told me she had loathed interviewing renowned North Vietnamese strategist General Vo Nguyen Giap in 1969—because the general out-maneuvered her. "I couldn't function as I usually do," Fallaci complained of the victor of Dien Bien Phu and Tet. "I had very little time. Then Giap, he dominated me, though we had time to make a fight. At a certain moment, we were shouting at each other. And when [Henry] Kissinger said he would see me because of that interview, I could not believe my ears. The Kissinger interview [was] even uglier . . . because it was so short, because he didn't open up. I need time to make an interview. And I need complicity. And I had neither."

Though she probably didn't mean it in the Giap context, Fallaci's comment points to one of the great secrets of the Q and A, its unspoken sexual element. Like love-making, interviewing requires attention, involvement, time—a willingness on the part of both subject and the interviewer to go with the moment.

One of my favorite interviews was with the Mexican novelist Carlos Fuentes in Chicago in February 1985. Our topic was revolution and literature in Latin America and Eastern Europe. There was a blizzard outside, so we sat around the Drake Hotel for two solid days drinking red wine and telling each other stories. The piece ultimately had the dreamy feel of a tryst, and it was that tone that carried the text along.

Here's Lawrence Grobel, one of the best in the *Playboy* stable, talking shop in *Writer's Digest:* "I sold encyclopedias for a short period of time and it probably taught me more about interviewing than anything I've ever done. . . . When you walk in, look around. See if they have paintings on the wall, something you recognize—a particular book, piece of furniture, anything you can relate to." Grobel describes coming into the room and immediately moving a piece of furniture or sitting on a certain chair that the subject hadn't intended for him. That's his way of signaling, "I'm not going to let you confine me." Grobel believes that interviews are always a power struggle between interviewer and subject. He's probably right. Every time you turn on the tape recorder, the bell sounds for another battle of wills. Who will control this encounter? Who will win this game? Lawrence Grobel has his little tricks. We all do.

I began with a degree from New York University in theater, and only later became a journalist. Originally, I'd hoped to be an actress. Or a playwright. Yet, by the time I'd finished school in 1966, the higher drama of 1960s politics overtook me and my first jobs as an adult were in the political realm—writing speeches, press releases, organizing things.

The problem was that politics interested me intellectually, but didn't suit me temperamentally. I hated the everyday lies that were endemic to the business, "the spin," as they call it now. I despised the manipulation, the falseness, the bad deeds rationalized by the dream of the good end. And so, at the age of twenty-three, I embarked on yet another career—reporting.

From the first, journalism was a great fit. As a writer, I could observe the political world, without being of it. I would witness, rather than exhort, which was fine. Like Chauncey Gardner in Jerzy Kozinski's *Being There,* I preferred "to watch."

And interviewing, that unique sub-specialty of journalism, particularly suited me. It used all I knew. Interviewing was the only area in print-reporting with a serious performance element to it. Even now, when I write up my Q's and A's, I constantly ask myself acting-type questions. Is the dialogue motivated? Does this sound real? Was I really "listening" to the interview subject?

Probably the most important decision an interviewer will have to make is in the choice of subject. This may sound terribly obvious, but I try to choose interesting people with something to say.

As such I scan the Sunday morning television news shows for signs of politicians who talk in something other than sound bites. I also read *The New York Times, The Washington Post* and more obscure publications like *World Press Review* and *Hollywood Reporter* for ideas. If I am interested in the president of Sri Lanka or the Mayor of

Ankara or Demi Moore, I might look up their clipping file on the database Nexis to see what sorts of interviews the potential subject has already given. . . .

What I look for in my subjects is an openness, a fluidity of language and honesty. With Q and A, because one has less room for interpretation, one either has to run with the piece—or kill the story. The interviewer has to be pretty certain that the subject is truthful. I once spiked a *Playboy* interview I'd spent much time on because I thought the actor in question might be using me to libel an actress he was feuding with. There was no way to prove or disprove some of his juicy assertions and I did not want to be party to anything so potentially shady.

Sometimes, my preliminary research will undo an assignment. [In the 1990s], a publication asked me to do a Q and A with ex-Watergate figure and now radio talk-show host G. Gordon Liddy. At first, I thought he might be fun. I mean, the guy is so edgy in his extremities and the fact that a former Watergate plumber is winning First Amendment awards is interesting. But when I read his autobiography, *Will,* and saw a recent *Playboy* "20 Questions" with him, I decided to bail out. To me, he seemed humorless, wooden, unreflective. The usually light and playful "20 Questions" feature dragged. I sensed this was an assignment that wouldn't work. At least not for me.

If, after a few pitches, a potential subject is truly and totally negative about an interview, I'll drop my pursuit of them. No point. If someone is going to act like you're dragging them to the Spanish Inquisition, they won't help you create the kind of material that will read well.

On the other hand, here's former *Playboy* editor Murray Fischer in *Alex Haley: The* Playboy *Interviews* describing how Alex Haley got Dr. Martin Luther King to sit down for a 1965 *Playboy* interview: "After a frustrating series of cancellations and three trips to Atlanta, he still hadn't met the man, and most interviewers would have given up. But Alex had taken pains to befriend King's secretary, and he finally threw himself on her mercy. He couldn't face his editor empty-handed again, he told her[,] and she sent him to a church barbeque King was attending. 'Let him see you there, but don't press,' she advised. He did what he was told, sitting there with a plate of chicken and potato salad till King finally took pity on him and came over to say hello, suggesting that they might talk for a few minutes over in his office. Their little chat stretched late into the night."

The second most important decision an interviewer must make is to commit to preparation. You should go into a session as prepared as any trial lawyer before a jury. Thus the interviewer should know the answer to any question he or she might ask, or at least have a vague idea of what the answer might be and have alternative follow-up strategies ready.

At the same time, the interviewer must be willing to be astonished. It is useful to come in with a line of questions and a rehearsed plan but it is important not to hold rigidly to it. If this is a play, it is an improvisational one. And just like in acting, the interviewer must be able to listen, to go with what is heard, to change course mid-interview.

Whether or not the interview will succeed will very much depend on the chemistry between the subject and the interviewer. That, in turn, depends on the level of preparation. An actor needs to know his lines, understand the motivation of his and the other characters. An interviewer needs to know all that is possible about the interviewee—through Nexis, books, clips, interviews with friends and relatives—before he or she ever turns on the tape recorder. Whenever I feel anxious about a particular interview, I combat my fears with aerobic research.

Even the toughest subjects will respond warmly to a well-prepared interviewer. The fact that I have confidence in my material makes me a strong questioner. Interviewing can be a bit like an intellectual boxing match. One had better enter the ring in top shape. As Oriana Fallaci, a more combative practitioner than I, once told me about her state of mind when she begins interviewing, "My insides are the insides of a soldier who begins to storm a hill."

Fallaci fights her fear with aggression. I control mine with tenacity and preparation.

Of course, the actual interview—the face to face—is the really vital part of the process. If the journalist doesn't get good material on tape, there's little that can be done to improve the story later on. As in documentary filmmaking, "If you don't have it on film, you don't have it."

Now, not all journalists think highly of tape recorders. Gay Talese, in his preface to *The Norton Book of Interviews,* rails against interviewers using the machine. "A tape recorder is to fine interviewing what fast food is to fine cooking," he suggests. "It permits the journalist to spend a minimum amount of time with the subject while following the question and answer path that leads to the undistinguished kind of article-writing that prevails today. The plastic rolls of tape record the first-draft drift of people's responses, and I think it has inspired laziness on the part of young journalists, and deafened them to the subtle nuances inherent in all exchanges between communicating people. What is being lost, in my opinion, is the art of listening . . ."

Gay Talese may be a nonfiction genius, but he's wrong on this. The very thing the tape recorder permits a journalist to do is listen. There are no taking-notes type distractions, no pens to run out of ink. Just you and the subject, interacting. I think this enhances listening. Now, there are journalists who are just lunkheaded and don't know how to listen, but that's not the technology's fault.

What is the technology's fault is how unreliable, regardless of price, most tape recorders have become. There was a time when I'd buy a machine and it would last two years. Two months now is lucky. I always bring two to an interview, just in case one fails, and frankly, one usually does. I've solved the tinny machine problem by buying my equipment with a service contract from Radio Shack—when the machine breaks down after five or fifty uses, I take it to the mall in whatever town I'm in and trade it in for a free new one. I always go into interviews with fresh, fresh batteries and pre-tested tape.

(One final note on mundane matters: I use ninety-minute premium brand tapes. That's because the interviewer wants long tapes, but the two-hour kind tears too easily. Anything less than the ninety-minute kind gives your subject too many breaks in the Q and A, too many opportunities to get off track.)

The first question an interviewer puts forward is key to the success of the interview. I spend hours developing my lead question. (Dan Rather once spent a whole month constructing a really good one for Richard Nixon.) It sets the mood. It also shows the subject, right off, that I've spent a great deal of time thinking about them, trying to understand what they do. And subjects, unless they are total fools, will respect a reporter for doing her homework.

I try to transcribe the tapes myself. Besides reminding me of what actually happened and giving me a sense of the tempo of the language, this allows me to feel the material. Call it Method Writing. I need it. And I'm not alone. Gabriel García Márquez told me during our 1982 *Playboy* interview that when he was writing *The Autumn of the Patriarch,* he returned to his native Colombia because he required "the smell of the guavas" to create his novel.

If you've prepared for and conducted the interview properly, the actual writing of it should sing.

Of course, I scan my raw material for a story line, a theme. . . .

Once the theme is clear, I hang the assembled material on the skeleton of the piece, bit by bit, till it is shaped. My first drafts are broad, long. With each draft, I whittle the material down further. At the end of the process, I read the story out loud, to see if the voices sound conversational, to check that it all sounds plausible.

Beyond these obvious pointers, the rest of what happens in a session is art, magic, and chemistry. I'd be an "id-jet" if I tried to quantify it.

BOB WOODWARD AND CARL BERNSTEIN

Bob Woodward was in his first year as a reporter at *The Washington Post,* working the night police beat, when he helped uncover the Watergate scandal. His reporting, along with that of colleague Carl Bernstein, would eventually lead to the indictment of forty government officials and the resignation of President Richard Nixon.

The Watergate story captured the Pulitzer Prize in 1973. A movie was made of Woodward and Bernstein's 1974 book, *All the President's Men.* In 1976 they published *The Final Days,* which chronicled the last days of the Nixon presidency.

Bob Woodward remains at the *Post,* where he is assistant managing editor. He has written or cowritten nine books, including *The Choice,* which profiles Bill Clinton and Bob Dole; *The Agenda,* about the early days of the Clinton-Gore presidency; and *The Brethren: Inside the Supreme Court.*

Carl Bernstein left the *Post* in 1976. He was Washington bureau chief and senior correspondent for ABC News for four years. He also worked briefly for *Time.* He dabbled in Web-based media as executive vice president and executive editor of Voter.com, until the company folded in February 2001. He is a contributing editor at *Vanity Fair.*

The names Woodward and Bernstein will forever be synonymous with investigative reporting. The identity of their famous anonymous source, dubbed Deep Throat, has never been revealed. This excerpt from *All the President's Men* deals with another source, known only as The Bookkeeper. Woodward and Bernstein had learned that a secret slush fund was used to finance the break-in and espionage at the Democratic National Committee headquarters in the Watergate building. In this passage, Bernstein uses several techniques to get his foot in the door and get a reluctant source to talk. The information he pries from The Bookkeeper will prove invaluable.

Sipping Coffee, Slowly

On the evening of September 14, Bernstein knocked at the front door of a small tract house in the Washington suburbs. Ever since he had lunched with the woman from CRP [Committee to Re-elect the President], he had had a feeling that the owner of this house was the person who had gone back to the prosecutors. He had asked around. "She knows a lot," he was told. The woman worked for Maurice Stans.

A woman opened the door and let Bernstein in. "You don't want me, you want my sister," she said. Her sister came into the room. He had expected a woman in her fifties, probably gray; it was his image of a bookkeeper, which is what she was. But she was much younger.

"Oh, my God," the Bookkeeper said, "you're from *The Washington Post*. You'll have to go, I'm sorry."

Bernstein started figuring ways to hold his ground. The sister was smoking and he noticed a pack of cigarettes on the dinette table; he asked for one. "I'll get it," he said as the sister moved to get the pack, "don't bother." That got him 10 feet into the house. He bluffed, telling the Bookkeeper that he understood her being afraid; there were a lot of people like her at the committee who wanted to tell the truth, but some people didn't want to listen. He knew that certain people had gone back to the FBI and the prosecutors to give more information. . . . He hesitated.

"Where do you reporters get your information anyhow?" she asked. "That's what nobody at the committee can figure out."

Bernstein asked if he could sit down and finish his cigarette.

"Yes, but then you'll have to go, I really have nothing to say." She was drinking coffee, and her sister asked if Bernstein would like some. The Bookkeeper winced, but it was too late. Bernstein started sipping, slowly.

She was curious. "Somebody is certainly giving you good information if you knew I went back to the prosecutors." Then she rattled off a few names that Bernstein tried to keep in his head; if she was mentioning them as possible sources, they must be people who either had some information or were unhappy with the way things were going down at the committee.

He went into a monologue about all the fine people he and Woodward had met who wanted to help but didn't have hard information, only what they had picked up third and fourth hand.

"You guys keep digging," she said. "You've really struck close to home."

How did she know?

"I ran the totals for the people. I have an adding machine and a deft hand." The way she said it was almost mocking, as if she knew she had been watching *Naked City* too much. She shook her head and laughed at herself. "Sometimes I don't know whether to laugh or cry. I'm an accountant. I'm apolitical. I didn't do anything wrong. But in some way, something is rotten in Denmark and I'm part of it." Then she started guessing sources again and Bernstein tried to keep the names straight in his head. She was glancing at his coffee cup. He tried not to look tense, and played with her dog. She seemed to want to talk about what she knew. But to *The Washington Post,* the enemy? Bernstein had the feeling he was either going out the door any minute or staying till she had told the whole story.

"My only loyalties are to Maurice Stans, the President's re-election and the truth," she said.

Bernstein had heard that Stans' wife was sick and in the hospital. He asked how Mrs. Stans was, and then inquired if the Secretary was going to end up a fall guy for John Mitchell.

"If you could get John Mitchell, it would be beautiful. But I just don't have any real evidence that would stand up in court that he knew. Maybe his guys got carried away, the men close to him."

What guys?

Her hands were shaking. She looked at her sister, who shrugged her shoulders noncommittally. Bernstein thought he had an ally there. The sister got up to get another cup of coffee. He took a gulp and handed his cup to her. She refilled it. Bernstein decided to take a chance. He removed a notebook and pencil from his inner breast pocket. The Bookkeeper stared at him. She was not going to say anything that they probably didn't know already, Bernstein told her, and absolutely nothing would go into the paper that couldn't be verified elsewhere.

"There are a lot of things that are wrong and a lot of things that are bad at the committee," the Bookkeeper said. "I was called by the grand jury very early, but nobody knew what questions to ask. People had already lied to them."

Sally Harmony?

"She and I have not discussed it. . . . But Sally—and others—lied." The Bookkeeper had worked for Hugh Sloan, and after he quit, she was promoted to work for Stans. "There were a few of us they were worried about who got promotions.

"Sloan is the sacrificial lamb. His wife was going to leave him if he didn't stand up and do what was right. He left because he saw it and didn't want any part of it. We didn't know before June 17, but we put two and two together on June 19 and figured it out."

She changed the subject. A few days earlier, the *Post* had reported that there was another participant in the bugging whose identity had not been disclosed; and that he had been granted immunity from prosecution and was talking.

The Bookkeeper started to speculate out loud: "Baldwin? He wasn't even on the payroll."

She tried two other names.

Bernstein shook his head. (He had no idea who it was.)

"It has to be one of those three," she said. "I'm pretty sure it's Baldwin."

Bernstein asked if she knew who had received transcripts of wiretapped conversations.

"I don't know anything about how the operational end of the espionage worked," she said. "I just know who got the money and who approved the allocations. And from what I can see, you've got all the names. Track a little upstairs and out of the finance committee," she advised. "It was the political people. . . . It won't make any difference. You've got to get the law on your side if anything is going to be done. The indictments are going to get the seven and that's it. The power of the politicians is too strong."

How many people were paid?

"Thirteen or fourteen from the fund, but only six or seven are involved. The grand jury didn't even ask if there were any payments that were extra-legal."

Did Stans know who received such payments?

"He knew less than I knew. My loyalty is to Hugh and Mr. Stans," she stressed. "For some reason, Mr. Stans feels we have to take the heat for a while." She had talked to Sloan that morning and he had mentioned a story in the New York *Daily News* that gave the impression that Sloan knew of the bugging operation. "I told him he should sue, but all he said was 'I want out.' The grand jury didn't ask him the right questions either, I guess."

Who knew all the answers to the right questions?

"Liddy and Sally Harmony. She has more information than I have. But she has never talked to me about what she knows. I urged her time and time again to do what's right. Sally got promoted, too." She was now working for Robert Odle.

Was Odle involved?

"Certainly not in knowing anything about the bugging. He's a glorified office boy, Magruder's runner. Jeb's definitely involved, of course. It was all done on the political side, that's common knowledge. All the people involved are with the political committee, not finance." But she wouldn't say who, beyond Magruder. Magruder was CRP's second-in-command. Bernstein started guessing, picking names that he remembered from the GAO list. Lang Washburn? He had forgotten that Washburn was in finance, not on the political side.

"Are you kidding? Lang's so dumb that the Monday after the bugging he called everybody in finance together to say that we had nothing to do with it. And then he asked Gordon to say a few words to the kids. At which point Gordon Liddy got up and made a speech about how this one bad apple, McCord, shouldn't be allowed to spoil the whole barrel."

Bernstein asked the sister for another cup of coffee and tried another name.

"Never. The White House got him out because he didn't like to do all the crazy things they wanted."

Who?

"Right under Mitchell," the Bookkeeper suggested.

Bernstein tried LaRue and Porter. She didn't respond. He tried again.

Silence.

What evidence did she have that Mitchell's assistants were involved?

"I had the evidence, but all the records were destroyed. . . . I don't know who destroyed them, but I'm sure Gordon did some shredding."

Was it hard evidence?

"It wouldn't positively say they planned the bugging; it wouldn't necessarily implicate them with this, but it would come pretty close."

How could she tell it linked them to the bugging?

"There was a special account before April 7. Back then, they were just expenditures as far as I was concerned; I didn't have any idea then what it was all about. But after June 17 you didn't have to be any genius to figure it out. I'd seen the figures and I'd seen all the people. And there were no receipts." Liddy was among those who received the money, she said. "Gordon's a case of loyalty to the President. He'll never crack. He'll take the whole rap."

The Bookkeeper was looking at Bernstein's coffee cup again, having second thoughts. "There are too many people watching me," she said. "They know I'm privy and they watch me like a hawk." She was convinced her phones were tapped.

How much money was paid out?

"A lot."

More than half a million?

"You've had it in print."

Finally it clicked. Sometimes he could be incredibly slow, Bernstein thought to himself. It was the slush fund of cash kept in Stans' safe.

"I never knew it was a 'security fund' or whatever they called it," she said, "until after June 17. I just thought it was an all-purpose political fund that you didn't talk about—like to take fat cats to dinner, but all strictly legal."

$350,000 in dinners? How was it paid out?

"Not in one chunk. I know what happened to it, I added up the figures." There had been a single sheet of paper on which the account was kept; it had been destroyed, the only record. "It was a lined sheet with names on about half the sheet, about fifteen names with the amount distributed to each person next to the name. I saw it more than once. The amounts kept getting bigger." She had updated the sheet each time a disbursement was made. Sloan knew the whole story too. He had handed out the money.

Bernstein asked about the names again. He was confused because there were about 15 names on the sheet, yet she thought only six were involved. Which six?

"Go down the GAO report; I think they've all been before the grand jury. They're easy to isolate; a couple have been named in the press but not necessarily in connection with this."

How were the funds allocated?

Telephone calls had something to do with how the money was doled out. Only three of the six had actually received money. "The involvement of the others includes answering some telephone calls," she stated.

Who were the six? he asked again.

"Mitchell's principal assistants. . . . the top echelon. Magruder is one."

He started throwing out more names. No use. He tried initials: if she told him their initials, she could truthfully say that she had never given Bernstein the names, and he would at least be able to narrow down the candidates. Early in the conversation, she had not answered when he had asked if LaRue and Porter were involved. He tried L.

"L and M and P, and that's all I'm going to give you," the Bookkeeper said.

Chapter 4

WRITING

What makes good writing? What makes a scene vibrant, a portrait evocative, an event unforgettable? Good writing is not magic, but it can feel magical. By mastering specific disciplines a writer can turn dry prose into living images.

In this chapter, a group of seasoned journalists describe techniques for writing well. Ken Fuson urges journalists to select details not simply because they add "color" but because they reveal meaning. Christopher Scanlan offers strategies for writing on deadline, and Paula LaRocque highlights the connection between good thinking and good writing.

John Hersey's celebrated essay on New Journalism, published in 1980, remains one of the profession's most illuminating pieces about writing creative nonfiction. Stressing the importance of accuracy, Hersey makes the impressive argument that even the most sterling prose cannot compensate for inaccurate reporting or the sin of deception. Finally, Donald Murray's essay pays tribute to one of the writer's most valuable allies: a perceptive and sensitive editor.

KEN FUSON

Here's what Ken Fuson of *The Des Moines Register* says about the kind of journalism that matters to him most: "We give people the facts—that's our job—but we don't always look as hard as we might to discover the joys and dreams and tiny triumphs of our neighbors. And so the world we portray in our pages often feels cold and mean and full of despair. . . . But if you look, you can still find . . . stories that give readers something important—a small sense of hope."

Stories that celebrate the human spirit have been a Fuson specialty for more than twenty-five years. At the *Register,* his stories won the 2001 Ernie Pyle Award for human-interest writing and the 1996 National Headliner Award for feature writing. At *The Baltimore Sun*, where he worked for three years, Fuson's rite-of-passage story about the making of a high-school musical, *A Stage in Their Lives,* won the ASNE award for nondeadline writing in 1998. He has written for *GQ* and *Esquire,* and his profile of quarter-back Brett Favre was chosen for the *Best American Sports Writing* anthology.

Fuson is a generous writer whose speeches at writing workshops are standing room only. He is modest and funny, but it is obvious that he thinks deeply about his craft. This selection comes from a talk Fuson delivered in October 2001 at The Poynter Institute for Media Studies, where he frequently serves on the visiting faculty. With his inimitable style and humor, Fuson runs down the advice he gleaned from his favorite writing "coaches"—including that master of the language, Yogi Berra.

What Would Yogi Do?

Here's the scouting report on my starting lineup of writing gurus:

1. William Strunk Jr. and E. B. White (*The Elements of Style*)
   Slender, no wasted motion, surprising power.
2. Jon Franklin (*Writing for Story*)
   Gives structure to the batting order.
3. William Zinsser (*On Writing Well*)
   The wily veteran still comes through.

4. Gary Smith (*Beyond the Game: The Collected Sportswriting of Gary Smith*)
   Every story a grand slam.
5. James J. Kilpatrick (*The Writer's Art*)
   Graceful and rock-solid; sure hands.
6. Susan Orlean (*The Bullfighter Checks Her Makeup: My Encounters with Extraordinary People*)
   So good, she makes it look easy.
7. William E. Blundell (*The Art and Craft of Feature Writing*)
   Has all the tools.
8. Walt Harrington (*Intimate Journalism*)
   Blessed with a deeper feel for the game.
9. William Ruehlmann (*Stalking the Feature Story*)
   Out of print, but can pitch with the best.

And my designated hitter:

10. Yogi Berra (New York Yankees)

The Hall of Fame catcher and Coors pitchman rarely gets his due as a writing coach, but a quick review of his verbal oeuvre (courtesy of *The Yogi Book*) reveals a man whose genius extends far beyond baseball.

• *What Yogi said:* "It's déjà vu all over again!"

Interpretation: Every story—well, most—has been done before. If you can't find a new one, strive to put your personal stamp on each story you cover. Roy Peter Clark of The Poynter Institute teaches a workshop in which he plays the piano and explains the relationship between music and writing. He makes the point that many of the songs that we associate with one singer (for example, Aretha Franklin's "Respect") were first recorded by another artist. Aretha took ownership of it.

In *The Good Times,* Russell Baker tells the story of Patrick Skene Catling, who leapfrogged over Baker for a promotion at *The Baltimore Sun*. Baker was outraged that Catling had been assigned to review the musical "*Oklahoma!*—and then I started to read, and outrage turned to wonder."

Baker writes: "His *Oklahoma!* review left me with an important lesson about newspaper writing which I tucked away in my head for the day when my luck might change: Don't settle for writing it the way it's always been written; dare to write it differently, and maybe you will write it better than it's been written before."

Remember Russell Baker the next time you're assigned to cover a spelling bee, the first day of school, or my personal favorite, the day-after-Thanksgiving shopping-spree story.

• *What Yogi said:* "You can observe a lot by watching."

Interpretation: The best advice I ever read about the power of watching came from James J. Kilpatrick in *The Writer's Art:* "This is the first secret of good writing: We must look *intently,* and hear *intently,* and taste *intently.* . . . We must look at everything *very hard.* Is it the task at hand to describe a snowfall? Very well. We begin by observing that the snow is white. Is it as white as bond paper? White as whipped cream? Is the snow daisy white, or eggwhite white, or whitewash white? Let us look very hard. We will see that snow comes in different textures. The light snow that looks like powdered sugar is not the heavy snow that clings like wet cotton. When we write matter-of-factly that *Last night it snowed and this morning the fields were white,* we haven't said much. We have not looked *intently.*"

Susan Orlean of *The New Yorker* supplied us with a one-paragraph demonstration of how the ability to observe, combined with a sense of rhythm, can produce music. This is from her story about a gospel-singing group (reprinted in *The Bullfighter Checks Her Makeup*). Read it to yourself, then read it aloud:

> I heard people at gospel concerts call eyeglasses "helpers" and a gravel road "a dirty road," and I heard an infant called "a lap baby," and a gun called "a persuader," and dying called "making it over," and an embarrassed person described as "wanting to swallow his teeth," and a dead person described as someone who was "having his mail delivered to him by groundhogs." Everybody talked about Jesus all the time. He was called a doctor, a lawyer, a lily of the valley, a lamb, a shepherd, joy in the morning, a rock, a road, peace in the evening, a builder, a captain, a rose of Sharon, a friend, a father, and someone who is always on time. I met a man named Porkchop and a man named Midget and a little boy named Royriquez Clarencezellus Wooten. I heard other gospel groups perform: the Christian Harmonizers and the Sensational Harmonizers and the Harmonettes and the Religiousettes and the Gloryettes and the Gospel True Lights and the True Gospel Singers and the Five Singing Sons and the Mighty Sons of Glory and the Fantastic Disciples and the Fantastic Soulernaires and the Fantastic Violinaires and the Sunset Jubilaires and the Pilgrim Jubilees and

> the Brown Boys and the Five Blind Boys and Wonder Boy and the Spiritual Voices. The concerts were like big public conversations. The exhortations that people called out to the singers most often were "Take you time!" and "Let Him *use* you!" The exhortations that Huey and Roger called out most often were "Do you believe in Jesus?" and "Can I get just one witness?" and "Are you with me, church?" and "You know, God is *able*."

As Yogi himself might say, she got all of that one.

• *What Yogi said:* "Nobody goes there anymore. It's too crowded."

Interpretation: Figure out which way the herd is headed—then go in the opposite direction. Chip Scanlan at Poynter mentions the famous example of how, when President Kennedy was assassinated, Jimmy Breslin interviewed the man who dug the slain president's grave. My guess is that Breslin, from the instant he arrived in Washington, D.C., set out to find the one story that nobody else had. That's one of the reasons his story still lives almost four decades later.

Why is it that Rick Bragg of *The New York Times* ("Somebody Told Me") can be sent to the megastories—the Oklahoma City bombing, the trial of Susan Smith, the schoolyard shooting in Jonesboro, Ark.—and always find the scenes and details that seem to elude others?

Because he veers away from the safety of the herd and actively looks for them.

When Dale Earnhardt, the stock-car legend, was killed . . . , Bragg joined the many reporters who went to Mooresville, N.C., Earnhardt's hometown. But Bragg found the perfect spot to explore the impact of this particular man. Here is his lead:

> His death brought a silence to the Wal-Mart.
>
> They heard it first in the electronics department, where, it being Sunday, the TVs were tuned to news of the Daytona 500. A pall, a sense of disbelief, spread through racks of Dale Earnhardt T-shirts, Earnhardt racing jackets and Earnhardt seat cushions, through the toy section with its stacks of Earnhardt "No. 3" model cars.
>
> Earnhardt, who lived just down the road from this town some 20 miles north of Charlotte, had hit the wall at Daytona, and been killed at age 49.
>
> After a moment, the silence broke. Women shrieked, and men cried.
>
> Then, slowly, they moved to the Earnhardt clothes and toys, and began to buy them all. By Monday, all that was left was a stack of seat cushions and one last box of toy cars. Acie Ellerbe,

assistant manager, tried to explain: Earnhardt was racing's Michael Jordan, a hero to the people here. . . .

Before Mr. Ellerbe could finish his sentence, the last toy car was gone.

Tip: If there's a television camera within 100 yards of you, somebody else out there is getting a better story.

• *What Yogi said:* "When you come to a fork in the road, take it."

Interpretation: Action always trumps inertia.

Write the sentence (if it stinks, you can fix it later). Do the story you've always wanted to do. Reach beyond your comfort zone to find the stories of people who are different than you. Ask the question that most scares you.

Tom Junod, the prize-winning *Esquire* writer, says most reporters eventually have to deal with the locked door—for example, the question that makes everyone uncomfortable, or the scene you would rather not witness, or the interview you would prefer to skip. The more locked doors you open, the better your story will be, he says.

A personal example: Many years ago, for a series about devotion, I wrote about a young couple that had been involved in a serious car accident on their wedding night. The wife was slightly injured, but the husband was paralyzed from the waist down. This was a long story, and I explored many sensitive aspects of their relationship, but I did not have enough courage to ask a critical question: Could these newlyweds still make love? I was too timid. As a result, the story wasn't as good, or as complete, as it should have been.

Unlock the door. It's always worth it.

• *What Yogi said:* "If you can't imitate him, don't copy him."

Interpretation: Please, Lord, just this once, let me write a sentence worthy of Tom Wolfe. Let my story flow like a Gary Smith profile, let me build suspense like Tom French, let me find the perfect details the way David Finkel and Tom Hallman always do. (While you're at it, Lord, change my first name to "Tom.")

Please, just one time, give me the intelligence of Malcolm Gladwell, the cleverness of Joel Achenbach, the craftsmanship of William Nack.

Let me see like Lisa Pollak and hear like Susan Orlean and write like Anne Hull. All I want is what John Hersey got when he wrote *Hiroshima*—the entire issue of *The New Yorker* devoted to my story, sold-out newsstands and a decision by the Book-of-the-Month Club to give the book to every customer, with this explanation: "We find it hard to conceive of anything being written that could be of more importance at this moment to the human race."

Doesn't usually turn out that way, does it? You can, and should, study the masters. Learn from them. Be inspired by them. But, as Popeye said, *I y'am what I y'am.* Your writing should reflect your own unique experiences and observations—what makes you you. Young writers often ask how they can develop their own voice or writing style. The answer is, by seeing and describing life as they alone experience it. Rick Reilly of *Sports Illustrated* says he never tries to use a description he has heard before. This is a worthy goal for all of us, and one of the reasons Reilly's columns always read so fresh and original.

• *What Yogi said:* "I really didn't say everything I said."

Interpretation: One of the scary truths about our business is that misinterpretations can happen and errors can be made, even when the reporter is diligent and the source is cooperative. Some reporters read passages to sources, particularly in sensitive stories (other reporters, especially the investigative types, consider this sacrilegious, so make sure you know the guidelines at your newspaper).

The point is: Are you sure? Is that what the person really meant? Did I hear them right?

Learn how to listen actively. Stephen R. Covey, in *The Seven Habits of Highly Effective People,* offers this tip: "Seek first to understand, then to be understood." Reporters who tape-record their interviews often are shocked at how often they interrupt sources.

Keeping quiet is a reporting tool, like looking up property records, that we can master with practice.

Listening with an open mind is just as important. Victor Merina, a teaching fellow at the University of California at Berkeley, conducts a workshop for journalists in which he shows how even the most careful reporters can make false assumptions about people based on race, fashion or surroundings. In one workshop, he asked reporters to describe him. They were wrong about everything from his ethnicity to the contents of his shirt pocket (business cards, not a cigarette pack). Be ever-vigilant. Never assume.

Our friend Yogi knew how frustrating it could be communicating his thoughts. As he told one reporter: "I wish I had an answer to that, because I'm tired of answering that question."

• *What Yogi said:* "It ain't over 'til it's over!"

Interpretation: Save something for the ending. Give the reader a treat for sticking with you (I'd like to attach a toll-free number at the end of my stories: *If you've gotten this far, call 1-800-GRACIAS for a free coffee cup*).

Reporters treat endings differently. In Jon Franklin's conflict-resolution story structure, the ending supplies the resolution of the conflict that was established earlier. I always know what my ending is before I begin writing—it gives me a destination.

Gary Smith, on the other hand, says he discovers the story's ending during the writing process. Do what works for you, but do it deliberately. Study the writers you admire. All of them, I'm certain, think as much about endings as beginnings.

Yogi did, too. Here's another quote: "You've got to be careful if you don't know where you're going 'cause you might not get there!"

• *What Yogi said:* "Slump? I ain't in no slump. . . . I just ain't hitting."

Interpretation: None. Just thought this might be a good line to dust off at your next job review.

CHRISTOPHER SCANLAN

As a former reporter and now a faculty member at The Poynter Institute, Christopher Scanlan has had both firsthand experience as a storyteller operating under deadline pressure and the benefit of studying the work of others. Before joining Poynter, he was a national correspondent in the Knight-Ridder Newspapers Washington bureau, a feature writer at the *St. Petersburg Times,* and a reporter at *The Providence Journal.* He is the author of *Reporting and Writing: Basics for the Twenty-first Century.* He edited the *Best Newspaper Writing* series for seven years and is coeditor of the collection *America's Best Newspaper Writing.*

In this selection, taken from *Best Newspaper Writing 1994,* Scanlan describes the difference between articles and stories and champions the use of narrative techniques not just in long projects but in everyday assignments.

Storytelling on Deadline

Twenty-two years ago, I was the police, fire, library board, and conservation commission reporter at the *Milford Citizen,* a small daily newspaper in a Connecticut suburb. This was my first newspaper job. I was 22 years old.

One weekend, I was sent to cover a drowning at a park outside town. It was a summer Sunday and the park was crowded with families who had come to escape the heat and frolic in the cool water of the lake.

There was no one in the water when I arrived, except for a Fire Department rowboat moving slowly across the smooth brown surface. Beneath the water, divers searched for the body of a teenage boy who had disappeared.

On the banks, families stood around, talking in hushed tones, all their games and Frisbee throwing halted by the accident. Even the children played quietly in the dirt, as if they too were mindful of the tragedy unfolding before them. Off to one side, by the cluster of police cars and emergency vehicles, the boy's family waited.

It took about an hour for the divers to find the boy on the lake floor. A diver surfaced and signaled to the men in the boat and then, suddenly, the boy's head and shoulders broke through the water.

I don't remember many details from that day, but the image of that dead boy is as clear as if I were still standing on the bank watching the rescuers carry his body onto the grassy shore. He was naked except for the long, sodden blue jeans he wore swimming. His chest was muscular and hairless and deathly white. He appeared to be sleeping. I scribbled observations in my notepad.

The boy's mother, a middle-aged woman who had waited, slack-jawed, chain-smoking, leaned on the hood of a police car now and beat a tattoo in the dust with her feet, an angry, futile rhythm.

I followed the rescue procession out of the park.

Back in the empty newsroom, I struggled for several hours to write a story for the next day's paper. This was in the days before word processors, and my desk sat beside a black Associated Press ticker. I was full of the experience, the images, the feelings, but I sat at my typewriter unable to get them onto the page.

I wrote lead after lead. I tried to describe the bitter staccato the boy's mother beat in the ground. Nothing satisfied me, and I ripped the abortive attempts out of the machine. The pile of crumpled copy paper grew in the wastebasket at my feet.

Eventually, I gave up. I surrendered to the wire service standard that clattered incessantly over that machine next to me. I don't have the clip, but I'm sure it came out something like this: "A 17-year-old Milford youth drowned yesterday at Lake . . . ."

I've never forgotten that experience because there was a story to tell that day and I didn't know how to tell it. I didn't have the tools.

Ten years later, two of us at *The Providence Journal* shared an assignment to write a front-page daily news feature. It had to be on the news, it had to be 20 inches long, and it had to be done by 8 p.m. We soon gave our new job a name: the "heart attack beat."

At the time, it seemed like the perfect name for a punishing assignment, but when I look back on the highlights of two decades in journalism, along with the lengthy takeouts and multi-part series that consumed weeks, months, and even years of my life, I keep coming back to a handful of stories I wrote during that year.

They are stories that haunt me to this day, because I think they embody the essence of the storyteller's craft: They convey important truths about what it means to be alive, and also because I know I did what at the time I thought was impossible—I reported and wrote them in a single day.

Learning to write well with the clock ticking may be the most important challenge that today's journalists face.

Unfortunately, in too many newsrooms, storytelling has become the exclusive province of the feature or project writer who is given space and time denied to other writers. Good writers, those who care about the craft and want to get better at it, chafe at the restrictions of daily deadlines.

They don't have enough time, they say, to gather the material they need—the telling quotes, the revealing detail, the senses of people, place, time, and drama—to write a story rather than an article.

Getting enough narrative information and being able to focus, organize, draft, and revise it into a story, all in the space of a working day, has to be one of the toughest high-wire acts of the news business.

But those are the kinds of stories I want to read in my paper. They are the stories I want to read aloud to my wife and daughters and clip and save for myself, stories that have the immediacy of life.

I've come to understand that what made the difference between the frustrations of my first newspaper job and the success, if not ease, that I enjoyed writing deadline news features a decade later, were a number of tools and strategies for reporting and writing the news. Some emerged in the crucible that is the deadline experience. Others came from insightful reporters, editors, writing coaches, and teachers, either through the good fortune of personal contacts in Providence, at The Poynter Institute for Media Studies and the *St. Petersburg Times*, and the Washington bureau of Knight-Ridder Newspapers.

Stories in the News

The police brief that Joel Rawson, my editor at *The Providence Journal,* handed me one Monday morning was only a couple of paragraphs long, but there seemed no doubt there was a story there. Over the weekend, an Amtrak train struck a teenage girl walking on the tracks. Local police credited a teenage boy with giving first aid that saved the victim's life.

Within minutes, a photographer and I were on our way. "From Jon to Lani, the Gift of Life," my 800-word account of the coming together of two very different teenagers, appeared on the front page the next day.

Newspapers are full of stories waiting to be told. Police briefs, classified ads, obituaries, the last two paragraphs of a city council brief; all may hold the promise of a dramatic story. Mine the paper, as Steve Lovelady of *The Philadelphia Inquirer* has been preaching for years.

The newspaper is just one fountain of ideas. Traditionally, the story was the "news," the event or development considered significant and worthy of attention. The challenge for today's journalists is to go beyond bureaucracy, beyond meetings, and to write stories that reveal the "joys and costs of being human," as Joel Rawson described it to his reporters.

- Examine how the "news" affects people's lives: a burglary, a bankruptcy, marriage, death, accidents. "The point is to stress the importance of getting true stories in the paper," says Jack Hart, writing coach at the Portland *Oregonian*. "Human dramas that go beyond the reports we usually run."
- Find the extraordinary in the ordinary stuff of life: graduations, reunions, burials, buying a car, putting Mom in a nursing home, or the day Dad comes to live with his children.
- Change your point of view. Not your opinion, but rather the spot from which you see the story. Write the council story through the eyes of the Asian who asks for better police protection in his neighborhood. Tell the story of the foiled suicide attempt through the cop who talked the jumper down.

After John F. Kennedy's assassination, Jimmy Breslin interviewed Clifton Pollard, the worker who dug the dead President's grave at Arlington National Cemetery. "One of the last to serve John Fitzgerald Kennedy, who was the 35th President of this country, was a working man who earns $3.01 an hour and said it was an honor to dig the grave." From that perspective, Breslin produced a haunting column that conveyed the nation's loss more poignantly than reams of eulogies from the high and mighty.

> At the bottom of the hill in front of the Tomb of the Unknown Soldier, Pollard started digging. Leaves covered the grass. . . . When the bucket came up with its first scoop of dirt, Metzler, the cemetery superintendent, walked over and looked at it.
>
> "That's nice soil," Metzler said.
>
> "I'd like to save a little of it," Pollard said. "The machine made some tracks in the grass over here and I'd like to sort of fill them in and get some good grass growing there. I'd like to have everything, you know, nice."

Report for Story

We don't write with words, writing coach Don Murray says. We write with specific, accurate information. When Joel Rawson assigned

Berkley Hudson and me to the daily news feature beat at *The Providence Journal,* he challenged us to bring back the sights and sounds of our city and state, not just who, what, when, where, and why, but how.

How did it look?

What sounds echoed?

What scents lingered in the air?

Why did people care?

• Get out of the office. Storytellers aren't tied to their desks. They are out in the streets. They're the reporters who show up before the news conference and hang around after it's over, the ones who interview the victim two weeks after the shooting. They know that stories don't end after the arrest or the election.

When Francis X. Clines was writing the About New York column for *The New York Times*, there were days he didn't know what he was going to write about. But, he said, if he could just go somewhere, he knew he'd be okay. "Reporters always want to witness when they write," Clines said after he won the ASNE award for deadline writing in 1989. "And when you do witness, then you know there's no way the story won't be interesting."

"You can't win the deadline writing contest unless you are where the story is," *Concord Monitor* editor Mike Pride noted when the ASNE judges gave the top deadline writing award to Colin Nickerson of *The Boston Globe* for his Gulf War dispatches in 1992.

• Look for revealing details that put people on the page. "In a good story," says David Finkel of *The Washington Post,* "a paranoid schizophrenic doesn't just hear imaginary voices, he hears them say, 'Go kill a policeman,' and 'You can't tell Aretha Franklin how to sing a song.'"

• Use the five senses in your reporting and a few others: sense of place, senses of people, sense of time, sense of drama. As a rookie reporter, I failed to adequately report the story of that teenager's drowning. Instead of standing there as a passive observer, I should have roamed the park, interviewing, eavesdropping. Approaching the family could have netted important details about the missing boy.

• Write while you're reporting. Listen for quotes, find details, uncover information that you know will be in the story. Reporting my story about the girl whose leg was cut off by an Amtrak train, I interviewed her parents. I asked her father what he did for a living. Engineer, he said. Then when he said his daughter should have escaped injury, I asked him to explain. I knew I was getting an expert's opinion that I could drop right into the story.

"By all rights," her father says, "she should have been safe." But Otey Reynolds is an engineer at Electric Boat and he knows that an object moving at a high rate of speed creates a vacuum and as air rushes in to fill it, it makes a wind. "And the wind sucked her leg under the train," he said.

Find a Focus

"The most important thing in the story is finding the central idea," says sports columnist Thomas Boswell of *The Washington Post.* "It's one thing to be given a topic, but you have to find the idea or the concept within that topic. Once you find that idea or thread, all the other anecdotes, illustrations, and quotes are pearls that hang on this thread. The thread may seem very humble, the pearls may seem very flashy, but it's still the thread that makes the necklace."

• Don't wait until you're back at your desk to figure out what your story is about. Find your focus in the field, award-winning journalist and author Richard Ben Cramer advises, so you can search for the details, scenes, quotes, that support it. The deadline storyteller must be a radar screen, forever monitoring for information that is the heart of the story.

By the time I reached the home of Lani Reynolds, the train victim, I had already obtained a police report rich with detail and had gleaned other nuggets from a variety of witnesses, including Jon Tesseo, the shy Boy Scout hailed as a hero. My notebook was filling up with quotes, facts, and revealing details, but I was still hunting for the element that would elevate this beyond the clichéd rescue story. Then Lani's mother, sitting on her living room couch, said this about the boy who came to her daughter's rescue: "He's a preppie, everything Lani disliked." And I knew I had found it. Don Murray calls the focus the "north star" that leads a writer out of the tangled woods of reporting.

• Good writers know that a story should leave a single, dominant impression. On deadline, finding a focus quickly is even more crucial.

An effective focusing strategy came to me one desperate afternoon in *The Providence Journal* newsroom as I battled to meet my deadline and the expectations of my editor for a newsy, well-written story. They are the two questions that help me keep track of the focus of my stories as I write and read and rewrite. To this day, I still write them at the top of my video display screen, even before the dateline. They are:

What's the news?
What's the point?

Answering the first question is usually easy. The second is often more difficult, but is more crucial. Forcing yourself to describe, concisely, what your story is about, its theme, may not only give you the focus; you also may hear the voice of your story.

Although by now I had my focus, rescue by an unlikely savior, I still didn't have a lead until I answered those two questions:

> Jon Tesseo is 17, the kind of boy parents look at and say, "Why can't you be like that?" Clean-cut, yearbook photographer, a Boy Scout nine merit badges from Eagle. Just the kind of kid Lani Reynolds couldn't stand.
>
> On Saturday morning, he helped save her life.

Plan on the Fly

Finding your focus will give you a destination. Now you need a map to get there. Some writers make a formal outline. Others jot down a list of the points they want to cover.

Writers are always looking for a new way to tell their story, to stretch the traditional forms, to experiment. Writing the lead often helps writers devise their plan of attack. Effective leads "shine a flashlight into the story," as John McPhee of *The New Yorker* puts it. It is the first step of a journey. Just as important, if not more, is the last step, the ending. Create your own form.

David Zucchino of *The Philadelphia Inquirer* says his deadline stories are "totally determined by the facts on hand, the amount of time I have, and the space. . . . The form is determined by the situation."

• Before you begin writing, make a list of the elements you know you want to include in your story. Number them in order of importance. Structure your story accordingly.

• Look for pivotal moments that make story beginnings dramatic and irresistible:

> When things change;
> When things will never be the same;
> When things begin to fall apart.

• "Think 'short' from the beginning," advises Roy Peter Clark, co-author with Don Fry of *Coaching Writers: The Essential Guide for Editors and Reporters*. It's a suggestion echoed in *The Elements of Style,* Strunk & White's indispensable guide: "You raise a pup tent from one sort of vision, a cathedral from another." Staying faithful to an 800-word length will help you jettison irrelevant information and avoid reporting detours that might be interesting but that will consume valuable time.

Once the writer accumulates a wealth of material—statistics, quotations, differing opinions—confusion often sets in. What does it all mean?

Clark offers several other strategies for keeping on track:

Conceive and re-conceive the story in your head.

Rehearse your lead on the way back to the office.

Give yourself three minutes to write a five-word plan to structure the story.

Lower Your Standards

The discovery of the story continues when you sit down to write it. Writers use the draft to teach themselves what they know and don't know about their subject. Saul Pett, a veteran feature writer for the Associated Press, once said, "Before it's finished, good writing always involves a sense of discipline, but good writing begins in a sense of freedom, of elbow room, of space, of a challenge to grope and find the heart of the matter."

• Write like hell, Clark says. Wait for the adrenaline to kick in.

• Put your notes aside before you start to write. "Notes are like Velcro," says Jane Harrigan of the University of New Hampshire, author of *The Editorial Eye*. "As you try to skim them, they ensnare you, and pretty soon you can't see the story for the details." Her advice: Repeat over and over, "The story is not in my notes. The story is in my head."

• Follow the advice Gene Roberts, legendary editor of *The Philadelphia Inquirer* and now managing editor of *The New York Times,* got from his first newspaper editor, a blind man named Henry Belk. "Make me see."

• Lower your standards. Of course, you and your editor must apply rigorous standards—of accuracy and clarity, among others—but ignoring the voice that says, "This stinks" is the first step to producing copy on deadline in time for revision. The wisest advice on the subject of writer's block comes from poet William Stafford: "I believe that the so-called 'writer's block' is a product of some kind of disproportion between your standards and your performance. . . . One should lower his standards until there is no felt threshold to go over in writing. It's easy to write. You just shouldn't have standards that inhibit you from writing."

That's not as paradoxical as it seems.

With 35 years' experience at deadline writing, AP correspondent Saul Pett said he stopped spending so much time on leads as he used to. "We make a mistake when we're younger. We feel compelled to hit a home run in the very first sentence. So we spend a lot of time staring at the typewriter. I'll settle for a quiet single, or even a long foul, anything that gets me started."

Rewrite for Readers

Good writers are rarely satisfied. They write a word, then scratch it out, or in this computer age, tap the delete key, and try again. "Nonwriters think of writing as a matter of tinkering, touching up, making presentable, but writers know it is central to the act of discovering," says Don Murray, author of *Writing for Your Readers: Notes on the Writer's Craft from The Boston Globe*.

The writing process isn't a straight line. Often the writer circles back to re-report, re-focus, re-organize. Good writers are never content. They're always trying to find better details, a sharper focus, a beginning that captivates, an ending that leaves a lasting impression on the reader.

• Role play the reader. Step back and pretend you're reading your story for the first time. Does the lead make you want to keep reading? Does it take you too long to learn what the story is about and why it's important? If not, are you intrigued enough to keep reading anyway? What questions do you have about the story? Are they answered in the order you would logically ask them?

• Shoot for a draft and a half. Write your story once through and then go back to polish, to re-order, to refine. If your time is limited, I'd argue that it's best spent on your ending. That's the last thing readers will experience. Make it memorable. The story of Jon and Lani ended this way:

> After Lani Reynolds was taken away for surgery Saturday, Jon Tesseo called Paul Gencaralla, the owner of the men's shop, to ask for a few hours [off]. He felt a little sick. Jon left the hospital and walked to a friend's house nearby. Before he got there, he was sick in the street.
>
> "He didn't get sick because of the gore," Gencaralla said yesterday. "An ambulance attendant had told him he didn't think the girl would make it. She'd lost a lot of blood. Jon said, 'I should have made a tourniquet.' What made him sick was the thought he didn't do enough."

Historian Will Durant once observed, "Civilization is a stream with banks. The stream is sometimes filled with blood from people killing, stealing, shouting, and doing the things historians usually record; while on the banks, unnoticed, people build homes, make love, raise children, sing songs, write poetry, and even whittle statues. The story of civilization is the story of what happened on the banks. Historians are pessimists because they ignore the banks for the river."

I know now that when I covered that tragic drowning 20 years ago, my biggest mistake was focusing on the river, or in that case, the lake, where rescuers were searching for the victim. The real story was on the banks, where his family waited.

PAULA LaROCQUE

"Packing a lead is like packing a suitcase," says Paula LaRocque. "You just put what you need in it. If you pack too much, the back will break."

As an assistant managing editor and writing coach at *The Dallas Morning News,* as a columnist for *Quill,* and as someone who has conducted writing workshops for scores of newspapers, LaRocque knows that the crafting of the lead, or beginning, of a story occupies a disproportionate amount of a writer's time—and, perhaps, it should. It does, after all, carry the burden of capturing readers. If a lead is not arresting, or if it is murky and confusing, a reader may stop reading. The goal of the lead—to entice, entertain, and inform—hopes for the opposite effect.

LaRocque is the author of *Championship Writing: 50 Ways to Improve Your Writing,* a collection of fifty of her columns from *Quill* In this one, published in July 1995, LaRocque talks about the "lead du jour"—the inclination for journalists to grow fascinated with a particular kind of lead to the exclusion of all others. Journalists need all kinds of leads, she says. Formulas serve only to narrow a writer's thinking and constrict creativity.

Hooking the Reader

Journalism seems always in the grip of one writing trend or another—especially for that all-important lead. Right now, the tension is between the summary news lead and the "story-telling" narrative lead. Suddenly summary is passé; the narrative is style du jour.

This bandwagon tootling on the "best" way to begin a story is so much hot air. Neither the summary nor the narrative lead is better. We need both, and more. We need whatever there is. A good newswriter's repertoire should include something besides what it now seems to contain—which is chiefly the five W's, the scene-setter, and the anecdote. Each can succeed as a lead, but none ensures success. That's because compelling leads are as individual as writing—and writing, in turn, is as individual as thinking. More than technique, we need intelligence and understanding, inventiveness and imagination. We need to connect, extend, associate, allude.

Writing is not much different from thinking—the better we think, the better we write. And to think well, we need room and intellect. Formulas not only narrow our room, they also constrict reason and imagination. Stories are infinitely various; so are the best writers. Accordingly, they write for this occasion, this story, only.

Here are some newspaper leads written for this occasion only, leads in which intellect combines with creativity to yield freshness and voice.

Ed Tunstall, covering the boxing scene in New Orleans, put this lead on an Associated Press story about a has-been fighter:

> Middleweight "Sailor" Danny Grogan, who never has been anywhere, is making a comeback.

Whitey Martin's AP lead about a boring and much-booed fight between Ezzard Charles and Jersey Joe Walcott included this sentence:

> At one point, the controversy became so heated they almost came to blows.

During the Vietnam War, AP writer Hugh Mulligan wrote this incisive beginning, brilliant in its deadpan brevity:

> Rama Dama Rau, Premier Ky's personal astrologist who predicted five years ago that the war would be over in six months, was drafted today.

Usually lackluster stories gain color and humanity in the hands of good writers. Former *Dallas Morning News* reporter Brad Bailey began a story about rodents in downtown buildings:

> Through with breakfast? Then let's talk rats.

And this bright lead topped Dana Milbank's *Wall Street Journal* story about a family of fat-free diet fanatics:

> Sam Karlin says his grandmother killed her husband and her children, and then took her own life. She did it with a knife—a butter knife.

There's nothing new about robbery and murder at the corner store, but Donald Myers's creative use of detail brought freshness, poignancy, and immediacy to this UPI story:

> The last sale Gustavo Cuello made in his La Chica grocery was a ham sandwich, and it cost 52 cents. He sold it to a killer.

Nonformulaic writers even know how to make a usually failed formula work. Lee Hockstader shows in this *Washington Post* lead, for example, that in the right hands, a quote lead can be effective:

> "Political impotence is finished!" Vladimir Zhirinovsky rasped at a polling station here Sunday as he cast his vote in Russia's legislative elections. "Today is the beginning of orgasm. The whole nation, I promise you, will feel orgasm next year!" As a campaign promise, it was only slightly more extravagant than the others Zhirinovsky had been throwing around on his way to the elections.

Tom French wrote the following lead for the *St. Petersburg Times*. Its run-on sentence and intricate structure would ordinarily create fuzziness. But it's so well executed, dramatic, and novel that it immediately provokes interest and curiosity.

> Much later, after nearly two years of searching for her killer, after the interviews at the station and the reenactments in the dark and the lie-detector tests and the growing list of blind alleys and one sudden moment of stupid good luck—long after all that, they finally arrested a man and charged him with rape and first-degree murder.
>
> An investigator asked a neighbor: "Does he look like a murderer to you?" The neighbor said: "What does a murderer look like?"

This *New York Times* lead by Lisa Belkin is made special by its utter simplicity and clarity.

> This is a murder mystery. The victim is a tree. Not just any tree, but a 500-year-old live oak, which Texans like to brag is "the most perfect tree in America." It is 50 feet tall. The branches reach out 127 feet. Its picture has hung in the Tree Hall of Fame in Washington. It is revered because of a legend that is probably untrue—that Stephen F. Austin made peace with the Indians in its shade. Anyway, that is why it is called the Treaty Oak. Marriages have been held under its canopy. Nearby cafes and office complexes have taken its name. Now someone is trying to kill it.

Too often, we talk about What Readers Want as though they were a breed apart. But we are readers—they want what we want. And what we want is to be enlightened and entertained, preferably at the same time. We find these leads pleasing in part because they promise information and diversion. They're novel, yet professionally mature, fair and appropriate. They capitalize on surprise, humor, whimsy, irony, economy, drama, and detail. Formula and fashion aside, that kind of writing is always right.

JOHN HERSEY

John Hersey is remembered as both a journalist and a novelist. But it was his reporting that made everything he wrote—fiction and nonfiction—so powerful.

His Pulitzer Prize–winning work of fiction, *A Bell for Adano,* was based on the true story of a small town in Sicily that was ravaged by World War II. In the novel, an Italian-American army officer defies his commander to secure for the town a replacement for the bell melted down by the Fascists.

Hiroshima, Hersey's most famous work of nonfiction, traces the lives of six people who survived the atomic bombing of the Japanese city. Published in *The New Yorker* on Aug. 31, 1946, the piece consumed the entire issue of the magazine. *The New York Times* ran an editorial calling attention to it, and the *New York Herald Tribune* called it "the best reporting" of the war. Albert Einstein was said to have ordered a thousand copies for distribution, and many newspapers eagerly sought to serialize it. It was later published as a book.

Hersey, who died in 1993 at the age of seventy-eight, worked as a war correspondent for *Time* and *Life*. He was an early opponent of the Vietnam War and was active in many causes, including those central to the craft of writing, such as anti-censorship, protesting government intimidation of writers, and copyright protection. In the autumn of 1980, he published an essay in the *Yale Review* examining the use of the devices of fiction in nonfiction writing. He warned of a blurring of the lines and took to task the so-called New Journalism and three of its practitioners: Truman Capote, Tom Wolfe, and Norman Mailer.

More than two decades later, as more and more literary journalists employ the tools of the fiction writer, there are new examples of a blurring of the lines. John Berendt's *Midnight in the Garden of Good and Evil,* which was published as a work of nonfiction, is actually a mix of fact and fiction.

In a way, Berendt is the perfect example of what so worried Hersey. The book, now sometimes referred to as a nonfiction novel, has made Berendt a millionaire several times over. As Hersey says, "The blurring of the crafts becomes respectable, fashionable, profitable, enviable. The infection spreads."

In this selection, Hersey's comments on Capote's work have been deleted and his discussion of Wolfe and Mailer greatly reduced. But the essence of Hersey's celebrated essay remains intact: A journalist should not confuse the freedom to use literary devices with the right to take literary license.

The Legend on the License

The imminent death of the novel is announced from time to time, but the very repetitiousness of the bulletins testifies to stubborn vital signs. I bring other news from the hospital. Journalism is on a sickbed and is in a very bad way.

The trouble did not begin but came out into the open with the appallingly harmful phrase Truman Capote used in 1965 to categorize *In Cold Blood.* It was, he said, a "nonfiction novel." The blurring of fiction and journalism sanctioned by that phrase is now widely practiced and widely condoned. This has not been particularly good for fiction; it may be mortal to journalism.

In fiction that *is* fiction, no holds need be barred. Novelists may introduce or disguise real people and real events as they choose. Tolstoy disguised all but the generals. Dreiser's *An American Tragedy* was suggested by an actual crime, but he did not feel the need to call his creation "a true-life novel." Malraux, who had an enormous influence on some of the novelists of my generation (e.g., Ralph Ellison), often depicted originals—among others, Chiang Kai-shek in all the splendid irony of his left-wing youth. E. L. Doctorow has had harmless fun with Morgan, Ford, and others. And so on.

The only caution in all this is the one so acutely perceived by Flannery O'Connor (in *Mystery and Manners*): "It's always wrong of course to say that you can't do this or you can't do that in fiction. You can do anything you can get away with, but nobody has ever gotten away with much."

In other words, there are tests. A test, for one thing, of quality; of art. Or, to put it more brutally for authors, a test of gifts. But the point is that always, in fiction, there is the saving notice on the license: THIS WAS MADE UP.

As to journalism, we may as well grant right away that there is no such thing as absolute objectivity. It is impossible to present in words "*the* truth" or "the whole story." The minute a writer offers nine hundred ninety-nine out of one thousand facts, the worm of bias has begun to wriggle. The vision of each witness is particular. Tolstoy pointed out that immediately after a battle there are as many remembered versions of it as there have been participants.

Still and all, I will assert that there is one sacred rule of journalism. The writer must not invent. The legend on the license must read: NONE of this was made up. The ethics of journalism, if we can be allowed such a boon, must be based on the simple truth that every journalist knows the difference between the distortion that comes from subtracting observed data and the distortion that comes from adding invented data.

The threat to journalism's life by the denial of this difference can be realized if we look at it from the reader's point of view. The reader assumes the subtraction as a given of journalism and instinctively hunts for the bias; the moment the reader suspects additions, the earth begins to skid underfoot, for the idea that there is no way of knowing what is real and what is not real is terrifying. Even more terrifying is the notion that lies are truths. Or at least these things used to be terrifying; the dulling of the terror that has come about through repeated exposure tells us how far this whole thing has gone.

Let me now drive my own stakes in the ground. I have always believed that the *devices* of fiction could serve journalism well and might even help it to aspire now and then to the level of art. But I have tried to honor the distinction between the two forms. To claim that a work is both fiction and journalism, or to assert, as Doctorow recently did, that "there is no longer any such thing as fiction or nonfiction; there is only narrative"—these are, in my view, serious crimes against the public. In a backward look in *The New Journalism* Tom Wolfe, citing a piece of mine from 1944, remarked, "Here we start getting into the ancestry of the New Journalism." The word "ancestry" makes me feel a bit like the Peking man, and in laying claim to authority in this field I prefer to think of myself as nothing more remote than a grandfather.

Now. After reading three recent publications—Tom Wolfe's *The Right Stuff,* an entertaining book, Wolfe's best so far; Norman Mailer's *The Executioner's Song,* a powerful work that unquestionably enhances Mailer's claim to the kind of literary top billing he has always so tiresomely whined after; and Truman Capote's "Handcarved Coffins," a gobbet of commercial trash by this once brilliant writer in his new collection, *Music for Chameleons*—I am one worried grandpa. These three hybrids clinch it. The time has come to redraw the line between journalism and fiction.

[I]

. . . Tom Wolfe's *The Right Stuff* is a vivid book, a tainted book. It gives an account of the Mercury phase of the United States space program, and its thesis is that test pilots of rocket aircraft, genuinely, and the seven Mercury astronauts, more ambiguously, shared an ineffable quality compounded of spiffy courage, arrogant recklessness, dry-palmed sass, and super-jock male potency (on earth they indiscriminately balled "juicy little girls," and in the sky they whipped around in Pynchonesque flying phalluses), to all of which Wolfe gives the catchy tag "the right stuff." Wolfe's style-machine has never run more smoothly than in this book. The writing is at times wonderfully funny. Some of the passages on flying are classy. A quick and easy read.

Then why tainted? Because Wolfe is the paradigm of the would-be journalist who cannot resist the itch to improve on the material he digs up. The tricks of fiction he uses dissolve now and then into its very essence: fabrication. The notice on the license reads: THIS WAS NOT MADE UP (EXCEPT FOR THE PARTS THAT WERE MADE UP).

. . . Wolfe's fiction-aping journalism, he wrote in 1973, "enjoys an advantage [over fiction] so obvious, so built in, one almost forgets what a power it has: the simple fact that the reader knows *all this actually happened*. . . . The writer is one step closer to the absolute involvement of the reader that Henry James and James Joyce dreamed of and never achieved . . ." Whew. That *is* a big advantage. But let's focus for a moment on much smaller things, such as that little word "all."

In defining the New Journalism, Wolfe wrote that a journalist need use just four devices of fiction to bring this amazing power to the page: scene-by-scene construction, dialogue, point of view, and what he called "status details." But the resources of fiction are by no means so barren as all that. One essential requisite and delight of fiction, for example, is the absolute particularity it can give to every individual, every character. Wolfe has apparently ruled this out; he is a generalizer. Let him find a vivid or funny trait in more than one member of a class, then without exception the whole class has it. Thirty-six military pilots show up at the Pentagon to apply for the space program; without exception they wear "Robert Hall clothes that cost about a fourth as much as their watches." "They had many names, these rockets, Atlas, Navajo, Little Joe, Jupiter, but they all blew up." All test pilots talked something he calls Army Creole. All seven astronauts went in for Flying and Drinking, Drinking and Driving, Driving and Balling. All Russian space vehicles were launched "by the Soviet's mighty and mysterious Integral"—though, as Wolfe knows, Integral was not a person or a state organ but a space ship in Evgeny Zamyatin's novel, *We*. "Every wife . . ." "Every young fighter jock . . ." "Everyone . . ." "Invariably . . ." "All these people . . ." "All . . ." *("All this actually happened . . .")*

Another big advantage over other writers that Wolfe apparently feels he has is that since he is using fictional modes, he is, even though dealing with nonfictional matter, freed from the boring job of checking verifiable details. If something turns out to have been dead wrong— well, that was just the free play of fancy. Some of the many details Wolfe should have checked but obviously did not are: The kind of car John Glenn drove. Whether Slayton, pictured as an active partisan at the meeting Wolfe calls the Konokai Seance, was even present. What operant conditioning means. The Latin name for the chimpanzee. What jodhpurs are. What cilia means. When the compass was invented. . . .

But there are disadvantages in the method, too, at least for the reader. One is the frequent juxtaposition of passages that are wholly made up with others that are only partly made up or, beyond the use of one of the four devices, not made up at all. Side by side, for example, are a long parody of an airline pilot's voice reassuring the passengers on the last leg of a flight from Phoenix to New York when the landing gear won't lock, and an account of how the test pilot Chuck Yaeger gets drunk, breaks two ribs falling off a horse on a moonlight gallop, doesn't tell the base doctor, and two days later goes up in an X-1 and buffets through the sound barrier, hurting so badly his right arm is useless. (Right stuff.) Both passages are funny, wildly hyperbolic, interchangeable in voice and tone. It is not hard to tell which of these is mostly made up (or is it wholly made up?). But what becomes not so easy, after many such oscillations, is to perceive exactly where the line between reporting and invention in any "real-life" episode actually lies.

This difficulty is immensely reinforced by the way Wolfe uses his third fictional device: point of view. At will, he enters the consciousness of his characters. We have the stream (or in Wolfe's case one has to say river) of consciousness of wives of astronauts, waiting out re-entry. We find ourselves in each astronaut's mind as he barrels across the sky. For an awful moment we become Lyndon Johnson. We may be dismayed to find ourselves suddenly trapped in a chimpanzee's head. Finally (James and Joyce certainly never gave us *this* pleasure) we are right there in God's mind, out of patience with John Glenn and barking at him, "Try the automatic, you ninny." Beyond the dicey issue of freely inventive recreation of thoughts and dialogue, long after their transaction, a further trouble is that Wolfe never makes the slightest attempt, which any novelist would make as a matter of course, to vary the voice to fit each character. What we hear throughout, ringing in every mind, is the excited shout of Tom Wolfe. Each astronaut in turn *becomes* Tom Wolfe. Without even a little jiggle of lexical sex-change each astronaut's wife becomes Tom Wolfe. Right Stuffers who are alleged to speak nothing but Army Creole are garlanded with elegant tidbits like *esprit, joie de combat, mas allá!* The chimp talks pure Wolfe. God help us, God becomes Tom Wolfe and with His sweet ear chooses the Wolfeish "ninny." . . .

While he has largely cooled his typographical excesses in this book (there are only three exclamation points, and no italicized words at all, on the first page), the aural and psychological overamplification is still very much there. The voice of every character, even that of a quiet woman like Glenn's wife, is Jovian. One can say that the charm in Wolfe is his enthusiasm. On nearly every page, though, this attractive quality sends him floating off the ground. When he is establishing the driving part of Flying and Drinking, Drinking and Driving, Driving and Balling, in which "all" the astronauts indulged, his excitement over their recklessness at the wheel leads him to write, doubtless in a *sportif* spirit: "More fighter pilots died in automobiles than airplanes." No time period. According to Navy statistics which Wolfe himself cites, there was a 23 percent probability that a Navy career pilot would die in an aircraft accident. Did one in four die on the road? In 1952, sixty-two Army Air Force pilots died in crashes in thirty-six weeks of flying at Edwards Air Force Base, 1.7 per week. Did two a week die in cars? The point is not that this little example of possibly humorous overkill announces in itself the death of journalism. The point is that this one happened to be readily catchable. How many others are not? Are they on every page? How can we know? How can we ever know? . . .

[II]

The case of Norman Mailer is much more complicated, because Mailer is so richly talented and so grossly perverse.

Readers know by now that the first half of *The Executioner's Song* is based on the horrifying story of two wanton murders in Utah by a bright, sick, witty, cowboyish paroled recidivist named Gary Gilmore, who, having been condemned to death for the crimes, staunchly insisted on being executed. The second half tells how the strong smell of money given off by this death-row drama drifted east with the weather systems and attracted New York's media vultures, the swiftest among them being one Lawrence Schiller, who had already picked the bones clean from other carrion: Jack Ruby, Marina Oswald, Susan Atkins, for examples. (Schiller had also—though Mailer finds it convenient to omit this from 1,056 pages which seem to leave absolutely nothing else out—arranged for Mailer to make bucks cleaning the dear flesh from the skeleton of poor Marilyn Monroe; and was, of course, to arrange the same for Mailer with Gilmore's remains.)

Besides nursing Gilmore along, making sure to keep the condemned man's death-resolve firm (else contracts might fly away), Schiller dug up a mass of background material, including the element that was eventually to attract the romantic fictionist in Mailer—the love story between Gilmore and a sad, dumb, compliant doxy named Nicole Baker, who had been married at thirteen, had been twice a mother and twice divorced by nineteen, had long been in and out of mental hospitals, and would do anything for her man, whoever he might happen to be, including "rubbing peepees" (for "Uncle Lee," at five), turning tricks (not exactly for a pimp, just for a nice guy who had some horny friends), ratting (to attractive cops), and attempting suicide (at Gary's request through the mail). . . . Schiller's pumping out of this pathetic Nicole is a shocking tale of commercial sadism from which Mailer, who later used . . . the material, manages to remain somehow serenely detached. One of the conveniences of having a book be both fiction and journalism is that when the journalist's money-grubbing dirty tricks begin to stink, the novelist can soar away on wings of art, far above it all.

Mailer does want it both ways. Had he, like Orwell with *Down and Out in Paris and London,* for instance, or like Solzhenitsyn in his first three books, simply called his work a novel and let it go at that, we could perhaps have lived with the immediacy of the reality underlying the fiction—remembering that some reality underlies every fiction. But no. This had to be labelled "A True-Life Novel." (Mailer has played this doppelgänger game before, of course. *Armies of the Night* was subtitled "The Novel as History, History as a Novel.") "I called [*The Executioner's Song*] a novel because it reads like one," Mailer has said in an interview (*The New York Times,* October 26, 1979). And it does. He is right. A powerful and moving novel. But also: "This story does its best to be a factual account . . . and the story is as accurate as one can make it." The book jacket praises the work as fiction and also calls it "a model of complete, precise, and accurate reporting." The legend on this license reads: THIS WAS MADE UP AND IT WAS SIMULTANEOUSLY NOT MADE UP.

It simply cannot have been both. What it cannot be, if we look closely, is "precise and accurate reporting." Asserting that it is can only mean sending journalism into the intensive-care unit.

There is a false syllogism at work here, having to do with a Wolfeish "all this actually happened." A: Gary Gilmore did kill, was condemned, did insist on being executed. B: Mailer has written an immensely detailed and artful novel about the Gary Gilmore case, in which he uses mostly real names. Therefore C: This must be reporting. Mailer puts it somewhat differently, though of course not diffidently. "God," he says (*The New York Times,* January 27, 1980), "was at least as good a novelist as I am."

The novel is presented in terse, highly charged paragraphs, like tiny chapters, which allow Mailer both to keep the point of view rapidly shifting among a very large cast of vivid characters—Mormons, families in their cobwebs, druggies and deadbeats, a whirligig mother of a murderer, straight victims and their heart-breaking survivors, Nicole and her procession of men, jailbirds, jailers, civil libertarians, lawyers, television and movie con men, and, of course, the fascinating psychopath at the heart of the yarn, as well as many others; and also to build a grim, gripping suspense. Since we know the outcome from the very beginning, this latter is a brilliant feat. It is a deeply disturbing story, told by a bewitching minstrel of the dark side of the soul. But let us not say that it is accurate reporting.

Mailer . . . freely admits that he has tinkered with dialogue. And here we go: Is a reporter entitled (was Capote, writing *In Cold Blood,* were Woodward and Bernstein, in *All the President's Men,* were Woodward and Armstrong, in *The Brethren,* entitled) to reconstruct extensive exchanges of direct speech from passages of action that had taken place long before the research—and claim that the published result is "precise and accurate"? Mailer evidently relied for bits of his dialogue on interviews of his own, many months after the events; but most of his raw material was at least secondhand, given to him by Schiller, who had extracted it, also mostly after the events, from the principals—so that the filtration leading to direct quotation is through three and (when the informant is repeating something another person has told him) even four sensibilities, to say nothing of a fallible memory or two or three. And then, on top of all that, for art's sake, Mailer has tinkered.

A more serious question is raised by what Mailer appears to have done with Gilmore's letters to Nicole. These are the stuff of old-fashioned melodrama—purloined letters. That is to say, a cub reporter for the *Deseret News* named Tamera Smith sweet-talked her way into Nicole's trust; Nicole asked Tamera to take the letters for safekeeping; Tamera promptly photocopied them without telling Nicole; and on Nicole's request returned the originals but not the copies. After Gilmore and Nicole had jointly attempted suicide, Tamera wrote a story partly based on the letters. Alerted by the story, the prosecutor's office then picked up the originals. And later "the carrion bird," as Mailer from his artistic distance calls Schiller, having clamped a money-lock on Gilmore's lawyers, bullied them into demanding the letters from the prosecutor under laws of discovery; and so got his hands (and eventually Mailer's) on them. Gilmore, the copyright owner, of course never gave his permission for the use of the letters. He never had a chance. He got four bullets in the heart.

The journalistic shadow on these letters, however, hasn't to do with this sordid history. The question is, rather, just how far Mailer moved them away from "precise and accurate" replication. What Mailer says about his editing of them in his afterword is wonderfully careful. He is frank to say he altered the interviews with Gilmore that Gary's lawyers taped, just as one would alter one's own remarks on a transcript: "The aim was not to improve his diction so much as to treat him decently." But watch the prestidigitator's hand very closely here:

> With Gilmore's letters, however, it seemed fair to show him at a level higher than his average. One wanted to demonstrate the impact of his mind on Nicole, and that might be best achieved by allowing his brain to have its impact on us. Besides, he wrote well at times. His good letters are virtually intact. . . .

It is true that Gilmore had a weird and interesting mind, and there is no way of knowing exactly where and how much Mailer meddled. One clue is in "voice." Granting that one's spoken and written voices may differ markedly, there seems such a gulf between Gilmore's articulation on the tapes and in his letters that we can't help wondering exactly whose brain it is, in the latter, that is having its impact on us.

First, from the tapes (altered for decent treatment):

> I seen that she wasn't on the list until just, you know, yesterday. . . .
> I guess perhaps they didn't quite take me literal. . . .
> They act like they're really doing something by giving you a big meal, but it ain't like the menu in the paper. You don't get it good, you know. . . .

And then this Mailerish voice in the letters:

> I'm so used to . . . hostility, deceit and pettiness, evil and hatred. Those things are my natural habitat. They have shaped me. I look at the world through eyes that suspect, doubt, fear, hate, cheat, mock, are selfish and vain. All things unacceptable, I see them as natural. . . . There are dead cockroaches in the corners. . . . I can hear the tumbrel wheels creak.
>
> What will I meet when I die? The Oldness? Vengeful ghosts? A dark gulf? Will my spirit be flung about the universe faster than thought? Will I be judged and sentenced, as so many churches would have us believe? Will I be called to and clutched at by lost spirits? Will there be nothing?. . . . Just an end?

Mailer may conceivably be able to produce photocopies of many letters like these with elevated language in Gilmore's longhand, but any reader who is the least bit interested in journalism will have grown suspicious long before reading them in print. . . .

In fiction, the writer's voice matters; in reporting, the writer's authority matters. We read fiction to fortify our psyches, and in the pleasure that that fortification may give us, temperament holds sway. We read journalism—or most of us still do, anyway—to try to learn about the external world in which our psyches have to struggle along, and the quality we most need in our informant is some measure of trustworthiness. *The Executioner's Song* may satisfy us as fiction—it does me—precisely because the author's voice is so pungent, so active, so eloquent, so very alive. But there is deep trouble when we come to the journalistic pretensions of this novel, precisely because the temperament of the reporter is so intrusive, so vaunting, and, considering the specific story being told, so hard to trust. . . .

Am I saying that we can accept what Mailer says as a novelist and cannot accept what he says as a journalist? Baffled by the impossibility of knowing when he is which, I am. When we read a novel, we are asked to suspend disbelief, and as soon as we close the book we can be expected in normal circumstances to bring the suspension to an end along with the story, for in fiction, as Auden wrote is the case in poetry (in *The Dyer's Hand*), "all facts and beliefs cease to be true or false and become interesting possibilities." But when we read an ambitious journalistic work, we are asked to believe, and to carry belief away with the book. This is a crucial difference.

Why does Mailer claim so much? He has repeatedly said over the years that he would rather be known as a novelist than as a journalist. In a *Paris Review* interview some years ago, which he liked well enough to include in *Cannibals and Christians,* he said:

> If what you write is a reflection of your own consciousness, then even journalism can become interesting. One wouldn't want to spend one's life at it and I wouldn't want ever to be caught justifying journalism as a major activity (it's obviously less interesting to write than a novel), but it's better, I think, to see journalism as a venture of one's ability to keep in shape than to see it as an essential betrayal of the chalice of your literary art. Temples are for women.

Disregard that last line. That was just Norman being a bad boy. But since the publication of *The Executioner's Song,* he has insisted over and over, that, yes, the book is both fiction and journalism. Asked how that could be, he said on one occasion (*The New York Times,* October 26, 1979): "A writer has certain inalienable rights, and one is the right to create confusion."

At the risk of taking Mailer seriously at a moment when we can see his tongue poking his cheek out, I would flatly assert that for a reporter that right is distinctly and preeminently alienable. If there is any one "right" a journalist never had to begin with, it is purely that one. This perversity of Mailer's brings us straight home: The widespread acceptance of *The Executioner's Song* as a "true-life story" is an ominous sign of journalism's ill-health these days.

[III]

. . . Our grasp on *reality,* our relationship with the real world, is what is at stake here. We have to grope our way through that world from day to day. To make sense of our lives, we need to know what is going on around us. This need plunges us at once into complicated philosophical issues, having to do with trees falling in distant forests. Can we always rely on what others tell us about what is "really" going on? A suspicion that we cannot has led to the great fallacy, as I see it, of the New Journalism, and indirectly to the blurring in recent years of fiction and nonfiction.

That fallacy can be crudely stated as follows: Since perfect objectivity in reporting what the eyes have seen and the ears have heard is impossible, there is no choice but to go all the way over to absolute subjectivity. The trouble with this is that it soon makes the reporter the center of interest rather than the real world he is supposed to be picturing or interpreting. A filter of temperament discolors the visible universe. The report becomes a performance. What is, or may be, going on in "reality" recedes into a backdrop for the actor-writer; it dissolves out of focus and becomes, in the end, fuzzy, vague, unrecognizable, and false.

The serious writer of fiction hopes to achieve a poetic truth, a human truth, which transcends any apparent or illusory "reality." And in good novels, the temperament of the author, as expressed through the complex mix of elements that writers call "voice," subtly becomes part of the impression of human truth that the reader gets. The fictionist may at times use real people or real events, sometimes deliberately remaking and transforming them, in order to flesh out imitation or make invention seem like reality. This sleight of hand works beautifully if the novelist is gifted, artful, and inventive; it is a disaster (and an open invitation to libel suits) when the writing is bad, when the invention is weak or nonexistent—in short, when fiction is not fiction.

Two kinds of grave social harm, beyond those already suggested, come from works like Capote's and Wolfe's and Mailer's.

The first is that their great success, whether in kudos or cash or both, attracts imitators. The blurring of the crafts becomes respectable, fashionable, profitable, enviable. The infection spreads. If the great Mailer can do it, so can any tyro, and the only certainty is that the tyro will fuzz things up worse than Mailer does. Headlines tell us that Capote has sold "Handcarved Coffins" to the movies for "nearly $500,000." The blurring has long since made its way into investigative journalism, which, of all forms of reporting, bears the heaviest weight of social responsibility. In *The Brethren,* the Woodward and Armstrong book on the Supreme Court which recently spent some time at the top of the bestseller list, the processes of filtration we have seen in the Mailer novel are similarly at work. Clerks vouch for Justices' subjective states, moods, thoughts, and exact words—mostly recaptured in distant retrospect. Chief Justice Burger refused all contact with the authors, yet: "Burger vowed to himself that he would grasp the reins of power immediately. . . ."

The second harm, related to the first, is far more serious. It is that these blurrings lead to, or at the very least help soften the way for, or confirm the reasonableness of, public lying. The message of Jules Feiffer's *Little Murders* is that tiny symbolic killings, done with the tongue, lead to big actual ones, done with guns. Habitual acceptance of little fibs leads to the swallowing whole of world-shaking lies. . . . Did we write off—I am afraid the vast majority of Americans *did* write off—being told in official announcements that bombs were being dropped on North Vietnam, when in fact they were being dropped on Cambodia?

It would be preposterous, of course, to hold Mailer's and Wolfe's . . . inventions responsible, retroactively, for lies told a decade [earlier]. But the point is that the two phenomena—the blurring of fiction and journalism, as Mailer and Wolfe and many others have practiced it . . ., and public lying, as Kissinger and Nixon and many others have practiced it (and some still do)—the two have had something like a symbiotic relationship with each other. Each has nourished and needed the other. Each in its way has contributed to the befogging of the public vision, to subtle failures of discrimination, and to the collapse of important sorts of trust.

But how could the blurring possibly be corrected at this late date? Hasn't the process gone too far? Isn't all this much too complicated? Aren't the shadings too subtle?

Not at all. It is very simple. To redraw the line we need merely think clearly about the legends on the licenses. All we need do is insist upon two rules:

The writer of fiction must invent. The journalist must not invent.

DONALD MURRAY

What is the role of an editor? What does a writer need from the editor? As Carl Sessions Stepp, a former Gannett editor who now teaches journalism at the University of Maryland, puts it, "Most writers would give the vowels on their keyboards for a good editor."

Yet it is a famously contentious relationship. The editor perceives the writer as a prima donna who cannot abide a single change in his or her copy. The writer regards the editor as a prose-butchering philistine. But the truth is that they need each other.

Donald Murray, the legendary teacher, writer, and founder of the coaching movement of editing, knows the value of a good editor. He has been one, and—like all writers—he is in need of one.

Murray is a columnist for *The Boston Globe* and professor emeritus of English at the University of New Hampshire. As a journalist, he has won a number of awards including the Pulitzer Prize for editorial writing in the *Boston Herald* in 1954. He has served as writing coach for *The Boston Globe*, *The Providence Journal*, and other newspapers. He is the author of two novels, and his poems have appeared in many journals, including *Poetry*. Some of his books on writing include *A Writer Teaches Writing*, *Learning by Teaching*, *Writing for Your Readers*, *Read to Write*, *Expecting the Unexpected*, and *The Craft of Revision*.

This essay on the writer-editor relationship was published in the *Cape Cod Times* and has appeared on the Web site of The Poynter Institute, where Murray has donated his literary papers.

What I Need from My Editors

I need editors.

Editors allow me to be more daring, to attempt to write what I have not written before in ways that may not work. If my assigned editors are not adequate, I develop colleague/editors who can help me keep learning to write. I recognize the time pressures on newspaper editors. I am not describing long psychiatric sessions but professional conversations designed to improve a specific piece of writing and the overall performance of individual writers. I realize I am describing the kind of editing you may only be able to do once a day or less, but in the long run this will save time because it places primary responsibility for clear, lively, significant writing where it belongs—on the writer. It may break the cycle of dependency—"If they are going to write my stories, I'll let' em." It may also create writer/editor relationships in which each person can speak in a shorthand when on deadline. They may have a context to which they can refer as they need.

Assignment. Most writers will produce better work if they are asked how they think a story should be covered. Writers may produce what the editor could have said, but if writers suggest the approach themselves, they will be more committed to it than if they are executing a command. The writer may need a few minutes to think and then respond, perhaps in writing. When writers are listened to, they may surprise themselves by what they say. I also need editors who give me a specific length and a firm deadline—and hold to it.

Change. When the focus or approach changes during the research or writing of a story, I appreciate an editor who will listen and consult on the implications for the final draft.

Response. Silence always means rejection. I need acknowledgment that my work and I exist, just like the good waiter's acknowledgment, "I have that large party to serve, but I'll get to you in a moment."

Encouragement. The better the writer, the more seriously the writer takes his or her craft, the more encouragement the writer needs. Talent and concern do not equal confidence, they equal insecurity. But the encouragement should not be vague praise—"great story"—but specific—"I learned from the way you turned those quotes into a dialogue." And it must be honest.

Understanding. It helps when editors say in a sentence or so specifically what they think the draft says. If the writer agrees, then they can move forward to other issues. If not, the misunderstanding needs to be resolved immediately, before going on. If they do go on, they will be talking about two different drafts on the same page. They will not understand each other.

An appropriate reading. Most serious conflicts between writers and editors occur when the writer expects one kind of editing and receives another. For example, the writer wants to know if the editor will allow the writer to try the approach the writer has sketched out in a rough first draft and the editor responds with a line-by-line final draft editing. The writer should tell the editor what kind of reading the writer needs, a quick scan to check the lead, focus, voice, form, order, documentation. A macro reading for pace, proportion and structure. A micro, line-by-line reading for voice, diction, syntax, accuracy, usage, mechanics and spelling.

What works. Writing is more often improved by identifying and extending what works than by correcting errors. I often know what doesn't work but I'm not sure about what works. I need an editor to tell me so I can play from my strength—which will often eliminate a great deal of error.

What needs work. I need to know what my editor thinks does not work in specific terms and why. Many times I begin to see solutions as soon as the problem is identified and do not need to be told how to solve it. Suggestions can be helpful but they also limit the writer's involvement. The writer should know more about the subject, the history of the story's writing, than the editor, and the solution should rise from the story, not from the editor's experience with other stories. I need room—10 minutes, 15 minutes on a column; a day, a week, a month on a book—to design, attempt and respond to solutions.

Collaboration. I work best if the editor allows me to collaborate on a story, suggesting what needs to be done and expressing confidence I can do it rather than telling precisely what to do. That may be necessary on some deadline stories but it is a failure of the writer/editor relationship. When an editor trusts me, I may be able to trust the editor. The boss/worker, officer/enlisted person relationship between editor and writer rarely produces good writing and even more rarely encourages a writer to improve.

Chapter 5

BEAT REPORTING

Covering a beat can be one of the most difficult jobs in the newsroom, but it can also be one of the most exciting. Both the curse and the blessing of being assigned to a beat is managing territory overrun with potential stories. The very riches of a beat present a burden of responsibility—and enormous opportunity.

The reporters whose essays appear in this chapter have covered a number of beats, from police to health to sports. Whatever their areas of coverage, beat reporters must learn to juggle the demands of the job. To that end, Edna Buchanan describes the value of having a friendly, media-savvy source. Diana K. Sugg talks about managing time and mastering her inclination toward perfectionism to avoid burnout in a high-pressure beat. Bill Plaschke opens a window into the world of sportswriting.

Unlike a general assignment reporter who covers a different topic every day, the beat reporter has a chance to master one subject over the course of time. As a reporter builds expertise on a beat, he or she can tackle ever more complex stories and begin to write with clarity and authority. The satisfaction that comes with achieving mastery is one of the rewards of this demanding job.

EDNA BUCHANAN

As a police reporter for *The Miami Herald,* Edna Buchanan covered more than five thousand murders, spent time with firefighters, cops, and criminals, and won the Pulitzer Prize for beat reporting. She chronicled much of her career as one of America's best-known crime reporters in her books *The Corpse Had a Familiar Face* and *Never Let Them See You Cry*. After eighteen years, Buchanan left the *Herald* to devote herself full-time to mystery writing. In fiction, she says, "You can make the good guys win and the bad guys get what they deserve—which almost never happens in real life." She nonetheless misses reporting. "There is something noble," she says, "about venturing out every day to seek the truth."

That job comes easier for the reporter who knows how to cultivate sources. In this selection, taken from her 1992 book *Never Let Them See You Cry,* Buchanan talks about a reporter's best friend: the source who is not only knowledgeable about the beat but understands the reporter's role.

"Fire!"

Yell "Help!" or scream "Rape!" and expect to be ignored. Yell "Fire!" and a crowd comes running. Fire kindles something deep and universal in the human soul. Fires are news.

Hair and clothes smelling of smoke, sinuses clogged, head pounding, I have covered hundreds of fires and had to run to escape or to rescue my car when the flames spread or explosions began. Paint factories and lumberyards catch fire a lot—so do failing businesses and old hotels. So do homes and high-rises.

It is healthy and advisable for reporters to view with suspicion warnings from most government officials, but it pays to listen to firefighters. At one burning paint factory, I argued with a fire department chaplain who insisted I retreat from the scene. He warned that explosions might occur inside the building and we could all be showered by dangerous debris. As I pooh-poohed the hazard and refused to budge, an explosion rocked the building. Debris rocketed into the air and I ran for my life.

After that, I started wearing a hard hat at fires.

Until fire hoses were trained on me, I did not appreciate their effectiveness.

On my first newspaper job, at the Miami Beach *Daily Sun,* where I shot my own photographs, I always wore dresses and high heels to work. That was before I knew better.

Fire erupted at a major oil facility on the MacArthur Causeway. Fuel-fed flames towered over the bay, making it a photogenic blaze. I rushed about, shooting the inferno and the firefighters at work. A tall construction crane stood abandoned nearby. Better pictures could be shot from that vantage point, I thought, and in my miniskirt and heels, I clambered awkwardly up into the cab.

The view was ideal. The fire, unfortunately, seemed to be spreading fast—in my direction. "Better wet down that crane!" the fire chief shouted. Before I could protest, they did. All I could do was try to shield the camera as, from all directions, pounding streams of water pummeled me about inside the cab. A TV camera crew caught the whole thing, much to their delight.

Fire attracts all sorts of people. Stu Kaufman was a little boy when he was chased away from a fire and told to go stand behind a rope with the media. "This is not your business," the man in charge sternly told him. Stu never forgot. He swore that someday it would be his business. He would run to fires, and they would tell him everything.

They did.

When he was a successful young businessman and reporter, he gave it all up to become public information officer for the Metro Fire Department. They gave him a beeper and the chance to do exactly what he had wanted to since childhood. He went to all the fires, disasters, plane crashes and major catastrophes and was told everything. He loved it. He went to bed at night afraid his beeper would *not* go off during the wee hours.

Relations between the press and Dade County's closemouthed and sometimes sullen firefighters were traditionally poor. Stu taught them that they had nothing to hide. People love firemen. Stu thrived on excitement. He loved heroes and wanted to tell the world about them. When planes crashed, when a busload of migrant workers sank roof down in a deep canal, when an exploding cocaine lab shattered a quiet neighborhood, when rescue workers used the "jaws of life" to cut a dozen injured motorists out of a multi-car pile-up, Stu was always there.

Unlike many people designated to deal with the press, he had heart, compassion and sense enough to recognize a good story. He also knew that when the department was wrong it was far more effective damage control to tell the truth right up front, rather than to lie and have the scandal snowball into a far bigger story as the outraged press tracked down the truth. Stu loved firefighting and reporting, passions that made him the best at his job.

He was still a radio newsman when I first encountered him. A wealthy couple was kidnapped by a man named Thomas Otis Knight. He forced them to drive to their bank and withdraw money. The victim asked bank officials for help and they summoned the FBI. The victim took the money the kidnapper demanded and returned to his wife, held at gunpoint in the car. The kidnapper and his victims drove off with the FBI right behind them.

Everybody assumed that once the gunman got the money, the couple would go free. The agents decided a rescue attempt would risk the safety of the victims. They decided simply to trail the car until the couple was released, then swoop down on the kidnapper. Agents followed the car until they realized it was taking too long. It all went bad in a remote area, on a desolate road. Knight shot both victims in the head, executing them before the agents could make a move. The killer fled into the underbrush.

It was my day off, and I had friends in for lunch. They went hungry.

Every reporter in the world seemed to be at the crime scene. Frustrated cops, dogs and FBI agents combed the brush in an intense manhunt. Reporters, photographers, and TV news crews gathered to interview the local agent in charge of the FBI.

Suddenly a cop shouted, "I've got 'im!" He had flushed out the killer, who had literally burrowed into the ground. Everybody ran, leaving the FBI chief standing alone, his mouth still open. Leading the stampede of running reporters was Stu, pounding after the cops and the guns and the dogs, tape-recorder mike clenched in his fist, breathlessly reporting as he ran. "They got 'im! They got 'im!" he shouted. He was not on the air live of course, but when it was broadcast later, his tape had the spellbinding urgency of news happening in your face. I loved it. Who *is* this guy? I thought.

I next saw him at a cargo-plane crash. Surly firefighters usually banned us from such scenes, but at this one, Stu seemed in charge. "Right this way," he said and led me up to the wreck. Who *IS* this guy? Still a radio reporter, he had become friendly enough to convince fire officials that what they needed was a better attitude toward the press. Next thing I knew, he was working for them, and he certainly made a reporter's life easier. Always accessible, he would put us in touch with rescuers at the scene, with the fire captains in charge, with the hero who revived a baby with mouth-to-mouth resuscitation. When he saw people in need of help, he made us aware of the story.

His energy and commitment were clear away from the fire scenes as well. He arranged funerals for fallen firefighters, friends and heroes. One fireman was driving his wife to a movie when he stopped to help a woman whose car had knocked down a power pole. He was electrocuted. A fire department paramedic drowned trying to save a girl trapped in a submerged car. A lieutenant died in a burning warehouse, another in the crash of his rescue truck while speeding to a false alarm. Stu cried every time.

When firemen told him how they hated to drive away after a house fire, leaving a burned-out family huddled on their front lawn at three A.M. with no place to go, he established a program called After the Burnout. Stu or a department chaplain would arrange to have the damaged property boarded up and coordinate with the Red Cross for shelter. Thanks to Stu, no burned-out family is left alone in the night.

After a teenage-arson epidemic, Stu set up Dade County's largest summer employment program for underprivileged youngsters. The kids wore shirts with official patches and went door to door, teaching their neighbors about smoke detectors, the importance of family escape plans and the dangers of children home alone. Stu knew that the best people to deal with neighborhood problems are neighborhood people. As important as the pay was the youngsters' sense of pride and self-worth. Many of them work for major corporations today.

Stu forgot no one. Every Sunday morning he and his children would visit headquarters to share a sack of bagels with the "unsung heroes": the fire department dispatchers.

Stu's official code designation was Staff 10. He was driving his radio-equipped county car to an airport incident one day when he heard an injury call: "A small child fell through a television set." The address that followed was his own.

He spun around on the highway median and raced toward home and family. Pedal to the floor, he heard a paramedic who had arrived at the scene. "Tell Staff 10 to slow down. It's just a small cut."

Stu even issued beepers to reporters, so Dispatch could alert us to major blazes. News agencies gave him their private frequencies so he could guide their photographers and reporters around traffic and police roadblocks to reach fires and disasters the fastest. Metro-Dade was the first fire department to set up its own photo van and shoot its own video. News photographers and TV cameramen taught firefighters how to shoot the best pictures until they arrived. A fireman shot still photos and video, then shared his pictures with the media. The van was equipped with a video recorder so footage could be copied and distributed.

Stu gave firefighters' discarded bunker gear to news photographers. He knows the best pictures are shot heading into the flames, over the shoulder of a firefighter using a hose. The resulting camaraderie sometimes saw photographers put down their cameras to help drag hoses. Stu set up a day-long news-media fire college for reporters—so we could experience what it was like to be firefighters and understand the job better when we wrote about it. We wore firefighters' gear, climbed tall ladders and ran in and out of burning buildings wearing oxygen tanks.

Nobody ever said you had to be rational to do this job.

Stu Kaufman was the best thing that ever happened to fire-fighting in Dade County. Too bad good things never last. After ten years, Stu had swallowed enough smoke, seen enough excitement and lost enough sleep. He felt that he owed more of his time and earning power to his wife and children and left to make big bucks in the corporate world.

I never smell smoke without missing him.

Only twice did I ever go home from *The Miami Herald* so late and so weary that I neglected to fill my car's gas tank though it was on "E."

Never again.

Major stories broke both nights, and I had to speed off into the dark, on empty.

I hate that.

Once it was a plane crash. Next time Stu Kaufman called at nearly four A.M. I knew it was bad when I heard his voice. The toughest one of all: a house fire, in Leisure City, more than forty miles south of Miami, west of Homestead Air Force Base.

Five dead. All children.

A summer thunderstorm was raging on the island where I lived. The rain was torrential, and no service stations were open.

My mind was already racing with everything I would have to do before the *Herald*'s first-edition deadline, eleven hours away. Hopefully I would find a gas station en route, but they are never there when you need them. I literally screamed in panic all the way, one eye riveted to the gas gauge, the needle flat.

Never had I driven for so long on empty. Never had I been so lost, for so long, on roads so dark, in the middle of rural South Dade farmland.

I had no idea where I was. For all I knew, I was speeding in circles. It was almost dawn when I spotted a farmworker and asked directions. The man had no idea where *he* was, much less where I was going.

By sunrise I feared that the fire crew would change shifts and go home before I found them. I finally stumbled upon their station and burst in, totally crazed, the needle now way below empty.

They were tightly wound too, for a reason that put everything back in perspective. The tragedy had been senseless. A ten-dollar smoke detector would have saved five young lives.

Their father, a big, burly, good-natured construction superintendent who loves children, was awakened by a noise in the night. He arose, walked into the living room and saw the sofa burning. Shouting to his wife to call the fire department, he tried to splash water on the flames. The pan he used melted. He was severely burned and ran out the front door, searching in panic for a garden hose. His wife tried to dial 911, but the telephone was dead. She ran out a utility room door to the backyard for a hose.

A nineteen-year-old son was awakened by his parents' screams as they searched in the dark for the garden hose. The dazed teenager, thinking it was time to go to work, sat up and saw an "orange glow from the living room." He ran to wake his kid brother, age thirteen. When he punched out a window, oxygen collided with built-up gases from the smoldering blaze. The entire room exploded. The blast threw the older boy partially out the window, but it hurled the younger boy and his dog back into the flames.

A neighbor heard the explosion, saw the fire and tried to reach the children, but the family pets, a bird dog named Whiskers and a boxer named Kane, attacked him. The parents restrained the animals as the neighbor trained his garden hose on the children's window. The father tried to reenter the house, but the intense heat drove him back. The fire was so hot that the leaves on a hibiscus tree in the front yard withered and blackened.

The first alarm came from neighbors, logged in at 2:53 A.M. A rescue unit and a pumper roared out of the station one minute later. Firemen could see the fire a mile and a half away, an orange glow below a towering column of smoke. The rescue unit arrived first, and a medic tried to climb in a window. Heat forced him back. The lumbering pumper arrived minutes later, and the crew began to beat down the flames. They arrived four minutes after the first call, but the house was gone in ten minutes.

I talked to the firefighter who found two dead children, ages five and six, in their bed, "beautiful little blond girls in long nightgowns. One was resting her head on her hands like she was sleeping." Two baby dolls lay nearby. He carried the girls out. The body of one of them left an eerie outline on her smoke-blackened bedsheet.

The thirteen-year-old boy died trying to escape. A window screen lay atop his body, in a back bedroom. His hands were cut. His pet dog, a miniature dachshund, lay dead at his feet. The room did not burn—everything in it melted. The two three-year-old girls, two of triplets, died cringing in corners, trying to hide from the flames.

Firefighters groping in the dark missed one of the triplets at first. The fire captain had nine names, and only eight were accounted for. Himself a father of five, he hoped the missing child had escaped, was frightened and hiding safely somewhere, but they found her after forty-five minutes, covered with soot, wedged in a tiny place between a mattress and the wall.

The parents, the nineteen-year-old son and the surviving triplet, a three-year-old boy, survived. The father was airlifted to a burn center.

A worn air-conditioner wire had ignited the sofa. The fire may have smoldered for as long as two hours, investigators said, then flames raced across wall paneling and erupted into an inferno.

Had there been a smoke alarm, investigators estimated, there would have been perhaps ten or fifteen dollars' damage, no more than a hundred—and no loss of life. None of the children were burned. All died of smoke inhalation.

As a result, Stu Kaufman established a smoke-alarm awareness program: Buy One, Get One Free. For each alarm sold, one was donated to a family unable to afford it. This tragedy touched Stu more than all the others. One of the dead girls, age five, had been visiting. From then on, when one of his children spent the night with friends, Stu would always make sure that the household was protected by smoke alarms.

Some time after, his ten-year-old daughter, already at a slumber party when he arrived home from work, called to say good night. Routinely, he asked about smoke alarms, and she said there were none.

Stu Kaufman spent the night outside the house in his parked car, on a fire watch.

You learn a lot covering fires—some things you wish you didn't know. Sometimes I feel like I've been on the beat too long and know too much. I avoid flying when I can, and when I can't, I wear no synthetics. Fire accompanies most air crashes, and I know that when polyester melts, skin comes off with it. So I wear cotton or wool and Reeboks. If I survive the crash, I can climb out and trudge for help.

I know that no fire department in America has a ladder that will go higher than ten floors, so neither do I.

In one city, I was booked into a twenty-seventh-floor suite. Hotel personnel could not understand why I insisted on something else, preferably on the third floor. Embarrassed, I finally confessed.

"Don't worry," the desk clerk cried, relieved that my problem was nothing more serious. "If anything happens," he promised, "the fire department helicopter will pluck you off the roof."

I don't want to be plucked off a roof. I want to be carried down a ladder by a husky fireman.

Sometimes I think I am the only person suffering from this neurotic mind-set—then I remember Stu Kaufman on his fire watch, spending that sleepless night in his car outside his daughter's slumber party.

Maybe we both have seen too much.

DIANA K. SUGG

Whether the assignment is police or politics, the environment or health, the "beat" reporter soon sees there are more stories to be told than one human could ever possibly write. How do you juggle the reporting of two or three or four stories at a time? What are the tools for staying organized, for developing sources, for balancing between deadline news stories and ambitious enterprise projects?

Diana K. Sugg is a health reporter for *The Baltimore Sun* who accepted her first beat assignment—night cops—thirteen years ago at *The Sacramento Bee*. Her beat coverage has been featured in *Crime on Deadline*, as well as *News Reporting and Writing*, a popular journalism textbook. She switched from the police beat to covering medicine in 1993, and her health reporting at the *Sun* has captured local, state, and national awards. Sugg covers a broad range of medical issues, but like the best beat reporters she also writes about the people behind the story: the young psychiatry resident scrambling to handle a load of children in the emergency room, the brothers offering their bodies to test sickle-cell treatments, the harpist who plays for the dying.

Sugg lectured on beat reporting at The Poynter Institute for Media Studies in September 2001 and is a member of Poynter's National Advisory Board. In this selection, drawn from her Poynter lecture, she offers straight talk on the beat writer's most vexing questions.

Conquering the Beat (Instead of Letting It Rule You)

If you're a beat reporter at an American newspaper, when you get to your desk each morning, you know what you're going to find: Your voice mail is jammed with 14 messages. The mail is stacked a foot high. The faxes cover your chair. And within a half hour, you'll be pushing aside whatever you had planned to juggle your daily crisis.

In my case, that might be a U.S. Centers for Disease Control and Prevention report that ranks Baltimore No. 1 nationwide in syphilis cases, or a groundbreaking Hopkins' asthma study in the *Journal of the American Medical Association*, or the man in the newspaper's lobby who says his mother's nursing home has taken away all the bells from patients, so they can't ring for help.

By lunchtime, I'll discover a thousand pediatricians are converging on Baltimore for a meeting. My editor is waving at me to come into her office. And I'm straining to hear a woman whispering in the phone. She's in a local hospital's AIDS unit, and a male nurse has just raped her.

You are a beat reporter. And you're the journalistic equivalent of the emergency room. You have too many stories, too little time. I'm not an expert, but a fellow reporter who's wrestled with beats for 13 years. Like you, I've ridden the high of a streak of great stories, those days when my stories are coming in one by one, ripe and ready for the front page. But just as many days, I've cranked out two dailies and three digest items, and I've come home hungry and frustrated, burned out from the stories I finished, guilty about the ones I never got to.

Like you, I have my list of stories, the great ones that excite me, the ones I plan to do once things settle down. I sometimes catch glimmers that I might be really good. But I also look at my stories sometimes and think they're junk. I feel the tremendous heft of the material I'm dealing with, and I wonder if I'm doing my beat justice.

I became a beat reporter by accident. Out of college, I worked for the Associated Press in Philadelphia and then the Spartanburg *Herald-Journal* in South Carolina. When I headed west to work a night GA shift at *The Sacramento Bee,* I was informed my first day on the job that I'd be working night cops instead. I was upset. I didn't want to be a beat reporter. I distinctly remember thinking: I don't know how to be a beat reporter.

It didn't take me long to learn the list of cop numbers by heart and turn into a hard-charging, story-cranking machine. But it's taken me years to see the big picture. That's what I want to discuss: how to handle your beat. You're not like other reporters, who are focused on one story at a time. The beat reporter is a cook creating a five-course French meal. You're a farmer growing crops in every field. You're the maestro conducting your own symphony. For every story you create, there are five others you're tracking, 10 wacky calls—and as many as 20 other potential stories you had to let go.

Much of the work of the great beat reporter doesn't show up in the paper. A lot of your work isn't the stories, but everything around those stories: how you handle your time, develop sources, balance long vs. short pieces, deal with your editors, your own perfectionism and thorny newsroom issues such as "cherry-picking." How you deal with these five crucial issues is a big factor in how successful you'll be.

TIME

This is perhaps your greatest challenge.

You never have enough. There's always another call, another medical journal, another city council meeting. Early on, it does help to take all this in. Go to as many meetings as you can, read as much as you can, meet as many people as you can. Every story will lead you to two more and help build sources. Doing these stories helps you build credibility and develop the facility to write about your beat. Even the stories you complain about having to do, you'll almost always wind up learning something from.

In many ways, the volume is a blessing. During the holidays or a slow week, when other reporters are struggling to find something interesting to work on, you can pick from among many stories. In fact, when you are a beat reporter, the kingdom of journalism is at your feet: investigative pieces, features, profiles, news analyses. It's all there for the taking.

But working too hard for too many days will lead to burnout. At *The Sacramento Bee,* I remember feeling so busy that I couldn't leave the newsroom to walk one floor up to the well-stocked cafeteria. I was living on Diet Cokes and Snickers bars. I toted the police scanner in the bathroom with me. I even landed in the cardiac unit twice.

And if you stay at a frenetic, cranking pace all the time, you'll never free yourself to do the great pieces everyone will remember. You are a farmer, but one field should be left fallow. What an editor deletes from a story is sometimes as important as what he or she leaves in. The same goes for you: what you choose to let go of can be as important as the stories you go after. These are among your toughest decisions. It helps to articulate a vision for your beat. As a health reporter in Sacramento, I honed in on the changes shaking the country's health care system, and I let go of many of the stories that didn't fit into that theme.

So you must be decisive. Be organized, and be ruthless. You have to learn to quickly sift through that voice mail and all the potential stories on your desk; otherwise, all your time to do other stories will get swallowed up. It may go against every cell in your body, but you have to acknowledge up front that you won't get to many of the stories on your beat. This isn't like college or other jobs you've had, where you tackled and finished all the work. This is a new country, where the clock is ticking. Your time is limited.

SOURCES

When the federal government shut down human subject research at Johns Hopkins Hospital several weeks ago, and employees were told not to talk to the press, the other health reporter at the *Sun*—Jonathan Bor—and I had to have the names and home numbers of Hopkins doctors who would comment. Those moments come for every beat reporter, and they're often after normal business hours. But we have to remember that sources aren't just for an emergency, or for the big investigative story.

Everyone on your beat should be a source. From the health commissioner to secretaries, these people keep you on top of what's happening. They help you see the big picture in a confusing study. They will get on the phone on a busy day to give you a quote. Take good care of them. Stay in touch with them. Look for the people who love gossip and newspapers, the ones who will warn you off a non-story. I found one police officer in Sacramento like that, who circulated in many divisions of the department. He tipped me off to shake-ups, compelling deaths, and other stories.

But when I first arrived in Sacramento, the situation on the police beat was raw. Many of the officers considered the *Bee* a liberal rag. They didn't like us, and they thought our stories were inaccurate. Some officers proudly told me they hadn't read the paper since the 1950s. Meanwhile, in the newsroom, I was told that the night cop reporter basically made calls from the office and filed briefs. You babysat the city at night and paid your dues until you could move to a "real" job.

What would you do?

I knocked on the door. I asked the night watch captain if I could talk with him. The police weren't used to seeing reporters around at night. They were suspicious of me. They complained about the paper. I used that to my advantage, presenting myself as a new reporter. I wasn't involved in past coverage, I wanted to be fair. I wanted to get to know them. I asked them what stories we had missed.

That first night, I ended up eating dinner with the watch captain. Over time, I started getting into the police station. Gradually, I spent more and more time there, until I would spend almost entire shifts there. It took months. The few cops who spoke with me were looked down upon. Some walked by me and never said a word. Some nights, I stood outside the station, buzzing the intercom, hoping someone would let me in. It was dark and cold, but I didn't leave. I figured some cop would walk by and take pity on me and let me in.

Gradually, detectives started to talk to me at crime scenes. They were quoted accurately in stories. They saw that I was willing to write about the good and the bad. They started to tell me about things ahead of time. Soon enough, I was trading information with them, and they were taking me behind the crime scene tape to get a look at a decomposed body.

The Gift of the Beat: Getting Up Close

Once you have that credibility and respect, you can move in for the bigger stories, the untold stories, the ones everyone will remember. This is the gift of the beat. By working in an area long enough, you can develop enough trust to get special access. After a year on the cop beat, for instance, I got permission to ride with the narcotics officers for three months. And when "Hopkins 24/7," the ABC documentary, had about 25 producers filming in every unit of the hospital, I was in the one place they were barred: the child psych unit.

This is a wonderful place to be. Special access is the place where no other reporters are. You're in another country, an unexplored territory. And you can get there, if you're patient. One night on deadline, my editor kept staring at a sentence in my story. It said that hundreds of elderly Marylanders were still caring for their now middle-aged disabled children. She pointed to it on the screen and said, "Go find one of those families and do a story on them." It took four months and dozens of calls to locate the one family who would let me in, but once they did, the story was beautiful.

The great thing about these stories is you can work them while doing your other stories. The first rule is to never accept a "no." I don't care what the barrier is—danger, patient confidentiality, or simply that they've never had any reporter there before. I don't care what it is; you can almost always work around it. You just have to be willing to work with them and try every angle.

Take the story I did last year in the Hopkins pediatric emergency room. I got a call that children with psychiatric problems were overwhelming the emergency department. The numbers were doubling at Hopkins, the University of Maryland Medical Center, and, as it turned out, hospitals across the country. Young psychiatric residents were on call all night, trying to handle these troubled children. I knew the only way to do the story was to get inside that emergency room.

But I was dealing with a double layer of confidentiality—not only was the story about children, but their problems were psychiatric. So I started with one meeting. I said I just wanted to talk about doing a story. I didn't expect them to agree to everything at once. I asked for something simple first. I let them get to know me. I met with everyone they wanted me to meet with. Finally, they agreed that I could follow a resident for one night. No camera, no children identified.

On the appointed day, I showed up at 5 P.M. to meet the psychiatric resident. By 6 A.M., she saw how committed I was to the story, and she asked if I wanted to follow her another night. That's what happens, once you're inside. They see you're not *Hard Copy*. They see you care. Soon, you're going several nights, and they agree to have a photographer. That work turned into an award-winning, 100-inch, two-page story, with photos, and everyone identified.

Extraordinary Stories Take Extraordinary Means

In sensitive stories, you have to be patient and be willing to calm people until the end. The Friday before the ER story ran, one of the Hopkins officials called me several times, upset about how Hopkins might look, trying to get its lawyers to block us from publishing. Also that week, I drove to every house and visited every family, read them the details on their child, in some cases showed a photo, explaining again this will be on the front page, even how big the pictures might appear. When people are in a vulnerable situation, and they have agreed to be in your story, make sure they understand. Double-check the details. Do right by them.

How you conduct yourself goes to the heart of how well you do. Realize that you are your own product, your own brand. When you're a reporter, your name is all you have. Do you want to be like Southwest Airlines, which is known as fun and efficient, or the airline that everyone hates? Are you the reporter who thinks he knows the story ahead of time, who forces the details into a preconceived mold, or do you listen to the people you're interviewing? Are you the reporter who confirms all the worst stereotypes about our business, or are you the one who surprises people with your honesty, integrity, and passion?

Don't think for a minute that the public doesn't quickly figure out which category you're in and deal with you accordingly. We like to think we find out about things through paper trails and computer databases. In reality, for so many stories, we're dependent on people, people who have come to like us, who know we'll be accurate and fair and human.

BALANCING LONG AND SHORT STORIES

It's easy to get lost in your beat. From education to crime to medicine, there's always a steady stream of stories. These dailies and shorter stories count: they build up your sources, they help you develop the skill of writing about your beat, they make you better qualified to write the bigger stories—and they often lead you to them. But you have to be careful: You could crank out pieces forever and not think much about longer stories. Except for my narcotics series, while I was on the police beat at the *Bee,* I didn't step back and look at what I was doing. That's my advice for you. Just as in life, you have to occasionally stop what you're doing and look around. Where are you? What track are you on? What's on the horizon?

Most of us know the enterprise story we want to do. We were working on another story when we discovered it. We drove back to the newsroom a little faster than usual. We excitedly told our editor. Maybe we started a folder. We did a little research. Then we took the fatal step: We put that story on our budget list. Too often, the story dies there.

This is my image of what happens: You're driving on a hot desert road in the Southwest. It's nearing noon and pushing 100 degrees. You're hungry, thirsty, out of gas. You're the reporter who's been cranking out the complicated stories that no one cares about, the must-do stories that are killing you, but you feel like they are getting you nowhere. Suddenly, you see a great story. It's like coming upon a beautiful gas station on that desert road. It's well stocked, with clean bathrooms, even a Pizza Hut attached. You want to rest, eat, stay awhile.

But then a daily comes up. Your editor asks you to go back down the road a little way and do that one story. It's only a few calls, a few hours, a few days. You can go back to the gas station soon. But then another story comes up, and you go even farther down that road, away from the gas station. Then another story shows up. Soon, you're so far away, you can barely make out that gas station, that story. Then one day, a few years later, you'll see that story on the front page of a major newspaper. And you'll wave to it. "Hi, story! Bye, Story! Good to see you!"

It's easy to say it's everyone else's fault: that you have too much work, too little time, that your editors are giving everyone else but you those wonderful clear weeks for projects. I used to do that.

About a year after I got to the *Sun,* I was upset about not doing some longer pieces, and I talked to the then-managing editor, Bill Marimow. He asked for budget lines. I brought him three. His response was: "These are great. Which order do you want to do them in?"

Do you know what happened? I walked back to my desk and the phone rang, and I got tied up in something else. I got swallowed, dragged down into the muck and mud of the dailies, the Medicaid nightmare, the all-important Hopkins study, all the stories you have to do, or you think you have to do. I felt too responsible for them. I didn't stop to think: Do I have to write this story today? Could I wait until we know more? Could a general assignment reporter cover it? Could I brief it? I didn't follow up on those three stories. I wrongly thought I'd get to them next week, or next month.

For a long time, I had the illusion that just over the next hill, in a few weeks, in a few months, I'd reach a clearing, a calm, beautiful oasis where no dailies could find me. I don't know how many times I've told sources or people calling that just after I finished these next few stories, I'd have time, things would calm down. But I am here today to tell you that you will never reach that clearing. I don't think there is one.

But every once in a while, there is a quiet morning, or a few hours when you can't get anywhere on your current story, and you can use that time to make calls on your longer one. Hoard that time. Take charge. Secretly, do a little here and a little there, until you've built up enough to say to your editor, "This is what I have. Give me two weeks, and I'll give you a great 60-inch story."

Don't complain about the stories you never get to. Get to them, at least a little bit at a time, so you can convince your editor to give you more time. Don't be like all the other reporters, lining up to complain that they never get to do a long story. You have your project, and it's partly reported. All you have to do is finish it!

The other thing that you must do, again, is be ruthless. Look at your stories. What are the best ones on your list? Why aren't you doing those right now? Often, on your beat, you get to know lots of people well, and they can sometimes guilt you into thinking you must do this or that story. But you don't owe any agency or any hospital or anyone a story—even if it's a good feature that will land on the front page.

You owe the readers great stories. That's it.

Think of the clothes in your closet, or your friends, or most things in life: it often boils down to a few that you truly like, your favorites. When you're getting overwhelmed, consider which stories you would do if you could only do three more stories in your life.

I recently did this. I'd missed time from work because of medical problems, so my mental backpack of guilt and stories was huge—ones I hadn't finished before I left, plus all the ones that stacked up while I was gone. I had this list of ones I felt I had to do. But one day, I just stopped. I thought about all the stories on my desk. Then I selected the best ones and went after them.

THE NEWSROOM

Getting Time with Your Editor

Every reporter needs to realize that this is a problem at almost every paper in the country. Wherever you go, you'll face this issue. So you have to find your own solutions. Wait in line to talk with your editor. Interrupt him or her. Try to make a weekly appointment. Learn your editor's habits, and find out the best time to approach him. Get the editor to the cafeteria, or walk somewhere to lunch. When you do get time with that editor, be prepared, have a laundry list of everything you need to run by him, and be efficient about it. But don't edit yourself so much that you're not talking about stories the way you need to.

If you're getting nowhere with your immediate editor, seek out someone else in the newsroom. Go to a reporter or another editor. I once found a wire editor a great source for brainstorming and talking about ideas. Whatever you do, make sure you're talking with someone. Some of the most crucial editing happens in the reporting phase, long before you ever begin to write your story.

Dealing with Other Reporters

Don't pay attention to what other reporters are doing.

As a beat reporter, you will be furiously working away, and you'll look across the newsroom and see other reporters taking long lunches. You'll see others getting months and months for a long project, when you can't even get three weeks for a story you believe is just as strong. You're better off not looking at that, not thinking about that, not comparing yourself to others. Your best defense is a good offense: Do your own good stories. You can't worry about what others are doing.

But anyone who's been on a big beat will soon discover that other reporters are going to do some of your stories. They will sometimes cherry-pick. The worst situation is an editor saying this: "Oh, you have to write 10 briefs and three dailies, so you can't do this big great Sunday story. We'll give it to this other reporter." Again, make sure you're quietly working on your own great Sunday story. If the story being given to another reporter is one you really want, make an argument why you should do it, and prove you can clear your decks and get it done. Do some reporting so it seems you're already halfway into it.

You need to keep in mind, though, that you'll never be able to do all the stories you want to do. Think of all the stories on your budget list you've never even started. Ask yourself: What is best for the paper? If a story needs to get in, and you can't do it, make sure someone else does it. Don't begrudge the other reporter. Don't be one of those reporters whose heart is shrunken into a seed by jealousy and bitterness.

My old editor, Gregory Favre, used to tell me, "You can't do it all, kid." And he was right. All you can do is your own good stories, one at a time.

Perfectionism

Most of us are conscientious. We're used to finishing every job we're assigned. But working a beat, you have to learn that you'll never finish it. At some point on the health beat, I realized that I could stay 24 hours a day, and I would never finish all the stories I wanted to do. I also realized that the paper wouldn't have room to run them all anyway. But it's hard to walk away. It's difficult to take that psychic burden of all the undone stories off your shoulders and let go of the guilt. But you have to, for your sanity, for your life. If you can't do it for those reasons, do it for your career. When I finished the story on the children with psychiatric problems in the emergency room, I was so worried about the stories that had stacked up, that I felt compelled to rush and do those. I didn't do a follow-up on the ER piece.

I like to believe that for every story you don't get to, there are always two or three others coming right at you. Think of the *I Love Lucy* episode, in which Lucy struggles to eat the chocolates in the candy factory. There are too many for her to stuff in her mouth. Or consider the analogy used by a character from HBO's *Sex in the City,* comparing men to taxi cabs: if you miss one, no problem, because there's another one right behind it.

Burnout

Too many reporters wait until they are so fed up and fried that they're on the verge of quitting. I urge you to stop before you get to that point. Think of the philosophy of a savings account. You have to pay yourself along the way, or you'll never make it. Take care of yourself along the way. If things are slow one day on your beat, go slow yourself, clean off your desk, update your phone numbers, go through files, and trash the stuff you're never going to use. Go to lunch outside the newsroom with colleagues you haven't talked to in awhile. When I left the *Bee,* a reporter walked up to me and said, "I think you're one of the nicest people in the newsroom, and I wish we could have gotten to know each other, but you always seemed so busy, I didn't want to interrupt you."

Take a mental health day. Go to bars with other reporters. Build vacations into your schedule. Go on fellowships. Get a master's degree. Look up some of your old stories and read them. Make sure there are a few people in your newsroom you can go to for a morale booster. Every once in a while, you just need to flop down in a chair, spill your guts, and get a little encouragement. And when you're really feeling bad about your job, I propose this quick fix: grab your notebook, get out of the newsroom and go interview someone. I promise you'll feel better.

The Diamonds on Your Desk

Lastly, I want to say something about inspiration.

Even when you love it, when you're cranking out great stories, this is a burnout profession. Just when you're ready to leave for the night, a crow with West Nile Virus falls dead in the Inner Harbor. Just when you've cleared a day to work on your weekender, Cal Ripken has back surgery. On Thanksgiving, your family is home together, and you're at the office vending machine, choosing between Snickers and Reese's peanut butter cups. A lot of times people don't like you. You doubt yourself. You think you're not doing enough. You think your writing is awful, that you've gone downhill. But before you get so demoralized that you're ready to quit, before you've planned your next career, think back.

Can you remember the interviews when, all in one moment, you got it? When the connections are all made, and it seems the person is talking to you in slow motion? When you know with every cell in your body, that this story is important, and that you are going to write it right onto the front page?

Have you come back, hot and sweaty in the summer, to the air-conditioned newsroom and opened your notebook, gently, like it was full of jewels you were free to arrange on the page? Have you been so absorbed in your story that you couldn't hear the photo editor shouting right next to you?

Have you ever driven back from an interview so moved by someone's words that you dare not turn on the car radio, for fear you'd break the stillness, lose the sacredness of the world that person has brought you into?

Do you still remember the stench of the woman dying of melanoma, and the husband who loved her so much that he still slept beside her every night? Can you still hear the brain tumor patient, who was brave enough to giggle in the MRI machine? Do you remember the 93-year-old woman who'd been brutally beaten, and how she managed to grasp your hand so tightly?

You carry those moments with you, and somewhere else, a reader does. In someone's home, your story is laminated in a photo album, or framed and hung on a wall. For years, they will remember the day you came and interviewed them.

Your stories may not turn out how you'd hoped. I always see them in my mind's eye, beautiful and shimmering and whole; once they're finished, they often seem like a piece of crude pottery. Maybe every story doesn't spark a great change, but we're the ones who are showing people a sliver of worlds they would otherwise never see—how hard a teacher works, why a teenager joins a gang, or maybe something as simple as not making assumptions about a misbehaving boy in a restaurant.

I will always remember the winter night a mother stood in her doorway, tears in her eyes, saying to me, "You tell them. You tell people it's not Michael's fault. We tried to discipline him. Mental illness is like any other illness. Maybe now people will understand."

Maybe now people will understand.

Don't dismiss the power of one story. Don't let all the tough things about your job cover over the diamonds on your desk. If you see stories everywhere you go, if you connect with people, if you care, take heart and follow your instincts.

And when you get back to your desk tomorrow morning, after you clear out the phone messages and scan through the faxes, dig out that great story you've wanted to do—and go for it.

BILL PLASCHKE

In the world of sports, scores and statistics are cold, hard facts—numbers that do not lie. But what about an athlete's personality, his penchant for partying? These are matters of interpretation, and a sportswriter must decide if and when they are important enough to be written about. Bill Plaschke, an award-winning sports columnist for the *Los Angeles Times*, has made that decision almost every day in fifteen years covering sports. If an athlete or coach or owner feels burned by a writer, the beat reporter can be shut out or, as Plaschke learned, physically threatened.

In this essay, written for the January/February 2000 issue of *Columbia Journalism Review*, Plaschke concludes that the best sports reporters take in everything and try to be reasonable—but they never back down.

Trying Not to Look Like a Vulture

I strolled through the Los Angeles Dodger clubhouse toward the outer door with a sigh. One hour until first pitch, and the hardest part of my day was done. I had mingled with the players, pitched through their paranoia, played catch with their insecurities, swung with their unusual humor, and gently bunted around their fears. Now I could walk upstairs to the Dodger Stadium press box and perform the absolutely easiest part of my job, which is writing about them.

Then I heard a shout. It wasn't the voice of a player. It was worse. It was the voice of a public relations man, the kind who only comes between sportswriter and player when they need separating.

"Plaschke! Plaschke!" shouted the Dodgers's Derrick Hall. "Raul Mondesi wants to talk to you."

Five feet from the door, I stopped and tensed. The last thing the moody Dodger outfielder wanted to do was talk.

A day earlier I had written that, even though it was only August, the disappointing Dodger season was essentially finished. I had written that problems ranging from upper management to the clubhouse underbelly were too great to overcome.

I had also noted what many in my town felt, that Mondesi is "a centerfielder who is too worried that everyone thinks he parties too much, which he does." I had added that, "Raul Mondesi sometimes acts as if his brain is dead." Maybe so, but the rest of him seemed very much alive on this August evening as he stalked toward me.

As a columnist who spent ten years as a beat reporter, I live by the philosophy that you rarely make an issue of a player's off-field behavior unless it affects what happens on the field. While this might seem constricting, it actually gives me the freedom to write about matters of legality and character—drugs and crime always affect what happens on the field—while gaining the trust of sources who know I won't sweat the other stuff.

In other words, marital problems are relevant only if a player is late to a game because he's being chased around the block with a frying pan. And if a player wants to spend all night in a bar, it's only an issue if he sleeps through the next day's first pitch.

So why did I write about Raul Mondesi's partying? Because earlier in the year he was arrested on suspicion of drunk driving the night before an afternoon game, and was subsequently held out of that game. He was eventually cleared of the charges, but not of the fact that thousands of fans who paid to see him play were deprived of that chance because he was partying when he might have been resting. I had chastised him in print once before, when he had been suspended from another game because he arrived late after another rough night.

As his glare broke the calm on this August afternoon, it was clear that he'd had enough.

"That's twice you get me!" he shouted as he approached me, his football physique stopping inches shy of my round middle-aged frame. "No more! No more!"

In the past when things like this have happened, I just stood there and said nothing, figuring that the best way to weather a storm is to let it pass. But experience has made me more brave, or self-righteous, or stupid.

"If you keep doing things off the field that stop you from playing on the field, I will keep writing about it," I said.

"You do this again, I'm gonna get you!" he replied.

"Just stay out of trouble," I answered.

"You want me to hit you now? I'm going to hit you now!" he shouted.

Mondesi stuck his right arm out, placed his right fist on my chest, and held it there.

"I'm gonna hit you, right now, right now!" he kept shouting.

Now I had been silenced. I wasn't moving. But I wasn't talking either. Friends always say I should not be worried if athletes hit me because I can sue them out of their signing bonuses. Easy for them to say. I wasn't just worried, I was scared.

I apparently wasn't the only one. Out of the corner of my eye, I saw sweat rolling down Derrick Hall's face as the publicity man started to plead. "Raul, please, please, don't do it, don't do it, we can work it out, we can work it out, please," Hall said.

Mondesi stood firm. I stood firm. Finally, the storm passed. Mondesi dropped his fist, shook his head, and walked back into a clubhouse filled with players who had been watching with glee.

"I thought you were dead," said Hall softly, wiping his face.

"It's still early," I said, wiping mine.

It's the part of sportswriting that nobody understands except the sportswriters.

Not the editors who only watch the athletes on TV. Not the readers who wear their jerseys to church. Not even family members, who hear stories of a terrible day that sound so unlike conventional journalism. It's the part about working large-shoulder-to-puny-shoulder with the professional athletes.

They are like any other sources for any other sort of journalist with the possible exception of: they are generally rich, insecure, sometimes uneducated, and often crude national heroes who have no need for anyone who would portray them otherwise.

Not that there aren't pleasant, civilized creatures among them. For every baseball star like Gorman Thomas, who once called me "a pimple," there is an Orel Hershiser, who once called my terminally ill brother to congratulate him on his high school graduation.

For every quarterback like Jim McMahon, who once blew his nose on a colleague, there is a quarterback like Brett Favre, who once gave me thirty minutes of funny childhood stories while sitting in a cold Green Bay office in his underwear.

For every golfer like Payne Stewart, who several years ago yelled at me for daring to ask why his partner had just walked off the course in the middle of the U.S. Open, there is a golfer like Payne Stewart, who softened into a sensitive and helpful man before his death.

Not that I blame any of them for any of it. Athletes are at their most vulnerable when dealing with the media. We're everywhere; we surround them as they are preparing for a game; we barely give them room to dress afterwards; and we're not looking to make friends, but front pages. An aide often separates politicians and businessmen and police from their questioners. Athletes are separated only by a towel, and sometimes not even that.

I have interviewed former Dodger manager Tom Lasorda while he stood underneath a shower. Arriving early for an afternoon game, shortly after a big breakfast, I was once confronted by Lasorda, who promised to give me a scoop if I would only sit in his office and eat pizza with him. Lasorda loves to eat, but hates to eat alone.

"But Tommy, I'm full," I said.

"Then no scoop," he said.

"Pass the pepperoni," I said.

Five pieces later I waddled into the clubhouse. Kirk Gibson began cursing me for correctly writing he wanted to be traded. A few lockers over, Jay Howell was waiting to yell at me for writing that his character was being tested. As I walked through the dugout heading for the press box I was met by Fernando Valenzuela, who pulled out a toy rope and tried to lasso my leg. I stopped at the dugout bench to talk to another writer and realized the tassels of my shoes had been cut.

When I finally reached the press box, I called the boss and told him I was finally sitting down to write my story.

"Oh, so you just got there," he said.

With the proliferation of TV and radio and Internet reporters, pro athletes often need to be rude and pushy just to catch their breaths. Some players will start a chorus of, "Vulture, vulture" when a pack of journalists enters their locker room. The secret to mining an environment so rich in human stories and inspiration is to convince the pro athletes that you are not related to the vulture.

The secret will never be taught in journalism school until the professor shows up with snuff under his lip and a towel around his waist. Rule one: Look the part.

Your boss may want you to wear a tie to work. But most pro athletes don't wear ties. In baseball, it's jeans. In basketball, it's hip slacks and sweaters.

Your parents may have wanted you not to curse. But most pro athletes curse. The more conjugations you have for each bleep, the better. There are drawbacks. For one, cursing can be infectious. I once heard my wife on the phone with her mother: "That was a great [bleeping] meatloaf recipe," she said.

But the theory is simple. The athletes are more comfortable talking to someone who looks and talks like them. That's 90 percent of sports reporting—standing around batting cages and end zones and practice courts, just talking. The best sports reporters are the people who are best at hanging out.

One late September afternoon, I was sitting in the dugout with Matt McHale, an accomplished reporter with the *Los Angeles Daily News*. Up walked Dodger Mike Scioscia.

"So, Matt, where do you spend your winters?" he asked.

McHale and I howled. It was a question that a player would ask another player, as they frequently only live in their team's city during the season. But it was a question that meant, when it came to being perceived as one of the guys, McHale had hit a home run.

"I spend my winter, uh, covering high schools," McHale said with a smile.

Rule two: You catch more flies with honey.

Be pleasant. Save your anger and indignity for the newspaper. When you criticize a player, you want him to think that such criticism is in his best interest, which it often is. He won't think that if he thinks you're a jerk. And then he won't talk to you. And then where are your readers?

There was once a game where Spike Owen, then a Seattle Mariner shortstop, hit his first home run of the season in the fourth inning but committed a game-costing error in the ninth. Standing in front of several reporters afterward, my first question to Owen was about the home run.

"What are you doing?" whispered a colleague standing behind me.

"Just wait," I whispered back.

Relaxed after talking for a few minutes about the homer, Owen was revealing and insightful when answering my next question about the error. You don't have to be a tough guy with the players to be a tough guy for the people who really count, your readers.

Rule three: Never back down.

Once a player thinks he can run you out of a clubhouse, you'll never feel safe there again. In the visitors' clubhouse in Yankee Stadium once, Mariner outfielder Steve Henderson began screaming at me. As often happens, his teammates also began snickering and glaring. Never do you see a sports team as united as when the target is a reporter.

I wanted to leave, but I couldn't. I wanted to interview other players, but because of this pack mentality, I couldn't. So I walked over to the box of Bazooka bubble gum and grabbed a piece. And another piece. And another piece. Waiting for the furor to die, I stuffed myself with gum.

By the time I felt comfortable asking anyone else questions, I could barely open my mouth. By the time I ran upstairs, it was twenty minutes to deadline, and I had not written word one.

"Are you going to make it?" shouted a worried desk person from the other end of the phone.

"Bfltmglfltis," I said, which, translated without the gum, means, "piece of cake."

Chapter 6

INVESTIGATIVE REPORTING

Investigative reporters want to change the world. They feel compelled to bring to light injustice, crime, or corruption. To this end they work long, sometimes tedious hours toward an uncertain goal. No matter what the focus of their curiosity, investigative reporters must be relentless and committed to raising questions no one else will ask.

As you will see in this chapter, the life of an investigative reporter is as difficult as it is rewarding. In different ways, these authors explore the question "why?"—why is a reporter driven to ferret out unpleasant truths and publicize them against strong opposition? Florence George Graves examines the ways in which personal history can inspire and motivate the investigative reporter. Leonard Downie Jr. argues that investigative reporters fight through problems like retaliation, self-doubt, and burnout because ultimately they are "activists," catalysts for change. Steve Lovelady stresses the importance of good editing, reminding us that even blockbuster reporting must be well written to be widely read and understood. Finally, Craig McCoy relates the dramatic story of a successful report that changed the behavior of police in his city.

Together, these readings paint a picture of investigative reporting as a difficult but noble calling.

FLORENCE GEORGE GRAVES

Florence George Graves is a veteran investigative reporter who helped break the Bob Packwood sexual misconduct story for *The Washington Post,* which led to the senator's resignation. She founded the muckraking *Common Cause Magazine,* which won a National Magazine Award for general excellence in 1987. As a resident scholar at the Brandeis University Women's Studies Research Center, she focuses on the intersection of sex, gender, and power in Washington politics and media. Her research and writing have been supported by numerous fellowships, including Harvard's Institute of Politics at the Kennedy School of Government, the Alicia Patterson Foundation for journalists, and the Fund for Investigative Journalism.

In this essay for the May/June 2001 *Columbia Journalism Review,* Graves talks about the choices investigative reporters make about whom to scrutinize and why. A reporter's own life story, she believes, can contain powerful motivations in the search for truth. Can that connection also be a hidden liability?

What We Investigate Is Linked to Who We Are

I can't remember which one of my stories about Senator Bob Packwood's sexual misconduct prompted Joan Valdina, a savvy octogenarian in my Unitarian Universalist church, to ask the question that would ignite—maybe "renew" is a better word—an investigation of my own psyche. I don't recall her exact words, but one Sunday after church, instead of offering a pat on the back for breaking the big story, she hollered something like, "I'd love to know what happened to you as a child that caused you to become an investigative reporter!"

What happened to me as a child?

It's hard for investigative reporters to know what really motivates them—their choice of stories, their determination to work day and night to nail down information. But given the sometimes awesome power invested in us to diminish some lives while enhancing others, occasional introspection doesn't seem too much to ask.

Had I repressed—as I feared my neighbor's question suggested—some dark childhood secret? I began torturing myself, almost methodically going through the file cabinet in my memory, dredging up emotional hurts, but nothing too traumatic turned up. If something in fact did "happen" to me, I think it was subtle, a slow realization that things are not always as they seem.

The same kind of thing, apparently, "happened" to other investigative reporters, including some of the best of us, such as Bob Woodward and Katherine Boo, both of *The Washington Post.* Both learned as children that people operate on different levels of reality. Woodward recalls working as a janitor in his father's law office in Wheaton, Illinois, as a high school student in the 1950s when curiosity led him through his father's files. There he discovered some of the best-kept secrets of the town's citizens and realized that "a public world and a secret world" could exist simultaneously. "Vivid" is how he remembers the "disparity," the "concealment" and "hypocrisy," he found in those files. Then, much later, while a Navy officer stationed at the Pentagon, he "saw a lot of communications traffic." The man who voted for Richard Nixon in 1968 began to develop hostility toward the Vietnam war. He began to believe "that something was grievously off the track," that "the government had misapplied its power." He was reading *The Washington Post,* liked its "deeply skeptical" sense of inquiry, and began to realize that journalism was one way to help make institutions accountable.

Kate Boo, whose Pulitzer Prize–winning work disclosed neglect and abuse in Washington's group homes for the mentally ill, notes that her mother "grew up poor and smart and proud," and Boo was "fascinated" by the way her mother's and her mother's siblings' choices in life were circumscribed by their economic circumstances. "Who knows what's inside us that makes us" choose certain stories, says Boo. But she acknowledges that "there's self-interest" in her focus on "the incredibly powerful stories in the lives of ordinary people." She says she gets "an enormous amount from the people I write about," including ideas about how to live a meaningful life.

Does that mean that Woodward and Boo aren't truly "objective" —journalism's supposed Holy Grail? Probably. In this matter I side with Jack Fuller, president of the Tribune Company's publishing operation, who wrote in his 1996 book, *News Values:* "No one has ever achieved objective journalism, and no one ever could." Fuller reminds us that "the bias of the observer always enters the picture, if not coloring the details at least guiding the choice of them." He then explains: "I don't use bias here as a term of opprobrium. One might have an optimistic bias or a bias toward virtue. It is the inevitable consequence of the combination of one's experience and inbred nature." Our goal, instead, should be "work of genuine intellectual integrity." This means journalists should link "the truth discipline in journalism with the highest standards in scientific and academic debate," and then apply the "Golden Rule"—to play square.

In 1992, I took my evidence suggesting Senator Packwood's pattern of misuse of senatorial power to *The Washington Post.* Woodward believes the *Post* "would have been remiss" if it had not taken on the story. Almost a year after the Anita Hill–Clarence Thomas hearings, the *Post* understood why Packwood's behavior was a public issue. Yet I can't tell you how many people I have met who have assumed some personal partisanship on my part, asking me whether Packwood had ever made an improper advance to me or whether I had ever experienced serious sexual harassment. The answers are "no" and "no," although certainly like so many women in the workplace, I occasionally had been subjected to obnoxious remarks. Does the fact that I am a woman make me more likely than a man to have recognized this particular kind of abuse of power? Of course. Should Woodward's Navy service during the Vietnam war have disqualified him from reporting Watergate? Should Kate Boo's observations about her mother's poverty have prevented her from reporting on the economically disadvantaged? Personal experience should not be a disqualification in journalism.

What happened to me as a child? I write with some trepidation about Waco, Texas, where I grew up. I have seen how easily reporters—even if unintentionally—stereotyped my hometown of more than 100,000 people, and consequently how easy it would be for a reader to project those stereotypes onto what I am about to tell you. Waco—"the heart of Texas"—is halfway between Dallas and Austin and just a few minutes from President George W. Bush's ranch in the tiny town of Crawford. Another tiny nearby community—Mount Carmel—was where David Koresh's Branch Davidian compound exploded in flames in 1993. This tragic event became known in the press and the culture as simply "Waco," leaving the town unfairly synonymous with weird people. I don't know anyone in Waco other than some local journalists who had ever heard of Koresh before the standoff, and the truth is that Waco is far more diverse than most people outside of Texas imagine. Its accomplished citizens include Dr. T. Berry Brazelton, the early childhood specialist, Ann Richards, the salty and liberal former Texas governor, and Robert Fulghum, the minister and author of

All I Really Need to Know I Learned in Kindergarten. So much for stereotypes.

And I am acutely aware of how dangerous it can be to focus on moments in time, to try to recall accurately childhood experiences through the lens of an adult. But sometimes that's our only choice.

Over the years I have wondered, on occasion, why I had been so determined—since the time I was a young child—to pursue the path of an investigative reporter. In elementary school I remember reading biographies of famous people and being especially taken by those of Ida Tarbell and Nellie Bly, two turn-of-the twentieth century muckrakers. I remember thinking, "That's what I want to do."

But why had their lives resonated with me, a baby boomer from a relatively prosperous Texas family, growing up when most women didn't consider professional careers? Looking back, I realize the extent to which growing up in Texas during the 1950s and 1960s shaped my future as a journalist. Negotiating life there helped me see just how skillfully people can operate on different, sometimes incongruent, levels, and how difficult it can be to figure out what is really going on.

I couldn't stop wondering about certain aspects of life in Texas. Why were there separate drinking fountains for "whites" and "coloreds" in public places? Why did my close friend's parents treat her decision to marry a Catholic as if there had been a death in the family? Why weren't Jews allowed to join the country club? Why should girls bother to excel in school if they were not entitled to use their knowledge in the world beyond the home?

I had difficulty reconciling all this. Church was a huge part of our lives, and there was not the slightest doubt that Jesus taught we should love our neighbors as ourselves, and that *everyone* was our neighbor (remember the Good Samaritan?). Our teachers told us how lucky we were to live in America, because everyone in a democracy is created equal and has equal opportunities. But it was obvious to me that there was a huge disconnect between what we were told and what people seemed actually to believe and do. I was constantly confused.

We had a housekeeper named Genner (pronounced "Gina") Hastings, a deeply religious black woman who worked at our home for many years, and I realize now that our relationship helped shape me. I loved Genner, and I believe she loved me—although I'm now open to the possibility that my perception of her love for me may have been mediated by the fact that she was paid by my parents to clean, cook, and help care for me and my four siblings.

But from my childhood perspective, Genner was a member of our family. She was a great cook who prepared much of our food, including specialties such as homemade mayonnaise, biscuits, and individual apricot pies that my brother almost inhaled as they came out of the oven. I happily planted wet kisses on her and she on me. Genner and I were so close that I remember feeling comfortable probing more deeply about skin color, which I gradually learned—from observation—divided us. Why was hers black and mine white? What did it feel like to be black? She knew these questions were asked out of a child's need to understand, and she answered them all matter-of-factly: God made some people white, some black, she explained. She waved off my efforts to engage her in what we would now call political discussions.

Yet I recall becoming mystified, disturbed—and even embarrassed—that many businesses even had back entrances that "coloreds" were required to use. When I would ask why, no one ever gave me an answer that made any sense. I once stole a sip from a "colored" drinking fountain, as if to dare the powers that be. What would happen? Would I get spanked? Would someone call the police? Would I get sick or perhaps even turn black? Nothing happened.

True friendship requires reciprocity, and as I got older and realized that Genner had a separate and very different life, I remember feeling the pain I thought *she* should feel. She went home to her tiny house in a dilapidated neighborhood on Sixth Street, while we lived in a spacious Georgian colonial with big white columns in a beautiful park.

As it turns out, I was reading the biographies of Ida Tarbell and Nellie Bly about the same time Rosa Parks had refused to give up her seat on the Birmingham bus. I realize now that during the early tumultuous years of that phase of the civil rights struggle, I was learning a profound lesson in how the personal can become political.

As time passed, the news was filled with stories about Selma and Little Rock and Martin Luther King. My heart went along on those walks for freedom. I was told that actually blacks were very happy, but the ungodly communists were stirring things up so the Soviet Union could then take over a weakened America. I might have believed that, but I knew the spirit, the humanity, of "the other," and I was sensitive to the inherent unfairness that flowed simply from the color of Genner's skin.

As I got older, I realized that I wasn't getting good answers to my many questions because there were no good answers, certainly none consistent with what I was taught at church and school. There seemed to be a tacit agreement to accept some things just as they are, what some writers call the "shared narrative," which can turn into unquestioned story lines dictating our lives.

I have come to realize, too, that my journalistic questions about Washington have been a variation on my efforts to penetrate childhood mysteries, an almost biological imperative to question the status quo. In the case of Senator Packwood, for example, why wasn't any major news organization tackling an obvious follow-up story of the Hill-Thomas hearings—the problem of sexual harassment on Capitol Hill? How had the Senator gotten away with behavior that had been rumored in Washington for almost two decades? As I reported the story, I began to realize that Packwood's exploitation of women fit into Washington's "shared narrative": for some, such behavior was simply a perk of power.

By now I know some answers to my neighbor's question about what "happened" to me as a child: I learned that a measure of truth can be right in front of you; that to see it you sometimes have to shift your focus or imagine yourself in someone else's place; and that finding it involves many types of searches, some of which take a long time. I learned to question authority, appearances, the majority's view, and the way things are always done; to be aware of the dangers of generalizing and of adhering to any fixed ideology.

These lessons became especially poignant for me during the past year when I found another personal relationship with a female of a different race sparking a whole new set of questions—personal, political, and journalistic. After many years of marriage, my husband and I traveled to China last year to adopt our daughter, Grace, now four. I think often about what is "happening" to Grace as she negotiates childhood. She asks "why" a million times a day. And I see more clearly how naturally children—who haven't yet learned the artifices of adults—can ask surprisingly penetrating questions about aspects of life we sometimes want to hide from or soften, or don't even see. Thanks to her, I have what seems like a million new questions of my own as I make plans to write about national and international issues that I previously was blind to. Sometimes my work may overlap with Grace's inevitable search for the truth of who she is and why she is here. Whatever she does in life, someday I'll tell her what I have learned: to be true to her own experience. To be guided not by some false idea of objectivity, but by intellectual honesty and the Golden Rule.

LEONARD DOWNIE JR.

In this selection, one of America's most accomplished journalists, Leonard Downie Jr. of *The Washington Post,* vividly describes the hurdles faced by investigative reporters. The excerpt is drawn from his book *The New Muckrakers,* considered one of the most influential works on investigative reporting since its publication in 1976. At the time of its writing, Downie was deputy metropolitan editor at the *Post* and had supervised its Watergate coverage.

Before becoming the paper's executive editor in 1992, he also served as managing editor, London correspondent, and national editor. His book *The News about the News: American Journalism in Peril,* coauthored with colleague Robert Kaiser and published in 2002, is an insider's look at the media. Told through candid interviews and Downey's own experience as a top editor, it is yet another important work of investigative journalism.

The New Muckrakers

Nothing could be more misleading . . . than the image of the investigative reporter as Robert Redford and Dustin Hoffman in *All the President's Men,* Woodward and Bernstein holding forth on a special hour-long segment of the *Today* show devoted entirely to them, Bernstein starring as a panelist at a national convention, or Woodward playing in a celebrity doubles tennis match as the partner of a Ford administration Cabinet member. In reality—especially during the years before Watergate when I worked as an investigative reporter for *The Washington Post*—investigative reporting has more often been lonely, frustrating, tedious, and emotionally draining work. Starting out doubtfully with a flimsy hunch or an improbable-sounding tip, the investigative reporter must find out what someone else does not want him to know. He must make countless telephone calls to persons who will refuse to answer his questions, hang up on him, or never return his calls. He must knock on doors that will never be opened for him, even when he knows the person he is after is inside, with the shade pulled down and doors bolted tight.

The investigative reporter must spend hours on end in dreary courthouse file rooms and other record repositories, searching through thousands of barely intelligible legal and technical documents to find small clues that often raise more questions than they answer. He must learn how to read and understand complicated lawsuits, real estate deeds and mortgages, thick books of government regulations on highly technical subjects, and involved financial records of private businesses—all with little help from experts in these fields who likely as not will resent his snooping or will try to mislead him. He must doggedly make his way through bureaucratic mazes to request other government records that may ultimately be denied him through a legal loophole or a stubborn cover-up, even after he has finally determined exactly what he is looking for, where it is kept, and who has custody of it.

With somewhat greater difficulty, the investigative reporter must be able to recognize and disregard more lies than are told to a police detective in an entire career on the homicide squad. Many of these lies come from very respectable people—government officials, top business executives, judges, and lawyers—people who would never be suspected of such duplicity. "Being lied to becomes so much a part of the investigative reporter's life," remembered Robert M. Smith, an investigative reporter for *The New York Times* in pre-Watergate Washington, "that once or twice a year he asks himself, 'Why is this guy telling me the truth?' "

From a precious few facts the investigative reporter must be able to project shadowy outlines of the truth and then flesh out that specter with little or no help from those who know the whole story. He must decide when he has enough information to go into print, despite continuing, genuine-sounding denials from important people the story may hurt. He knows that everyone who has refused to talk to him while he was working on the story will now be waiting for just one small mistake they can pounce on with dramatic public indignation. Great apprehension washes over the reporter as the story is finally finished and he waits to see how it will stand up the next morning in the glaring light of day.

The investigative reporter must face the fact that his stories *will* hurt people. While he was working on his story, these people were the enemy—the "targets" of his investigation. They had betrayed the public trust or wronged some individual. They had lied to him or refused to tell him their side of the story. But following publication, after weeks or months of tense investigative reporting, these same people may suddenly reappear before the reporter's eyes as ordinary, frail beings like himself—people with loving families and friends and human hopes and aspirations. When, during the mid-1960s, I wrote a series of articles about systematic injustices, administrative chaos, and incompetent judges in the District of Columbia's federally supervised local court system, judges I had known well stopped talking to me and passed the word that I had maliciously betrayed and humiliated them. After the Justice Department and Congress subsequently imposed several major reforms on the D.C. court system, I was told that the former chief judge, who was replaced in a shakeup, was left a "broken man" and that his grown sons vowed to take physical revenge if they ever ran across me.

The investigative reporter must be ready for the targets of his stories to strike back in any way possible to try to ruin his reputation, estrange his editors, or gag his sources. Lawyers who practiced in D.C. courts, for example, instigated a local bar association investigation of me and my sources of information, rather than looking into what I had revealed about conditions in the courts. Lawyers and judges who were suspected of having cooperated with me were ostracized by the rest of the legal community. Several judges on the court met with my editors to try to convince them that my stories were malicious distortions that should be retracted in print on the *Post*'s front page. Another series of articles I wrote revealing corruption among officers of several local savings and loan associations cost the *Post* hundreds of thousands of dollars in revenue lost when the city's entire savings and loan industry retaliated by withdrawing all its advertising from the paper. Other investigative projects drew the usual obscene letters and phone calls and veiled threats to me and harassment of those persons who were believed to have been my sources.

At *The Washington Post,* everyone involved in the reporting, writing, and editing of the Watergate stories suspected that all our telephones were tapped, that at least Woodward and Bernstein and probably executive editor Benjamin Bradlee and publisher Katharine Graham were being followed constantly, and their private lives thoroughly investigated for any hint of something that could be construed as scandal. Indeed, friends of Richard Nixon, at what appeared from the White House tapes to be the specific direction of the President, did challenge the licenses of the *Post*'s television stations in Florida. White House aides publicly branded Bradlee as a Kennedy family "coat holder" who they said was working ruthlessly to destroy Nixon. Bob Woodward was accused of abusing in an unpatriotic way contacts he may have made with White House aides while he was a Navy liaison officer there. There were whisperings in Washington that Carl Bernstein might be trying to avenge his parents, who had been active in the labor movement and were accused during Nixon's Red-baiting years of being Communist sympathizers. Someone Bernstein had never met before tried to sell him marijuana on a busy downtown Washington street in what appeared suspiciously like a set-up.

It also has since become known that other investigative reporters disliked by the Nixon administration were the subjects of telephone taps, FBI investigations, and Internal Revenue Service tax audits. Elsewhere in the country investigative reporters working on local stories have been ordered to appear before judges and grand juries to explain what they have been up to and who their sources are. Some have been jailed for refusing. In an outrageous act of retaliation, two members of the 1975 Pulitzer Prize–winning *Indianapolis Star* investigative reporting team that exposed police corruption and inefficiency in the prosecutor's office in the Indiana capital were themselves charged with bribery in an obviously trumped up case concocted by the police and local prosecutor.

In most instances, however, retaliation against investigative reporters takes more subtle, although sometimes even more effective, forms. Sources simply dry up overnight. Friends the reporter has made over years on a beat suddenly turn away from him. He gets a cold, unproductive reception from officials he contacts for the first time but who already know his name and reputation. It becomes more difficult for the investigative reporter to find information and put stories together. His editors become displeased with his decreased production, and the reporter begins to doubt himself, sliding into a professionally paralyzing depression. It has happened to me and to investigative reporters who have worked with and for me.

The alternative to these dark periods for the normally manic-depressive investigative reporter are the adrenalin-pumping highs, produced by what Robert Smith called "the thrill of the chase," and the subsequent feeling of triumph over great adversity when an investigative story of some impact is finally finished and published. The need to experience such satisfaction again and again can turn the best and most determined investigative reporters into scandal-hungry fanatics who live for the next front-page victory that only the raking of more muck can produce. "It's almost a perverse pleasure," Bob Woodward admitted. "I like going out and finding something that is going wrong or something that isn't the way other people are saying it is, and then putting it into the newspaper."

For most investigative reporters, just seeing their latest exposé in print on their newspaper's front page is soon not enough. They want outrage in reaction to the injustice they have exposed and some evidence that something will be done about it. Someone must be indicted, forced to resign from office, or defeated at the next election, and Congress or the state assembly or the city council must pass remedial legislation Nothing can depress an investigative reporter more than to have his stories met with silence. He would sooner spend time in jail for not revealing his sources than be ignored. Seymour Hersh regularly solicited officials' reactions to his own exposés for follow-up stories for the front page of *The New York Times* and freely expressed his outrage when it seemed that little would be done. Other reporters have slipped information to prosecutors to help induce indictments. Still others, like Miriam Ottenberg of *The Washington Star,* who during the 1950s and 1960s pioneered investigative reporting of consumer fraud, have actually helped write and lobby for corrective legislation in Congress. Becoming an active, and sometimes brash, advocate can damage a reporter's reputation for fairness and warp his perception of his purpose. It can lead him arrogantly to justify his own overstepping the bounds of propriety to uncover wrongdoing by others.

STEVE LOVELADY

What is the role of the editor of investigative journalism? For more than two decades, Steve Lovelady edited one of the most acclaimed investigative reporting teams in American journalism, Donald Barlett and James Steele. For twenty-two years at *The Philadelphia Inquirer* and later as editor-at-large for Time Inc., Lovelady guided dozens of other writers as well, all struggling to reduce reams of data and interviews to incisive, powerful stories.

In this essay for the May/June 2001 *Columbia Journalism Review,* he presents one of his most valuable tools for helping a reporter find focus. It is an effective exercise for any writer of in-depth stories, be they investigations or features.

Twenty-Five Words or Less (and Other Secrets of Investigative Editing)

The success of any investigative story or series rides or falls on how early the editor becomes a collaborator in the process. By editor, I mean the lucky soul who will be doing the manuscript editing at the tail end of the process. There are four points at which he or she can become involved:

1. At the initiation of the story itself;
2. During the reporting;
3. After the reporting but before the writing;
4. And, finally, of course, in the actual line editing or, if necessary, restructuring of the manuscript.

Involving your editor in all the stages, one through four, will save a world of grief for both editor and reporter. (Among other benefits of proximity, the reporter may even drop his paranoia enough to think of the editor as a partner!) Involving your editor in stages two through four is next best. Even involving the editor just in stages three and four often works.

But involving the editor—or, if you're the big boss, calling in the cavalry—only in stage four? That's a sure-fire recipe for disaster. The magnitude of the disaster can be measured by the frequency of the following utterances: "Whose goofball idea was this in the first place?" (referring back to stage one). "The reporting has more holes in it than a presidential position paper" (referring back to stage two). "If I had known this is what you had, I would have suggested we approach it *this* way. . ." (referring back to stage three). Or all of the above.

Far too often for me, over the course of twenty-six years as an editor at newspapers and five as an editor at magazines, it has been all of the above. And I like to think that this experience has taught me something. What it has taught me is that if I can have only one of the four stages, I will take stage three—the sit-down between editor and reporter, after the reporting but before the writing.

That, my friends, is where the rubber meets the road. It is where the editor finds out if the reporter has the faintest clue how to climb the mountain of documentation and notes he has assembled and emerge at the top with a sharply worded, crisp, briskly told tale. Often, even the best reporters and most facile writers need help at this stage, and it is no wonder. After all those interviews, after weeks or months of document-digging, trail-sniffing, blind alleys, discoveries, dry holes, and amazing finds, synthesizing all that material is a daunting task.

What I like to give the reporters in this post-reporting, pre-writing session is what I call the twenty-five-words-or-less test. This is not my idea. (Few of my more effective practices are; I'll steal from anyone.) As far as I can trace, it originated with David Belasco, the former Broadway producer. Belasco spent much of his working day receiving supplicants: would-be playwrights who wanted him to produce their script, or their idea for a script. And whether the work in question was a one-act play with a single character, or a four-act play with twenty-six characters and seventeen subplots, Belasco would tell these supplicants, "If you can't write your idea on the back my calling card, you don't have a clear idea." So I stole that, and I tell the reporter sitting in my office, "Look, I know you spent nine months and $XXX,000 of the newspaper's money chasing this thing to ground. But I want you to sum it all up for me in twenty-five words or less. Take your time. Go walk around the block, or go out for a drink, or whatever, if you want. But then come back and give it to me in twenty-five words or less. And you're not allowed twenty-six."

Believe it or not, this works. You, the investigative reporter, may well think your project is far too complex, far too nuanced, far too important to be reduced to a twenty-five-word nut. I can only tell you this: in the course of editing eleven Pulitzer Prize–winning stories or series and, in the magazine realm, two National Magazine Award winners and three finalists, I have yet to run across the story too complex or too nuanced or too important to be summed up in twenty-five words or less. And once the reporter-writer submits himself to that discipline— thinks it through and comes up with the twenty-five words —a magical thing can happen.

Three things, actually. Presto, the heart of the story—the incisively stated, powerful topic paragraph—has been essentially written. And, in all likelihood, a blueprint has been revealed for how to go about constructing the entire story or series. And—just as important—it will quickly become clear if there are holes in that mountain of assembled data on which you are both staking your careers.

You can't ask for much more than that.

In most investigative projects, alas, none of this happens. And that's too bad. For I believe that the reason many a worthy project in the end leaves few ripples in the pond into which the stone was thrown is not that it was poorly reported, not that it failed to deliver the goods, not that the idea was flawed; but, rather, that weeks and months of superb reporting were tossed down the drain by tedious writing and uninspired editing.

And that, in turn, is not just a failure to execute stage four well but almost certainly a breakdown in the process at stage three. For two years, I served as a Pulitzer judge, sorting through 200 to 250 entries in a given category. These stories were so important to the newspaper that published them that it had nominated them for the ultimate accolade. Yet I cannot tell you how many times my fellow judges and I would throw up our hands in exasperation and ask, "Can *you* figure out what they're driving at?" That is a terrible waste —of the reporter's effort, of the newspaper's money and newshole, and of the editor's ulcer. Gene Roberts, my boss and mentor for seventeen years at *The Philadelphia Inquirer,* used to put it this way: "Nobody ever won a Pulitzer Prize because of the first twenty or thirty column-inches of a major story. But hundreds have *lost* a Pulitzer because of those first twenty or thirty inches." I have no doubt he is correct.

I also have no doubt that if your story befuddles those judges, it also almost certainly befuddled your readers. And that's the real crime.

I want to touch on one other thought, and that is what happens to the story once a polished, agonized-over, and carefully crafted manuscript is delivered. The editor of that story, or series, fully as much as the reporter—no, more than the reporter — then has the task of carrying the baby safely through a woods full of dangers.

That woods is . . . your own organization. There are so many ways to trip up a great story—from layout and makeup that does not give the story the pride of place that the effort deserves, to timid copy-editing and lawyering that eventually blankets the story like a new snowfall blurring a rocky landscape.

At this point you are no longer the coach; you are the blocking back. The reporter is the ball carrier and the story is the football. To mix a metaphor, this is where you, the editor, have to, without declaring so—God, *never* declare so—become a guerrilla warrior protecting the project from all the inevitable internal forces that serve to blunt its impact.

Frankly, over the years, in the always perilous process of getting an investigative story or series ready for print and, finally, into print, I have had to make more shoestring catches to save a story from well-intentioned but ultimately wrongheaded editors—both above and below me—than from reporters themselves. But that, my friends, is another story.

CRAIG McCOY

Craig McCoy is city editor of *The Philadelphia Inquirer.* During twenty years at the paper, he has worked as city hall bureau chief, as New Jersey bureau chief, as an urban affairs reporter, and as an investigative reporter. In this last role, he was part of a team that reported on how the Philadelphia Police Department mistreated crime victims. The reporting on that subject, especially regarding the mistreatment of rape victims, won the Scripps Howard Foundation's award for public service and the Selden Ring Award for investigative reporting. It was twice a finalist for a Pulitzer Prize in public service.

In this essay for the January/February 2000 *Columbia Journalism Review,* McCoy reveals how the reporters identified the story and overcame numerous obstacles to publish pieces that the Philadelphia police were determined to suppress.

How We Got That Story: The Buried Rapes

For much of 1998, the *Inquirer* wrote articles about how Philadelphia's police department had camouflaged crimes in its statistics, in a long-running ploy to make the city look safer than it was. As evidence mounted, some police officials conceded that cheating on crime stats was deeply entrenched in the culture of the department. But they insisted that crimes like murder and rape were exempt from such tactics.

Yet one case the newspaper had uncovered in 1998 involved a woman's claim that a loan shark had beaten and raped her in front of several men. That charge, we discovered, had been downgraded to a peculiar code—"investigation of person," a noncriminal classification—in a precinct notorious for fiddling with crime reports. We were intrigued.

By the end of 1999, we were able to report that the Special Victims Unit had buried thousands of rape and other assault complaints in bureaucratic dead zones—including two cases involving a murderer and serial rapist who is still at large. The women in these cases never realized that their complaints had been sidetracked.

After reporting on the case of the woman and the loan shark—the police later acknowledged she had indeed been raped—we began pushing to find out if the deep-sixing of her complaint was an isolated episode or part of a hidden trend. New rounds of citywide crime statistics, meanwhile—some leaked to us, some public—were showing a big increase in rapes, and for most crimes. It was clear to us that this surge was not the result of some crime wave, but of a turn toward more honest reporting by police, who were under public pressure to do so after our 1998 stories.

We began to wonder: What were the human stories behind those figures? How many solvable cases have been swept under the rug? What happened to the victims?

We had learned how to locate victims and decipher the tedious paper and electronic trail of police documents through our work in 1998. Through court files, leaked investigative reports, and other sources, we began to find a number of rape complaints that had come in to the sex crimes unit but never emerged as reported crimes.

But finding such rape complaints was far easier than sorting them out, separating those with a solid foundation from those open to a charge that they were fabricated, as sometimes happens. When a case felt substantial to us, we tried to corroborate the woman's story with friends and family, with witnesses and neighborhood anti-crime volunteers, with current and former beat police and detectives. We had to ask detailed and intimate questions that focused on the issue of consent.

We quickly learned that the victims most likely to be dismissed by police tended to be poor, transient women, with histories of drug abuse or petty criminal records. We found women without telephones or fixed addresses. One was interviewed in prison, another at the corner bar. But we found middle-class victims too, working women who lived in downtown Philadelphia.

There were issues of confidentiality, of course. All the women were assured from the start that we would not publish names or identifying details without their permission. Ultimately, several agreed to be named, and even photographed at the scenes where they had been raped. In case after case, victims signed forms giving us access to their emergency-room records—invaluable, neutral, contemporaneous accounts.

We also interviewed police, from patrol officers to police commissioner John F. Timoney. From the moment he had arrived, in early 1998, Timoney was one of Philadelphia's most popular public figures—a blunt reformer who exuded crime-fighting confidence. But while he was open to media scrutiny in general, Timoney was reticent when it came to the rape squad.

When we sought to question him about specific cases, his spokeswoman faxed us this reply from Timoney: "What part of 'I'm not going back over last year's crimes' don't you understand? We are NOT going back to review or revisit the work of others to satisfy your [word deleted] interest." When we pursued patrol officers and detectives, sometimes at their homes, the commissioner and the police union both complained.

We kept knocking on doors, however. First we hit on the homes of former supervisors and investigators from the rape squad. We found George Pennington, now a police chief in a small Pennsylvania town, and he was brutally frank about how things worked. He told us on the record how the squad—overburdened, understaffed, and pressured to make its stats shine—had routinely ditched complaints. They were from victims who "didn't fit a certain profile," who weren't "people of substance," or who lived in rough sections of the city that an investigator might not want to visit. "They wanted the rapes down," Pennington told us. "Basically, it was public relations."

While some police officers agreed, often ex-commanders insisted that virtually all sexual-assault complaints were recorded as crimes. But our reporting and review of crime-by-crime data debunked that assertion. So did a response to a Freedom of Information request that we had filed in 1998 and amended in early 1999. That response stunned us, and gave us a wedge to ask more-pointed questions. Released after prodding from *Inquirer* lawyers, the FOIA data included a big chunk of the buried history of the Special Victims Unit.

For example, we got copies of correspondence between the FBI and the unit about the squad's dramatically high rate of labeling rape complaints "unfounded" in its early years. The FBI was critical, but the unit was unapologetic. In one letter to the FBI, the unit described the scenarios of false rape complaints, including reports of rape "by extraterrestrials, evil spirits, television or movie stars, etc."

The unit did respond to the FBI's concerns, however—by simply switching tactics. It began dumping cases in other ways, such as "Code 2701"—a non-crime category called "investigation of person," which patrol officers normally use for pedestrian stops. Over the years, thousands of complaints sent to the Special Victims Unit were coded 2701.

The dumping of rape complaints, we found, sometimes hampered investigation in dramatic ways. We were able to demonstrate one such occurrence. Our inquiry began when an anonymous caller, almost certainly a cop, described two 1997 attacks—never disclosed to the public. The caller told reporter Clea Benson that these assaults appeared to be the work of the same man who had committed other rapes, and then gone on to murder a woman in 1998.

The caller provided leads to one case—the rough address of the attack and the month it occurred. With those details, we located the complaint in the department's massive and anonymous incident database, which the city had reluctantly begun releasing to the media several years ago. The case had been classified Code 2701. By cross-checking the facts we had already gathered with a commercial database listing of everyone who had lived on the block in recent years, we were ultimately able to ID the victim and order a copy of the initial police incident report, for the standard $15 fee, one of hundreds we bought over the last year.

The report's narrative made clear the horror of the attack: the woman had reported that she awoke in bed inside her ground-floor apartment with a stranger on top of her. The man sexually assaulted her for hours. Around dawn he fled. She theorized that he had slipped into the apartment through a narrow opening in window burglar bars.

The woman declined to talk with us, although her lawyers did. But searches of real estate records and visits to the crime scene, meanwhile, led us to many friends and former neighbors, all of whom told the same tale: that the police had viewed the victim with suspicion, "like she was the perpetrator," as a friend of the woman put it. Indeed, one of the officers who responded to the crime told us, in an interview in her home, that the victim "looked like a woman who thought every man should want her." Through sources in the department, we learned that the rape squad had decided that the window opening was likely too narrow for anyone to slip through, and so coded her case "2701." Translation: her story was a fantasy.

Meanwhile, we were also able to find the second case that the anonymous caller had given us a tip on. Other sources gave us enough detail on that case to find it in the police database. It, too, had been dumped into Code 2701.

Around that time a downtown serial rapist—linked to a murder of a Penn doctoral student in May 1998—had struck again, raping another student after removing burglar bars. Amid public uproar about his attacks, 500 people jammed a town meeting in a church to hear an FBI "profiler" provide a psychological sketch of the killer. Afterwards, reporter Michael Matza watched as a tearful woman in her twenties pressed her hand into the FBI agent's hands, asking him questions. By night's end, the woman and her father had returned with Matza to the *Inquirer*'s office, where she poured out her story well past midnight.

She turned out to be the woman in the second case that the caller had alerted us to. And she was grateful, she told us, that we wanted to hear her story. Then she pulled a chilling snapshot from her handbag, a photo of her face taken days after the intruder had choked her unconscious inside her apartment. It was a devastating image—the whites of both eyes flooded with blood from broken blood vessels. The rape squad coded the case Code 2701, and passed it to detectives who classified it as a burglary.

After we questioned the police department about her case, police conducted a new round of DNA testing on underwear that had been taken from her apartment. Semen on the underwear, it turned out, matched the DNA of the serial rapist-killer.

Within days of that lab test, police conducted another round of DNA testing on hair samples taken from the apartment of the woman whose window opening police had deemed too narrow for anyone to enter. Detectives never conceded that the window was large enough. And the DNA sample tested positive. She, too—Code 2701 and all—had been a victim of the serial rapist-killer, who is still at large. After these stories and our series on the larger problem, readers reacted quickly. Women's groups in Philadelphia urged the department to exhume the buried cases, called for a shake-up in the rape squad, and successfully demanded city council hearings on the unit's performance. Commissioner Timoney has pledged to add more detectives to the unit. The commissioner, who once told us he lacked the time or resources to examine old complaints, has also begun a review of cases going back five years—the statute of limitations on rape.

Chapter 7

OFF THE STRAIGHT AND NARROW: SPECIALIZED STORY TYPES

Creative nonfiction, obituaries, features, and columns all face the same test: does the story connect with readers?

This chapter explores a variety of specialized story types and the ways in which each strives to touch readers' hearts as well as their heads. Tracy Kidder, writing about creative nonfiction, insists that the point is to make the truth believable, not to lead a reader to believe anything that is not true. Suzi Parker, who began her career writing obituaries, recalls the ample evidence that what she wrote really mattered to people. John Tierney believes the biggest challenge in feature writing is learning how to surprise your reader. James Bellows writes about his attempt to revitalize a newspaper through—of all things—gossip. Though the forms they use are different, these writers employ the same formula for success: to speak intimately to readers, one must rely on emotion, insight, and humor.

TRACY KIDDER

"One of the exciting things about being a journalist," Tracy Kidder has said, is "you get to get outside your own life and into the lives of other people, and you're constantly surprised." One of the most accomplished practitioners of creative nonfiction, Kidder takes up residence in the lives of ordinary people living in ordinary places and captures what he sees and hears using the tools of the fiction writer: dialogue, character, scene, and plot. The result is intimate and, yes, surprising.

In his Pulitzer Prize–winning book *The Soul of a New Machine,* Kidder took readers inside the lives (and basements) of computer hackers and engineers. He dwelled in a teacher's classroom to produce *Among Schoolchildren;* in a nursing home for *Old Friends;* on both the physical and emotional plane of a construction site for *House;* and in the shoes of a police officer and other residents of Northampton, Massachusetts, for *Home Town.*

In the following essay from *The Fourth Genre,* a collection edited by Robert L. Root Jr. and Michael Steinberg and published in 1999, Kidder says the nonfiction writer's "fundamental job is to make what is true believable." Too often, he warns, practitioners of creative nonfiction bend the rules of journalism and warp that objective, writing not what is true but inventing facts to fit their own truths.

Faith, Truth, and the Facts

When I first started trying to write in this genre, there was an idea in the air, which for me had the force of a revelation: that all journalism is inevitably subjective. I was in my mid-twenties then, and although my behavior was somewhat worse than it has been recently, I was quite a moralist. I decided that writers of nonfiction had a moral obligation to write in the first person—really write in the first person, making themselves characters on the page. In this way, I would disclose my biases. I would not hide the truth from the reader. I would proclaim that what I wrote was just my own subjective version of events. In retrospect, it seems clear that this prescription for honesty often served instead as a license for self-absorption on the page. But I was still very young, too young and self-absorbed to realize what now seems obvious—that I was less likely to write honestly about myself than about anyone else on earth.

I wrote a book about a murder case, in a swashbuckling first person. It *was* published, I'm sorry to say. On the other hand, it disappeared without a trace; that is, it never got reviewed in *The New York Times*. And I began writing nonfiction articles for the *Atlantic Monthly*, under the tutelage of Richard Todd, then a young editor there. For about five years, during which I didn't dare attempt another book, I worked on creating what many writer friends of mine call "voice." I didn't do this consciously. If I had, I probably wouldn't have gotten anywhere. But gradually, I think, I cultivated a writing voice, the voice of a person who was well-informed, fair-minded, and temperate—the voice, not of the person I was, but of a person I sometimes wanted to be. Then I went back to writing books, and discovered other points of view besides the first person.

Choosing a point of view is a matter of finding the best place to stand from which to tell a story. It shouldn't be determined by theory, but by immersion in the material itself. The choice of point of view, I've come to think, has nothing to do with morality. It's a choice among tools. I think it's true, however, that the wrong choice can lead to dishonesty. Point of view is primary; it affects everything else, including voice. Writing my last four books, I made my choices by instinct sometimes and sometimes by experiment. Most of my memories of time spent writing have merged together in a blur, but I remember vividly my first attempts to find a way to write *Among Schoolchildren,* a book about an inner-city schoolteacher. I had spent a year inside her classroom. I intended, vaguely, to fold into my account of events I'd witnessed in that little place a great deal about the lives of particular schoolchildren and about the problems of education in America. I tried out every point of view that I'd used in previous books, and every page I wrote felt lifeless. Finally, I hit on a restricted third-person narration.

The approach seemed to work. The world of that classroom seemed to come alive when the view of it was restricted mainly to observations of the teacher and to accounts of what the teacher saw and heard and smelled and felt. This choice narrowed my options. I ended up writing something less comprehensive than I'd planned. The book became essentially an account of a year in the emotional life of a schoolteacher. My choice of the restricted third person also obliged me to write parts of the book as if from within the teacher's mind. I felt entitled to describe her thoughts and feelings because she had described them to me, both during class and afterward, and because her descriptions rarely seemed self-serving. Believing in them myself, I thought that I could make them believable on the page.

Belief is an offering that a reader makes to an author, what Coleridge famously called "That willing suspension of disbelief for the moment, which constitutes poetic faith." It is up to the writer to entertain and inform without disappointing the reader into a loss of that faith. In fiction or poetry, of course, believability may have nothing to do with realism or even plausibility. It has everything to do with those things in nonfiction, in my opinion. I think that the nonfiction writer's fundamental job is to make what is true believable. I'm not sure that everyone agrees. Lately the job seems to have been defined differently. Here are some of the ways that some people now seem to define the nonfiction writer's job: to make believable what the writer thinks is true, if the writer wants to be scrupulous; to make believable what the writer wishes were true, if the writer isn't interested in scrupulosity; or to make believable what the writer thinks might be true, if the writer couldn't get the story and had to make it up.

I figure that if I call a piece of my own writing nonfiction it ought to be about real people, with their real names attached whenever possible, who say and do in print nothing that they didn't actually say and do. On the cover page of my last book I put a note that reads, "This is a work of nonfiction," and listed the several names that I was obliged to change in the text. I thought a longer note would be intrusive. I was afraid that it would stand between the reader and the spell that I wanted to create, inviting the reader into the world of a nursing home. But the definition of "nonfiction" has become so slippery that I wonder if I shouldn't have written more. So now I'll take this opportunity to explain that for my last book I spent a year doing research, that the name of the place I wrote about is its real name, that I didn't change the names of any of the major characters, and that I didn't invent dialogue or put any thoughts in characters' minds that the characters themselves didn't confess to.

I no longer care what rules other writers set for themselves. If I don't like what someone has written, I can stop reading, which is, after all, the worst punishment a writer can suffer. (It ought to be the worst punishment. Some critics seem to feel that the creation of a book that displeases them amounts to a felony.) But the expanded definitions of nonfiction have created problems for those writers who define the term narrowly. Many readers now view with suspicion every narrative that claims to be nonfiction, and yet scores of very good nonfiction writers do not make up their stories or the details in them—writers such as John McPhee, Jane Kramer, J. Anthony Lucas. There are also special cases that confound categories and all attempts to lay down rules for writers of narrative. I have in mind Norman Mailer and in particular his *Executioner's Song,* a hybrid of fact and fiction, carefully labeled as such—a book I admire.

Most writers lack Mailer's powers of invention. Some nonfiction writers do not lack his willingness to invent, but the candor to admit it. Some writers proceed by trying to discover the truth about a situation, and then invent or distort the facts as necessary. Even in these suspicious times, writers can get away with this. Often no one will know, and the subjects of the story may not care. They may not notice. But the writer always knows. I believe in immersion in the events of a story. I take it on faith that the truth lies in the events somewhere, and that immersion in those real events will yield glimpses of that truth. I try to hew to what has begun to seem like a narrow definition of nonfiction partly in that faith, and partly out of fear. I'm afraid that if I started making up things in a story that purported to be about real events and people, I'd stop believing it myself. And I imagine that such a loss of conviction would infect every sentence and make each one unbelievable.

I don't mean to imply that all a person has to do to write good narrative nonfiction is to take accurate notes and reproduce them. The kind of nonfiction I like to read is at bottom storytelling, as gracefully accomplished as good fiction. I don't think any technique should be ruled out to achieve it well. For myself, I rule out only invention. But I don't think that honesty and artifice are contradictory. They work together in good writing of every sort. Artfulness and an author's justified belief in a story often combine to produce the most believable nonfiction.

SUZI PARKER

The obituary beat was once the domain of worn-out reporters whose legs or ambition had given out. Reporters too tired (or too complacent) to go out and gather information in the field were put out to pasture. Every day, they sat at their desks and simply recorded the information phoned in by funeral homes or relatives of the deceased.

But the elevation of obituary writing to an art form has changed all that. Finely crafted essays depict the deceased honestly, in all their idiosyncratic glory. And suddenly, the beat is sought after by writers of all ages and experience. After all, the best obituaries find a home on page one. And the first thing many newspaper readers turn to is the obituary page.

Suzi Parker is a freelance journalist who began her career writing obituaries and whose provocative writing has since become familiar to readers of the online magazine *Salon*. She wrote numerous articles about the investigations surrounding Bill Clinton in his (and her) hometown of Little Rock. Her work has been published in the *Economist*, the *Christian Science Monitor*, and *The New York Times Magazine*. In this selection, which appeared in the May 3, 1998, issue of *The Washington Post*, she describes her first two years in journalism, as the "Angel of Death" at the *Arkansas Democrat-Gazette*.

When Death Was My Muse

Death had its perks.

One Thanksgiving, I received an 18-lb. sugar-cured ham. A trio of mourners once gave me a huge lush fern. During the Christmas season, I received a shiny, colored tin of expensive chocolates and a sparkling brass holiday ornament. Then there was that time I ate a free lunch at the downtown Masonic temple and got a guided tour of the building—all because I wrote obituaries.

I never planned to write about death, especially in my first job out of graduate school. It wasn't on my Top Ten list of things to achieve before turning 30. With two degrees in journalism, I expected to be out in the field, chasing fires, investigating illegal activities in seedy motels and tracking down politicians' illicit business dealings and messy personal lives. I wanted to be Lois Lane. I wound up as Elvira.

My college dreams of Pulitzer Prizes hadn't prepared me for an obituary beat. Sure, I thought I could deal with death. Reporters imagine, some even thrive on, the worst—a multiple homicide, a plane crash killing 200 people, a blaze that wipes out an entire family. Big stories on the front page, leading to bigger "perspective" pieces and prestigious awards. Alas, I had to write biographies of the dead.

I was working at the *Arkansas Democrat-Gazette*. As stories about President Clinton often have noted, this is a small city in a small state. The proverbial six degrees of separation between any two people shrink to about half a degree. Everybody seems to know or have some connection to everybody else. Gossip is an honorable pastime, and obituaries are an agreeable way to catch up with old acquaintances.

For two years, I listened to sobbing, dignified, laughing, distraught—and sometimes just plain crazy—survivors, all the while trying to decipher truth from grief-induced fantasies. Unlike so many of my newspaper colleagues, I never had the option of hearing the stories of my subject firsthand. For that I needed a Ouija board—and nightly deadlines never allowed for that kind of indulgence.

My editors even sent me to study under the guru of obituary writing, Jim Nicholson of the *Philadelphia Daily News,* and learn the secrets of retracing the lives of the weird, the wacky and the wealthy. I came back asking all the right questions: What did they eat? What did they wear? What was abnormal or unique about them? Did they spend their lives trying to develop a cure for some disease? Or did they ride the rails with hobos? And how exactly did the deceased come to be named Velvet Couch?

When my day was done, I had buried a father who never spent enough time with his family, a Bohemian mother dying from cancer who did biblical scenes in needlepoint on every pew in her church, a lonely artist who raced into a burning house to rescue her five cats. I immortalized them in one column of newsprint and went home exhausted, wondering who would die during the night. I never worried about whether I would have something to write about the next day.

Death became me. I received kudos and memos from superiors. To friends and strangers, I was known as the Obit Girl. I was the hit of any party, naturally dressed in black. As I held my glass of wine, co-workers, one after the other, would ask, "Oh, Angel of Death, who died today? How did they die? How old were they? Tell us everything." Morbid curiosity ruled, and I, the Spice Girl of the Dead, possessed all the answers about those souls departed for the afterworld.

More than once I heard from seasoned crime reporters, "I don't know how you do it. Amazing. I could never do it."

Truth is, I really didn't know how I did it. I often woke up at 3 A.M., sweating and paralyzed by dreams of the dead. I told no one that, as a child, I had feared death, funerals, hearses, caskets—and that I still held my breath whenever I drove past a cemetery. Even now, I go out of my way to avoid a funeral procession on the highway. I hid my sadness for the families I interviewed. My colleagues didn't know that at the end of the day I sat in my car, blasted the radio and let the tears gush from my eyes.

In my two-year tenure on the obit desk—before I burned out and asked for another beat—I learned that death plays a funny game. For each byline, my mortality stared directly back at me. Every story toughened my heart a little more and numbed my emotions. I began to feel nothing except the wet tears on my face at the end of a long, draining day. Every night, I crawled into bed believing that, in the end, death wins.

But after the crying stopped, I pondered this job and realized that I, in fact, liked death's generosity. Besides the gifts, it provided me with local fame, and sappy, yet completely sincere, fan letters and phone calls. My obituaries often were printed in funeral programs, glued into scrapbooks and laminated as bookmarks. Sources, even funeral directors, called to inform me when a fascinating or prominent person was at death's door. Some people phoned and begged to reserve a space in the column for their dying loved one. Over time, my colleagues no longer considered obit writing a lowly clerk's job. For all the tears, nightmares and eventual burnout, they could see that I had connected with readers—day in, day out—on a deep, personal level. Death had given me new life.

JOHN TIERNEY

What really makes great feature writing is great thinking, and *New York Times* writer John Tierney is an extraordinary thinker. His column, The Big City, was often Topic A around watercoolers in Manhattan. His *New York Times Magazine* article "Recycling Is Garbage," in which he argued that recycling is one of the most wasteful activities in America, attracted more letters than any article ever published in the magazine. He is coauthor, with Christopher Buckley, of the novel *God Is My Broker,* an ecclesiastical satire and parody of the self-help industry that tells the story of a failed Wall Street trader who becomes a monk and receives stock tips from God.

Creativity is the mark of Tierney's work. Before joining the *Times* in 1990, he spent ten years writing for magazines, among them *Atlantic Monthly, Discover, Esquire, Health, Newsweek, Outside,* and *Rolling Stone.* His habit of thinking rigorously about ideas leads him to find unconventional approaches to his stories.

Creative ideas—and their genesis—were the subject of a talk Tierney gave to a class of students at Yale University, an edited transcript of which appears in William Zinsser's 1995 book *Speaking of Journalism* and is excerpted here. Too often, Tierney says, reporters and editors deliver stories that contain no surprises; they merely fulfill some preconceived idea. But the best stories come from the pursuit of questions to which neither the reporter nor the editor knows the answers. Tierney obviously lets his curiosity drive his reporting and writing. The result is that the reader, like the writer, embarks on a journey of discovery.

Finding the "Take"

For me the biggest challenge in feature writing is to find the angle—or, as it's sometimes called, the "take." Most stories originate with the idea that there is an interesting person or phenomenon or trend, and the trick is to think of a particular way to tell that story. A rule I try to remember—I've heard it attributed to the editor Byron Dobell—is that "a story should be a verb, not a noun." It shouldn't just be about a place or an institution; something should be happening there.

Early in my career as a magazine writer I got an assignment from *Esquire* that turned into a debacle. It was to write a story about Phil Knight, the founder of Nike. He was a man who had used a waffle iron in his garage to make the first sole of a running shoe that revolutionized the business. He was worth about $400 million. It seemed there ought to be something there to write about. But I never figured out what the take was; I never got beyond the nouns "Nike" or "Phil Knight." I couldn't even manage a simple profile, because when I went to see him I was unable to extract a single interesting quote. That's when I learned that the worst question an interviewer can ask is: "Can you tell me an interesting anecdote?" The person might have a million of them, but his mind will go absolutely blank. You can silence any raconteur with that question.

During that process my editor sent me a piece that Tom Wolfe had written for *Esquire* about Robert Noyce, who was one of the fathers of Silicon Valley. It began with the fact that Noyce grew up in Iowa and lived in Grinnell, a town that was founded by Protestants fleeing the sinful ways of the East; they went to Grinnell to start a new society. Wolfe's take was that these software engineers in modern California had the same attitude toward the East—they were puritans appalled by big New York corporations with extravagant hierarchies and lavish perquisites. In Silicon Valley it wasn't customary for the president of a company to have his reserved space in the parking lot. One day a visiting executive from New York was brought to the company by a chauffeur, who sat outside waiting, and the engineers were shocked that a company would assign one person to waste his time sitting in a car. It went against the religious values of Silicon Valley.

Anyway, that's how Wolfe saw it, and I remember resenting his story because it didn't have a quote from any software engineer saying that was how *he* saw Silicon Valley. It was all Tom Wolfe's idea. But later I came to think Wolfe was right to impose that perspective on the story. Even if the software engineers never talked about religion, Wolfe was justified in arriving at his own take on the subject, just as he had been entitled to say that astronauts had to have "the right stuff." I doubt if that phrase even occurred to the astronauts until they read Wolfe's book, and then they probably realized that he had captured the spirit of their program in a way they couldn't have.

In general, I think, the writer is more interesting than the person he or she is writing about. That sounds arrogant, and I don't mean that you shouldn't realistically portray the people you're covering or that you should intrude yourself into their story. But the reason you're a writer is that you have an interesting way of looking at situations. At least you have a fresh perspective. Most people who have been doing something for a long time become completely accustomed to the weirdnesses of their lives. You should always be faithful to representing how people feel, what they think and what they say. But I don't think you have to look at it from their point of view. That took me a long time to realize. I could hear the voices of the people I had interviewed saying, "That's not the way it is." And after a certain point I thought: I don't care; this is how *I* see it—which may be a more valid perspective.

I'll give you a small example. I did an article for my paper, *The New York Times,* about the boat basin at 79th Street on the Hudson River, which has been the subject of countless stories over the years describing the colorful bohemians and old salts who live there. My story compared them to the city's homeless squatters. These people were squatters on public land, which the city spent $2 million to fix up, and I wondered: Why do they have a right to stay there? The city is kicking the homeless out of the parks; why do these boat people have special rights? Well, my article got taped up on the fence at the boat basin and was annotated with 36 refutations. At one time that would have bothered me, but I knew that my facts were accurate and that my perspective was valid. The boat people had their own perspective: They had a right to be there because they had been there for ten years and it was only proper that the city should pay for them. But I think a more interesting question for the reader is: Why are your tax dollars going to give someone a low-rent place in a public park?

. . . I quoted the boat people's lawyer and their point of view, but I didn't give them 50 percent of the article. The gist of the piece was going toward "Why don't they pay any property taxes?" . . .

The most obvious way for a writer to approach any broad subject—any big institution or trend—is to find one person or place or event that stands for the whole story. Of course that's a cliché; there's even a word for it—it's called synecdoche. But in reporting many feature articles, the most important element is the considerable amount of time you spend trying to find the one person who makes a good story.

I was sent to Africa with another reporter to do a series about AIDS, the ultimate "noun" of a story. We had a whole continent and tons of statistics and studies, but we needed something specific—one tale. I went to Zambia, and I noticed that many articles about AIDS referred to a practice that was spreading the disease, called ritual cleansing. But the reference was always just one or two sentences. So I started asking about the practice. It wasn't an easy trail to follow; I would be in a village, and someone would know someone who had engaged in ritual cleansing, and they'd say, "You go about six miles and you'll see a big tree and then you turn left." Finally, in the capital city of Lusaka, someone put me onto a case. It took a week of badgering people before I got to that person's house, in a shantytown, but it turned into a good story. Here's how it starts:

> LUSAKA, ZAMBIA—Sanford Mweupe now looks back wistfully on the uncomplicated days when he had only two wives to worry about. So do the two wives. Domestic life has been strained ever since the events delicately referred to in the household as "the confusion."
>
> Last year, after his brother died, Mr. Mweupe was chosen by the family's elders to perform a ceremony called ritual cleansing. According to the tribal tradition, the brother's two widows had to be purged of their husband's spirit by having sex with a member of his family.
>
> The problem was that Mr. Mweupe's brother had died of AIDS, and the widows quite possibly were infected as well. Mr. Mweupe's wives pleaded with him not to go ahead, but the elders insisted he cleanse the widows and then also take them as wives. He heard warnings from modern doctors, but a traditional healer assured him it would be safe.
>
> So Mr. Mweupe became confused—a not uncommon reaction on a continent where a virus has suddenly intruded into tens of millions of lives. Fatal diseases are never simple anywhere, but it is hard to imagine any quite as complex as AIDS in Africa.
>
> In places like this capital city, where it appears that a fifth of adults are infected, AIDS is a family disease that touches virtually everyone in some way. It confronts Africans not only with death but with challenges to their cultural foundations: their ancestral beliefs, their marital roles and familial obligations, their conceptions of morality and sexuality.
>
> "What could I do?" Mr. Mweupe, a soft-spoken 52-year-old, said one recent afternoon in his living room. "I was bound by tradition."

Once I found that man, it was fairly straightforward to tell his story and give readers a vivid look at what was happening in Africa. All the effort was in finding him.

At one point I was assigned to do some pieces about the Times Square redevelopment—another noun, and a vague one. I came upon a building, at the corner of 42nd Street and Broadway, where the tenants were being evicted. It was almost empty, and I just went in and wandered around, and there, separately, I came upon two ancient Times Square institutions—the radio host Joe Franklin and a press agent named Dick Falk. On one level those were easy stories, once I found the two men—the idea of these two entrenched Broadway types getting kicked out. The problem was to find a fresh way of looking at them. God really is in the details in this kind of story.

Joe Franklin has been written about forever. But to me the funny thing—my take on it—was that the city is trying to clean up Times Square, and it has to get Joe Franklin, who has the messiest office in the world, to move. I don't claim that this take was a revolutionary insight—you might think it was so obvious as to be trite. But at least it gave me a way to write about Joe Franklin and the redevelopment of Times Square. It enabled me to select which details to mention and which quotes to use. When you have a lot of quotes from people who talk at great length, you have to choose the right ones. In Joe's office everything in the world was there, and trying to convey that was what I loved:

> The New York State Urban Development Corporation has achieved a major triumph in its long and troubled campaign to clean up Times Square. This week its lawyers are forcing Joe Franklin to clean out his office.
>
> Mr. Franklin is renowned as Broadway's greatest nostalgist and television's most durable host—his 39-year-old syndicated talk show is listed in the *Guinness Book of World Records*—but some acquaintances think his most remarkable achievement is the clutter in his one-room office. The debris sits above the northeast corner of Broadway and 42nd Street, in a building whose tenants are being evicted to make room for a new office tower.
>
> The mounds of coffee cups and unanswered letters long ago engulfed the desk and surrounding floor, squeezing Mr. Franklin and his secretary into a clearing by the doorway with one chair. They would take turns sitting. They kept working there this week as movers began carting off, among other things, 12,500 sheets of vaudeville music, 10,000 movie reels, and an undetermined number of unopened press releases from the Eisenhower era.
>
> "I've told them not to throw out anything," said Franklin, who is 62 years old. "The key word to me is 'someday.' It's my solace: someday I'll get to it. This way I also get a thrill that a

> neat man can never have—the thrill of finding something that was irretrievably lost."
>
> He rummaged through a pile and found a shopping bag where he had filed a 1971 issue of *The New Yorker,* which had a profile of him, called "Broadway Joe." He pointed to the description of his office: "It has that quality that goes beyond mere grime and disorder." Mr. Franklin nodded happily. "I love that description," he said.
>
> Mr. Franklin said he thought of the room as the "prototype of what an office should not be," and his secretary, Sophia Orkoulas, agreed. Ms. Orkoulas, a 21-year-old actress, looked surprised when asked to describe her filing system.
>
> "Well, we don't have drawers where you keep paper inside and stuff like that," she explained. "There really isn't much of a system. We just remember what section of the floor we put something. I thought about organizing things once, but this is the way Joe likes it."
>
> Ms. Orkoulas said there wasn't really any need for a supply cabinet because there were not really any supplies. When they needed a pen or a paper clip they rummaged on the floor for a used one, and when they needed to write something they could always find an old letter or an announcement with an unused side.
>
> "We used to have some blank sheets of paper," she said, "but we ran out."

The secretary said all that with an absolutely straight face. It's only when you go back and look at your notes that you realize how absurd it is.

. . . I had a similarly chaotic experience with the other tenant in the building, Dick Falk, whom I later wrote about in another story. He was a man who could talk happily for three hours straight—one disjointed story after another. I walked out of his office exhausted; I didn't know how I was going to produce anything coherent from the interview. But later something occurred to me as I was telling friends about Falk. By the way, that's often a good way to figure out the take. As you tell your friends about a story, notice which details interest them and which direction you find yourself following. Anyway, in talking about Falk I found myself focusing on how amazed and delighted he was to have a reporter wander uninvited into his office. For once this PR man wasn't out there begging for publicity, but he was making news anyway because he was the last tenant in the building. And it occurred to me, as I waded through all the ridiculous press releases he had given me, that it was odd he hadn't written a press releases about this reasonably newsworthy situation. So that theme became the frame of my story. It began with a straightforward two-paragraph lead, followed by the longest sentence I've ever gotten into the *Times:*

> The 12 floors of the Longacre Building are empty these days except for the security guards and Richard R. Falk. He is the same age as the building, 79, and has been known for decades as the mayor of 42nd Street. He opposes the $2.5-billion redevelopment of Times Square, which is supposed to begin with the demolition of his building, and he has refused to move out of his one-room office on the third floor.
>
> What Mr. Falk has done so far during his solitary entrenchment against the New York State Urban Development Corporation's project makes for a moderately unusual story. But what he has not done so far is truly extraordinary.
>
> So far Mr. Falk, who proudly claims to be the model for the loathsome public-relations man in *Sweet Smell of Success,* who currently estimates that he has generated five tons of press clippings and supplied gossip columnists with made-up quotes from 10,000 clients, who in his quest for publicity has carried a cross up Broadway, dressed a model in a bikini of frankfurters, gotten March 21 declared "Fragrance Day" and tried to check a trained flea named The Great Herman into the Waldorf-Astoria Hotel—so far Mr. Falk, by his own admission, has not sent out a single press release about his plight. . . .
>
> "It's just facts," he said disdainfully of his situation. "It's 100 percent real. I can't write a press release for that. You need a press agent when you have something that's 50 percent real. You make it a little fantastic or humorous, bring in enough pseudo-facts, and the papers will buy it. I always say that everything I write is guaranteed to be 50 percent true."

The article goes on to recall some of Falk's publicity exploits, brought off with his self-described "demonic frenzy" on behalf of legions of Broadway restaurants, nightclubs and would-be celebrities, and concludes by going back to the opening theme:

> "The press is coming to me," he said. "I just can't believe it. All my life I'm looking for space in the papers, I'm dying for it, and now it's falling on me. Without creating anything, I'm in *The New York Times!* To be in the *Times*—you're immortal, almost. Do you know how many millionaires would die to get a story in the *Times?* It took me 50 years, but I made it. I'm going out in style. This is it. This is my epitaph."

> He was asked if he had any suggestions for how the epitaph should read. Of course he did.
>
> "Famed Flack Who Exploited and Promoted Stars and Shows Finally Gets His Reward."

In writing feature articles it's important to be able to change directions. The best stories are often the ones that surprise you. Writers tend to go into stories with a preconceived idea and to stick with it. I try to remind myself to stay flexible. When the world chess championship between Karpov and Kasparov was held at the Macklowe Hotel, an editor at the *Times* got the idea: Just go over there and see what it's really like, these two guys locked in combat. Just go watch them. I went, and all I saw was two guys sitting at a table. I couldn't come up with anything to say. Later I was hanging around the hotel's pressroom, where the grandmasters gather, and it struck me that what was much more interesting was the kibitzing going on—all these guys sitting next door and commenting on the moves. So I stole an idea from one of my favorite books, *One-upmanship,* by Stephen Potter, and wrote a piece about chess kibitzing—tips on how to kibitz, which I gleaned from some of the grandmasters in the room:

> "Always give yourself an escape," said Bruce Pandolfini. "If you're not sure whether a move is good or not, say, 'That's interesting' or 'That's worth taking a look at.' If it really looks wrong, say, 'I'm not *quite* sure that's sound.' You can get away with saying that a move gives a 'spatial edge' or a 'powerful attacking position' as long as you don't specify what edge or what attack. Or you can just generalize with something like 'Black seems rather defensive here.' How can anyone argue with that? It may not mean anything."

. . . What I give myself credit for in that chess story is the idea of asking those kibitzers, "What are the rules of kibitzing?" As soon as they heard it they got excited. I also called a lot of other people—heads of chess clubs in different parts of the country—and asked them. Many of them couldn't think of any rules, but a few got into the spirit as I egged them on.

. . . I was lucky enough to have an editor who was open to a different story. That's not always the case. There are editors who not only insist that they know exactly what the story is; they also think they know exactly how to write it. A friend of mine got an assignment from a magazine editor who told him that the story had to begin with three anecdotes, then state the theme, then have a section about this and a section about that. Such formulas are stifling to the writer—and ultimately, of course, to the reader. It you can plot the story so explicitly before you do any reporting, how interesting or surprising can it be?

But good editors realize that the best stories are the ones they didn't ask for. They realize that *they're* not out there on the street. When I sit in on story idea meetings at the *Times*, it's interesting to see the situation from the editor's perspective. Someone might make an offhand suggestion that will turn into a story idea after 20 seconds of discussion. Obviously the editors don't know much about the topic or how the story's going to turn out; they only know that it's an interesting topic, and they trust the reporter to find the right angle. They realize that the reporter knows more than they do, and they can be dissuaded if you come back and say, "There's no story there." But of course it's always better if you can then suggest another story—one that you *did* find.

JAMES BELLOWS

The gossip column is not the most respected institution in American journalism. But for getting the attention of official and unofficial Washington in the post-Watergate era, it could not be beaten. Brought in to rescue the financially ailing *Washington Star* in 1975, editor James Bellows created The Ear—and with it a buzz that confirmed Washington's preoccupation with gossip. The legendary Bellows details his delight in setting Washington on *its* ear in his 2002 memoir, *The Last Editor: How I Saved The New York Times, The Washington Post and The Los Angeles Times from Dullness and Complacency*. Bellows, of course, did not rescue those papers, but worked for their competitors in the glory days of newspapers when major cities supported at least two.

The seven-day-a-week Ear, written by two reporters and edited by Bellows, was a bit like a runaway train, and even Bellows admits the column was not always accurate. Across town, at the rival *Washington Post*, editor Ben Bradlee, a frequent target of the column, called it "sneering, impugning, belittling and ridiculing." In a letter to Bellows, he concluded that the editor of the *Washington Star* had become "something of an authority on what is shoddy and disgraceful in journalism." And, he might have added, widely read.

The following excerpt is from *The Last Editor*.

The Ear

In January 1975, I was off an another suicide mission, this time to try to save the venerable *Washington Star*. The *Star* had been the preeminent newspaper in the capital during the years of World War II. It had an illustrious history and a great lineup of writers. But newsprint was scarce during the war, and the *Star* had used most of its space for advertising; *The Washington Post* used theirs for the news. Also, the *Star* was the victim of nepotism: The three families that owned the paper used it as an in-house welfare system. And nepotism led to stagnation. Besides, when TV arrived, afternoon papers had the life expectancy of fruit flies because people got their news at nightfall from television.

Another thing that damaged the *Star* was the increased prestige *The Washington Post* gained from two youngsters named Woodward and Bernstein who happened to unseat a president.

Still, I couldn't dream that the city of Washington didn't have enough people who read without moving their lips to support two newspapers.

So the year after Nixon left town on a rail, I arrived. A Texas multimillionaire named Joe Allbritton, who had made fortunes in funeral homes and banking businesses, had bought the paper and hired me to become its editor. He knew of the changes I had wrought at the *New York Herald Tribune* in its glorious final days and thought I could bring similar incandescence to the *Star,* perhaps with a better outcome.

Joe found me at the *Los Angeles Times,* which I affectionately called the "velvet coffin" because of the generosity it showed its editorial staff. I was the associate editor in charge of "soft news," and one of the popular features I had introduced was a gossip column by Joyce Haber.

"Are you going to start a gossip column in Washington, Jim?" I was asked at a farewell party.

"Oh, I don't think so. Gossip is trivial. Washington is a serious place."

That's how I saw it, in my naïveté. Washington was sober, solemn. Look at all that white marble, the Library of Congress, the Capitol dome. Boy, did I have the wrong number.

On my first trip to the capital, I attended a couple of dinner parties and observed, to my astonishment, that Washington *ran* on gossip. Everyone loved to talk about everyone else. Who was doing what to whom? A famous Washington hostess summed it up when she said, "If you don't have anything nice to say about someone, come sit by me."

Gossip made the Washington world go round.

So I decided that maybe a gossip column wasn't such a bad idea. I discussed it with the other *Star* editors, especially the talented head of our soft news section, Mary Anne Dolan. She suggested a perky Brit named Diana McLellan who could write with wit and flair.

I called Diana McLellan to my office.

"Diana," I said, "we are going to start a gossip column and you're going to write it."

She was aghast.

"Mr. Bellows, gossip isn't very nice. It's tacky and tawdry. There would be a public outcry. People would cancel their subscriptions. It would inflict pain. There's nothing you can say that would make me write a gossip column."

"We begin next Monday," I said.
"I'll get on the phone," said Diana.

Women's Wear Daily had a well-read column called The Eye. We called our column The Ear.

I knew it would take two people to do the job. The column would run without a byline, seven days of the week. I thought it would be controversial and people would want to see it daily. Two writers would assure that we'd never miss a day; not illness, vacation, rain, nor sleet would halt the column. So Louise Lague, a tall talented reporter, joined up the next day as Diana's partner.

The Ear was the wickedest thing to hit the capital since the Nixon administration. It was audacious. It was insolent. It was fun. And it quickly became "must" reading throughout Washington.

Did Ethel Kennedy buoyantly drive her convertible up the curb at Roger Mudd? . . . Did a southern congressman get pinched for propositioning a lady cop? . . . Did a prominent senatorial widow get arrested for shoplifting in Georgetown? . . . The Ear learned of these succulent happenings. Reporters in the *Star* newsroom, scrambling to save the paper, fed these items to Diana and Louise. Congressional staffers were good sources. Also, disgruntled bureaucrats. Also, certain politicians with a sense of humor, if that isn't an oxymoron. Also, hairdressers and florists. Gossipers all.

Sometimes the column would bother its subjects. When The Ear printed something that annoyed Washington's mayor, Marion Barry, he had all the cars towed from outside the paper's offices.

But there was a measurable statute of limitations of people's irritation with The Ear:

Busy people forgave you faster than idle ones.
Southern congressmen forgave you before northern ones.
Writers and editors forgave you when they could pay you back.
Cabinet members forgave you sooner than senators.
Academics *never* forgave you.
And Kennedys got even.

The success of The Ear was a testament to the fact that Washington was at heart a small, provincial, southern town. It might have been the Capital of the Free World, but it loved its gossip. John F. Kennedy once said, "Washington is a combination of northern charm and southern efficiency." It was also a combination of dish and dirt.

I urged Diana and Louise to include coverage of the media, and it was fun to treat reporters as though they were movie stars. They loved it. I trace a lot of today's media self-importance to the unaccustomed attention we gave them. Robert Redford played a Washington journalist. Now there are a dozen Washington journalists playing Robert Redford.

We started to send out little gold ear-shaped lapel pins to the people who were mentioned in the column. Some were enraged at having been kidded in the column, but the sheer cheek of the thing soon got to them. Eventually most of the honorees cheerfully wore their ears. At first, people assumed the lapel pins meant the wearer was deaf, and they would raise their voices. That's all we need in Washington—more raised voices.

For a few years we held an annual Ear Ball, to which we invited everyone who had ever been mentioned in the column. This generated some wildly variegated crowds. G. Gordon Liddy showed up, fresh out of prison; members of the party leadership; White House speechwriters; hairdressers, interior decorators, and local socialites . . .

The success of The Ear was a testament to more than Washington's provincialism. It was also a testament to Diana McLellan's wit and vivacity. Diana was the daughter of an RAF brigadier general who eventually became defense attaché for the British embassy in Washington. She grew up all around the world, including Wales, Rhodesia, and London. "You become more aware of what makes things work when you have to confront things new all the time" (not unlike constantly changing newspapers). As a teenager she was an art student. "I wasn't going to be a writer at all. I was precocious and snobbish," she said.

Louise Lague was Rhode Island–born, left-handed, five-eight, green-eyed, and of French-Canadian descent. Only 26 when The Ear was launched, she was a bright and funny writer but wary of hurting people's feelings. Her motto: No scolding, no finger-pointing, but lots of verve, italics, and exclaiming. It was always: "How *heartwarming* to see Senator So-and-So taking his secretary to lunch at the Jockey Club! *That* is appreciation, darlings!"

So before there was *Thelma and Louise* there was Diana and Louise, who came close to the edge, but never drove off. Diana and Louise rarely went to parties, as most gossip columnists do, relying instead on personal contacts and the stream of phone tips that flooded in. In fact, at first few people knew who actually wrote the column. The big weapon in their closet was the message machine. In those days, before everybody had one, theirs was a treat to listen to. I remember them setting it up before they'd go out to lunch, and when they came back, there'd be a stream of whispered murmurs on the machine.

"Through some outrageous fortune," recalls Louise, "we could pretty much tell what was true and what wasn't." (I wish I had known that when I was carefully vetting the column each day.) "The day we were asked to judge a dog show, I knew this thing was *big*."

In a short time, Diana and Louise's identity became the worst-kept secret in Washington, right up there with the guest list for the Lincoln Bedroom.

And with their help, gossip stepped out of the closet and became almost respectable. Diana's explanation for the popularity of chatter: "It's because we don't have *opinions* to gossip about anymore."

The biggest celebrities in Washington were Ben Bradlee and his lovely roommate, Sally Quinn. The movie blockbuster *All the President's Men* was lighting up Washington's screens at this time. Ben Bradlee, the charismatic editor of *The Washington Post,* was a combination of all that is admirable in journalism and pop culture. He and Sally Quinn were the beautiful people of the Potomac. So we started making them regulars in The Ear. We called them "The Fun Couple."

It was nothing personal.

All right, perhaps I was a little annoyed at how *The Washington Post* always referred to the *Star* as "the financially troubled *Washington Star*." For a while I thought that was our name: *The Financially Troubled Washington Star.*

And you must understand something else.

After Watergate, Ben Bradlee was a huge, heroic, larger-than-life figure. Jason Robards had just won an Academy Award playing Ben on the screen. Robards/Bradlee was a noble, witty, astute editor in power stripes. . . .

Ben Bradlee could be forgiven for being a little puffed up by the attention. So when The Ear targeted his Achilles' heel it must have been particularly annoying. But after all, he was cavorting about with a much younger woman in his own newsroom. Did he expect that to go unnoticed?

On top of that, much of the news about Bradlee and Quinn was coming to us from his own newsroom. Ben threatened to fire anyone caught leaking information to The Ear, but still it came.

Some of the leaks may have been inspired by jealousy. Sally Quinn was not uniformly adored in the *Post* newsroom. Some of her fellow journalists grumbled that the stories she brought in would not have been assigned to her if not for her relationship with the editor.

Most people gave Ben a wide berth. And here, The Ear had the temerity to make fun of His Eminence. The Ear would do to Ben Bradlee what Nixon and Colson never managed to do—needle and embarrass him. But, of course, I had an advantage over Nixon: He only had the FBI, the CIA, and the IRS; I had Diana and Louise.

Ben was the perfect target for us, and I took delight in tweaking him. Not because I didn't like him—I admire Ben enormously—but because it worked wonders for the *Star*. When you are the second paper in a market, you have to position yourself against the first paper—you have to be sassy and irreverent, and you have to get people talking.

As I said to Joe Allbritton when I moved to Washington:

"We can't be a pale copy of the *Post*. That's not how it's done."

"How's it done?"

"We've got to get them to jump into our pond. We've got to make waves. We've got to liven things up."

The Ear, featuring Ben and Sally, was one of the ways of getting the *Post* into our pond—of livening things up.

We could see them wincing . . .

In 1975 the *Star* had run a series of articles on gays in pro football. The pieces were shepherded by the sports editor, Dave Burgin, who had worked earlier at the *Trib* and went on to become the editor of *The Orlando Sentinel,* the *Oakland Tribune,* and the *San Francisco Examiner,* among other papers.

Spurred by our gay pigskin series, the Chicago columnist Mike Royko had written a great column on the phenomenon. He observed that the macho guys who watch football on TV were now finding it disturbing when their favorite quarterback patted the tight end on the rear.

I wanted to run the Royko column in the *Star,* since it had grown out of our stories. But Royko's column was syndicated exclusively to the *Post* in Washington. So I called my pal Ben.

"Ben," I said, "I'm sure you don't intend to run the Royko column in the *Post*. You won't want to promote our series."

"So?"

"So I'd like to buy the column for the *Star*."

"I'll call you back."

When Bradlee called back he sounded a little aggressive.

"Okay, you can run the Royko column, but you'll have to say: 'With the permission of *The Washington Post.*' "

"Fair enough, Ben. I'll just— "

"That's not all," said Bradlee.

"What else, Ben?"

"For *one month* you don't run my name or Sally's in that damn column of yours!"

I agreed.

"Oh, Ben— "

"Yeah?"

"Maybe you'd better send me a letter confirming the deal."

When I received the letter, I posted it on the bulletin board. The newsroom erupted in laughter and it was a big score for our side.

Ben Bradlee had been brought in to do for the *Post* what I was later brought in to do for the *Star*—brighten it up. Ben's career was a little like mine, only with security. Back in the Eisenhower years (if you will cast your mind back), the *Star* was being knocked off its upholstered throne by *The Washington Post.* Eugene Meyer, the *Post*'s owner, turned over a growing daily to his son-in-law Phil Graham, who was without newspaper experience. Graham had married Katharine Meyer, the only one of Meyer's kids who was attracted to journalism. In 1959 Phil Graham bought *Newsweek* magazine. When he died in 1963, Kay Graham assumed the leadership of the *Post*. She took *Newsweek*'s Washington bureau chief, Ben Bradlee, to lunch at the F Street Club and asked him what he wanted to do with the rest of his life. His answer has become the stuff of legend: "I'd rather be managing editor of the *Post* than anything in the world. I'd give my left one for the job." History does not record whether Ben was ever asked to make this ultimate gift of loyalty. (There is a possible answer to this intriguing question in [an] e-mail from the *Star* associate editor Ed Yoder: "Re the story about Ben's left one, at Bradlee's retirement party at the *Post,* Kay told the famous story and then quipped, 'I accepted his offer.' ")

The *Post* was prospering at that point, but it had grown dull and flabby, a typical concomitant of financial success, I have observed.

Ben was installed at the *Post* as deputy managing editor in 1964 with the understanding that he would get the top job when Al Friendly retired. But Friendly was in no hurry to go. It might have been a long wait had not Walter Lippmann and Friendly lunched one day. Over the appetizer, the columnist said: "Al, you shouldn't be an administrator all your life. You ought to start writing again." Friendly was persuaded to step down. And just 90 days after joining the *Post,* Ben Bradlee became its managing editor. Yes, Virginia, there *is* a Walter Lippmann.

Now we come to the question of accuracy and The Ear.

I must admit that The Ear wasn't always accurate.

Once The Ear ran a rumor that President Carter had bugged the house where the Reagans were staying as they waited to assume the presidency. That wasn't correct.

Then there was the item about the former secretary of state Dean Acheson having been spied at a Georgetown dinner party. Only it turned out that at the time of that particular party, Mr. Acheson was regrettably deceased. Diana made it all right with a correction: "Mr. Acheson is a teensy bit dead," she apologized.

"Oh, the shame of the first few public screw-ups," recalls Diana. "Louise and I each blamed the other in private, but if you personally wrote it, you had to set it straight. If our victim was inappropriately indignant, we added enough details to our correction so that he wished to God he'd kept his mouth shut."

Whenever The Ear made a mistake, Diana McLellan would write a correction—what she called "a grovel." She wrote with such wit that her corrections were as entertaining as her mistakes. And more lethal.

Ben Bradlee blistered us for our mistakes.

"Their record for accuracy is the worst I've ever seen!" he exploded. "They never call to check out what they print about me. They're unbelievable!"

Art Buchwald had worked for me on the *Trib,* and he was an old friend of Ben's. The ideal mediator. He arranged a lunch for the two of us at a hotel far from the center of town. You couldn't have the editors of Washington's two big dailies be seen eating together.

I explained to Ben that The Ear was just a device to get the *Post* into our pond. Ben was still fuming because The Ear had reported that his sons had had a run-in with the law—something about overparking. I acknowledged our mistake and apologized. I agreed the kids were off limits.

And that was about it for our landmark lunch. Two checks.

Then there was the time The Ear accused *The Washington Post* of killing a column that accused a U.S. senator of repeatedly seducing a blonde constituent. Why did the *Post* spike the column? Perhaps because during the 1976 pressmen's strike, when the *Post* presses were damaged, the good senator had let the *Post* print their paper on the presses of his suburban daily. And so the *Post* was returning the favor. Said The Ear:

> *Take care of your chums and your chums will take care of you . . .* You must have heard by now that a Virginia constituent has accused Sen. Harry Byrd, her very own senator, of seducing her thrice while she begged him for help in finding her deserting husband. It's all in a Jack Anderson column this week, and it ran in over 900 newspapers, but *not* the *Post,* darlings. The Knowledgeables are saying that's because the senator's own sweet little rag printed the *Post* when they were having their Troubles. Ear is astonished.

My phone rang as soon as our first edition hit the streets.

"That's a cheap shot!" barked Bradlee.

"Wait, I'll look at it," I said.

"I just wanted to tell you that personally," said Ben and hung up.

I looked at the column and it seemed a little strong. I killed the last two sentences, which ascribed an ignoble motive to the *Post.* Then I called Bradlee back. But he wouldn't take my call. I got his secretary.

"I'd like to speak to Mr. Bradlee."

"He's all tied up, Mr. Bellows."

"Tell him I think perhaps Ear should run a correction."

"He's all tied up, Mr. Bellows."

"Explain to Ben that a correction would repeat in *all* editions a charge that has only appeared in *one* edition."

"He's all tied up, Mr. Bellows."

"So ask him if he wants to drop the whole matter or have it corrected."

"He's all tied up, Mr. Bellows."

"Tell him I apologize and we've knocked out the bottom line."

"I'll tell him, Mr. Bellows."

"Have him call and tell me what he wants me to do."

Ben never called back.

When the *Star* died, Ben Bradlee hired Diana McLellan to write a gossip column for *The Washington Post.*

"What the hell," Ben told a reporter who questioned his adopting a feature that had given him so much pain. "We can't afford not to take somebody's good idea."

But I ask myself: Would Jason Robards have done that?

Chapter 8

BROADCAST JOURNALISM

Broadcast journalists and print reporters confront at least one similar challenge. They both have to connect with an audience. TV and radio reporters, however, use two tools the newspaper writer lacks: moving pictures and sound.

In this chapter, three veteran television reporters talk about the unique difficulties and opportunities created by the broadcast medium. Robert Krulwich reveals his secrets to storytelling on camera. Jeff Greenfield describes the test of stamina that live coverage of a presidential campaign can become—and did, memorably, in November 2000. Jim Wooten, who has covered many of the world's most horrifying news events, examines the sense of detachment that is necessary to do the job—and tells the dramatic story of the one time that detachment failed him.

ROBERT KRULWICH

New York magazine called him "the man who simplifies without being simple." He takes complex subjects—economics, technology, science—and explains them in a way that is both clear and entertaining. ABC News correspondent Robert Krulwich has reported on AIDs, genetics, parenthood, and that world-famous American cultural icon, Barbie. He has appeared on two Peter Jennings children's shows, one about the war in Bosnia and the other on drugs. He is regularly on *Nightline* and reports for *ABC World News Tonight, Prime Time Live,* and *Good Morning America*. Before joining ABC, Krulwich was a correspondent for CBS News. He is also a regular contributor to PBS. He won the 1991 George Polk Award for his *Frontline* report "The Great American Bailout," an investigative story on the savings-and-loan scandal; a duPont–Columbia University Award for "The Best Campaign Money Can Buy"; and a national Emmy for a *Frontline* on business and computers. His ABC special on Barbie, a cultural history of the doll, also won an Emmy.

Krulwich says finding your own voice in television—your own "sound"—is important. It can mean the difference between keeping listeners tuned in—with their eyes and ears—and losing them. In this essay for the Fall 2000 issue of *Nieman Reports,* a magazine produced by Harvard University's Nieman Foundation for Journalism, Krulwich describes the sound he strives for: that of an interesting neighbor with a memorable story to tell.

Sticky Storytelling

I tell stories on television. I tell them long (on *Nightline* and *Frontline*), I tell them medium (on *Prime Time Live*), and I tell them short (on the evening news), and like any storyteller, I want my audience's complete attention while I am on the screen. But what I really want is a couple of hours after I've finished, I want some of them, half would be nice, to remember what I've said; not all of it, just the gist, maybe an image, a thought, something sticky enough to carry my message a couple of beats past my performance.

Everybody knows TV news is ephemeral. But the sad truth is news on network TV has become so smooth, so polished, the typical story moves through the audience like a suppository. In. Out. "What did he say?"

I will be standing on a street corner, waiting for the light to turn, and somebody with a big smile will come up to me and say, "I saw that thing you did on TV yesterday about the— "

I wait. I tense.

"About the— "

About half the time what the person recalls, I never said, or some other reporter said, or it was sort of what I said but skewed in some unfathomable way, or whatever memory sparked this exchange flickers, dims, and ends: "That thing, you know, you said yesterday, it was— " (long pause).

"Well, thanks," I say, unhelpfully.

On the radio (I used to work for National Public Radio), this is not a problem. Radio reporters learn to write with calculated vividness, pushing the listeners to paint images in their own heads so they unwittingly become co-authors of the story. On the radio, a story well-told sticks for days, years.

TV is harder. Good television reporters have to learn how to work the room. On television, the audience is two, five, seven, fifteen feet away staring back across a couch, a bed, a kitchen table. This distance matters. Consider: A newspaper reporter puts words on a page and that page is usually eighteen inches from the reader's nose. How many children, spouses, and pets can squeeze into those eighteen inches? Between the TV and the viewer there can (and will) be a Barnum and Bailey circus of "Watch me instead!" distractions. Every good television reporter knows the real job is to grab the audience's eyes and hold them tight through the storm.

How do I do that? I begin with an observation: TV news has a very familiar form. It is authoritative, cadenced, smooth, dispassionate, articulate. It doesn't gulp or waffle or giggle. It is a speech pattern that carefully announces that it is *not* normal conversation; it is News. News on TV has a sound, a sound designed to create credibility. I talk this way, it says, because what I am saying is True and Important. Now listen.

The problem is that sound has become so familiar that at some level that composers would understand, it has become very easy *not* to listen. We know these tones, this writing style, these image sequences so well, we don't have to pay attention. We know the beat.

The opportunity here is obvious. If most reporters are modeling themselves on Walter Cronkite and Jane Pauley, what I do is model myself on no one. Instead, implacably, incorrigibly, I try to sound like myself, like the ordinary me.

If I were sitting next to you on a bus and we got to talking about something that I know about, something exciting (to me) like a tax proposal, a scientific discovery, something difficult, but something I'd want to explain, on television I try to sound exactly as I would on the bus. True, on TV I have the advantage of pictures and graphics and snippets of interviews, but I work hard to create a sequence that feels improvised, as fresh and intimate as an accidental encounter.

This means: (a) whenever I sound too much like Pauley or Cronkite (who are good, by the way, icons, even), I consciously shift down, to take the "News" out of my voice, and (b) I cut and arrange my images so that they do not flow normally. I want surprise. I want to create a pattern that is instinctively unfamiliar, so that at a level the audience may not be aware of, there is a touch of suspense. What's he going to do, say, now?

Sometimes this works. A few months ago, I was on the A train in New York City, my hometown, three o'clock in the afternoon, when the guy across from me, in full hip-hop garb, the gold chain, three earrings on the right lobe, big pants, leans over and he says, "Hey, didn't I see you on TV talking about the—"

"Yes?"

And he delivers a perfect condensation of a story I did on Dolly the cloned sheep's cells. He remembered the whole thing. It is moments like these that make me want to dance off the train, bow deeper than I ever would for an Emmy, and touch the hem of Stephen Jay Gould. It doesn't happen often, maybe three out of every ten encounters, but on TV (as in baseball) .333 is a pretty good average. Way good enough for me.

JEFF GREENFIELD

What is it like to cover a story live on television for eight to twelve hours? Every four years, TV news correspondents face that scenario as they broadcast the presidential election. In this selection, CNN's Jeff Greenfield, host of *Greenfield at Large* and senior analyst for *Inside Politics,* shows how he prepares to fill all that airtime. He begins by memorizing minutiae about the candidates, information from which he can improvise commentary appropriate to every possible election outcome.

Greenfield is the author or coauthor of nine books and writes a column for *Time*. He has won numerous awards over the course of his career, including three Emmys for his work on *Nightline* specials and an ABC prime-time special on Ross Perot. In November 2000, when the Al Gore/George Bush contest stretched on long past election night, Greenfield found himself hosting the network's nightly special election program for thirty-seven days. That experience is chronicled in his 2001 book *Oh, Waiter! One Order of Crow!* from which this selection is drawn.

Bellwethers, Factoids, and Thirty-seven Days

There is no single way to prepare for eight or ten or twelve hours of continuous coverage. Some of my colleagues spend Election Day working the phones, calling old contacts around the country and inside the campaigns. Others assemble enough research material to complete a doctoral dissertation on the campaign. (My colleague Judy Woodruff invariably arrives on the anchor set with a mountain of five-by-eight cards that contain the names, ages, family and political histories, and blood types of every candidate for every office in the land. Then the live coverage begins; someday, she has promised me, she will actually get to look at one of these cards while we are on the air.) My own practice is to go over as many facts and anecdotes as I can possibly cram into my head. Once they are more or less locked in, I reduce them to a word or two that I can jot down on a note card next to the name of a state. I then list the states in order of their poll-closing times, and go over this list so often that I don't need to look at the written notes once we hit the air.

On some Election Nights, all the preparation in the world won't provide more than a moment of genuinely interesting analysis, except for the hard-core political junkies—the folks who watch C-SPAN 2 for erotic arousal. In 1996, for example, the Clinton-Dole race—and I use that term loosely—never really changed from April to November. Viewed over time, the polling data looked like an EEG of a brain-dead patient, as flat as the Kansas horizon. But on this Election Night, I had come loaded for bear. You want historical ironies? On an election night in 1970, exactly thirty years earlier, the fathers of *both* Al Gore and George W. Bush had lost their races for the United States Senate. You want a dramatic contrast? On his fortieth birthday, Al Gore was a United States senator who had competed in the presidential primaries and was a clear contender for future national office. On *his* fortieth birthday, George W. Bush was a moderately unsuccessful businessman with a losing race for Congress behind him who awakened to the knowledge that he had a drinking problem.

I also came prepared to drop in short "factoids" about each state, once we were able to project a winner—little gems to illuminate the greater meaning of the numbers, preferably within ten or fifteen seconds. My producer-assistant Beth Goodman and I gathered these items under the "iceberg" theory of preparation. Just as eight-ninths of an iceberg never appears above the surface, the great majority of what I gathered would never see the light of day—but you could never tell before the fact what elements would be useful. Here's part of what my checklist had to offer:

- No Republican has ever won the White House without winning Illinois.
- No Republican has ever won the White House without winning Ohio.
- Missouri has voted with the winner in every presidential election in the twentieth century, except for 1956 (it went for Stevenson that year by two-tenths of 1 percent of the vote); Delaware has voted with the winner ever since 1952. These two states have a legitimate right to be considered bellwethers. (I also checked *Safire's Political Dictionary* to make sure I knew what the hell a bellwether was—it's a male sheep, who leads his flock into and out of pastures—often wearing a bell around his neck.)
- If Gore in fact lost Tennessee, that would make him the first candidate to lose his home state since George McGovern lost South Dakota to Nixon in 1972. If he won the presidency despite that

loss, he'd be the first victor to lose his home state since Richard Nixon in 1968 (who claimed New York State as his residence then).

- If Gore won Michigan, talk about the classic New Deal–New Frontier state, the place where Democrats once began every fall campaign in Detroit's Cadillac Square, where blue-collar union workers rallied to the cause. Democrats lost the state to Nixon in '72 over busing, lost to Reagan in '80 over recession and inflation and crime. Bill Clinton regained it for the Democrats, and if Gore holds on, note the power of good economic times. Remember to mention that the United Auto Workers' contract made Election Day a paid holiday from work. If Gore lost Michigan, have that quote handy from his 1992 book *Earth in the Balance,* where he calls for the elimination of the internal combustion engine—and note how many of those UAW members liked to hunt.
- And speaking of guns, note how much money the National Rifle Association spent on issue advertising in places like Michigan, Ohio, West Virginia; note how energetically NRA President Charlton Heston campaigned in those states.
- For the Senate races, too, there was ammunition ready to fire at the drop of a projection. When Hillary Clinton was declared the winner in New York—something we would probably do the moment the polls closed at 9 P.M.—have ready the story of Eleanor Roosevelt. Shortly after FDR died, one of his closest aides, Interior Secretary Harold Ickes, had implored Mrs. Roosevelt to move back to New York and run for the United States Senate. She declined. Now, more than half a century later, aided by the son of Harold Ickes, the First Lady, who was said to have communed with the spirit of Eleanor Roosevelt, was about to claim that seat for herself.
- When Jon Corzine was projected as the winner in New Jersey, talk about the successes and failures of deep-pocket candidates of the past, and note how a twenty-four-year-old Supreme Court decision about campaign-finance laws encouraged the emergence of multimillionaire candidates, past and present. In Minnesota, department-store heir and perennial loser Mark Dayton looked like he would win a Senate seat; in Washington, dot-com millionaire Maria Cantwell might knock off Senator Slade Gorton. (If that happened, give a capsule history of Gorton's career—he won in 1980, lost his seat in '86, won the *other* Senate seat in '88, cruised

to reelection in '94, and lost in '00—the first politician ever to win and lose *both* Senate seats in his state.)

- If seventy-nine-year-old Delaware senator William Roth fell to Governor Tom Carper, talk about the rhythms of political life: Roth had won his Senate seat thirty years ago because the incumbent senator, John Williams, had retired at age seventy, having advocated a Constitutional age limit on senators—a plan Roth had strongly supported. Now, his age was his undoing; a fact dramatized when he had briefly passed out in front of the TV cameras while campaigning.
- And then there's Missouri, where Senator John Ashcroft might wind up losing to a dead man: Governor Mel Carnahan, killed in a plane crash just three weeks before the election. The acting governor has promised to appoint Carnahan's widow, Jeanne, to that seat if more people vote for Carnahan than Ashcroft, and she has agreed. Ashcroft had built a small lead in the closing weeks of the campaign, but how the hell do you run against a widow who has just lost a husband and a son? Missouri was also the state where almost twenty-five years earlier, a young Congressman named Jerry Litton, on his way to claim victory in a Senate primary, was killed along with his family in a plane crash.

There were other matters to consider as Election Night began. Some were of great moment—past elections filled with Electoral-vote melodrama, like the John Quincy Adams–Andrew Jackson battle of 1824 (the last time the son of a former president had won the White House). Some were of a more personal nature. For instance, I took great satisfaction from the fact that Larry King would be along every hour for a short interview segment. Not only was he the most familiar and popular personality on CNN, but those segments would afford ample time for a bathroom break, and/or a chance to bolt down food or drink. Speaking of which: Once again I had neglected to bring a change of shirt and tie with me—an omission that made any attempt at refreshment during the night an excursion into danger. I happen to be the victim of a condition that renders me at times all but incapable of bringing food from plate to mouth without a substantial fraction of sustenance winding up on my clothes. And these times generally coincide with moments when I am about to appear on camera.

One short vignette from my past will illustrate this: In 1985, I was one of a group of ABC News reporters assigned to produce pieces during the three-hour-long Super Bowl pregame presentation. A few days before the event, we were told to come to the stadium wearing the outfits we'd be sporting on game day, in order to record the opening shots for the pregame show. On my way to the stadium, I spotted a colleague enjoying lunch at an open-air Mexican seafood restaurant. I joined him, carefully covering myself with so many napkins that I resembled a papier-mâché dummy. I finished my meal, paid the bill, removed the protective covering—and spotted one last tempting bite of seafood enchilada. I picked it up, put it in my mouth . . . and World War III exploded. Only the providential presence of a nearby While-U-Wait dry cleaning establishment prevented me from appearing on national TV disguised as a Jackson Pollock painting.

(One of my exasperated producers once said to me, "Greenfield, the next time we have a lunch break during a shoot, either order melba toast or bring along a full-body condom.")

There was, finally, one other question on my mind: Just how long would we be here? We were committed to staying on the air until we knew who the president would be, and what the makeup of the new Congress would be; but the House and Senate were both in play, and we might well have to wait until the West Coast results were in to know how those battles would come out. Similarly, with the presidential race up for grabs, we might well have to wait until Oregon and Washington reported in to learn who'd won. In the last close presidential contest, the Ford-Carter race in 1976, the networks had to wait until after five o'clock in the morning, when Mississippi finally went for Carter by fewer than fifteen thousand votes, until signing off. That wouldn't work for me at all; my plan was to get off the air, get back to my Atlanta hotel, throw my things together, and catch a 6:30 A.M. flight back to New York. Why? So I could join my friends for our regular Wednesday lunch. No one can accuse me of lacking a sense of priority. As I sat down to join Bernie Shaw, Judy Woodruff, and Bill Schneider at the faux-oak anchor desk, I hoped we would know the outcome well before five o'clock in the morning.

As I said: who knew?

JIM WOOTEN

Jim Wooten has been a reporter for more than thirty years. He is the author of three books, a former staffer for *Esquire,* and former Washington correspondent for *The New York Times*. As an ABC News correspondent, he has filed stories from more than forty countries and five continents. He has covered the war in Bosnia, the civil wars in El Salvador and Beirut, the Sandinista revolution in Nicaragua, Israel's invasion of Lebanon, and racial unrest in South Africa. But the seven days he spent covering the exodus of refugees from Rwanda to Zaire in 1994 have never left him. In this 1994 essay for the *Columbia Journalism Review,* he explains why.

Parachuting into Madness

We landed in mid-morning, schlepped our gear across the tarmac, strolled to the airport fence—and watched a little girl die. She was about six years old but so wasted from cholera it was hard to tell. Her mother laid her beside the road, knelt to touch her one last time, then lifted her face and fists to the African sky and screamed.

This was my introduction to a week of reporting on the exodus of nearly a million refugees from the horrors of Rwanda to the hell of Zaire: ten thousand minutes of my life, each soaked in death, all coagulating into a reality that would penetrate every defense I'd ever devised against personal involvement in a story. My career had taken me into most of the darker crevasses of our times—big wars and small, famines and floods, revolutions and riots, all manner of disaster and destruction all over the world—usually on one of those short-notice, short-term assignments that suddenly land a reporter in the thick of a crisis with little time for reflection. Parachute journalism is honest work but it is neither glorious nor glamorous and it is not neurosurgery. It requires only stamina, a strong stomach, and the knack for putting some distance between the facts and the emotions. Over the years, working so often in this mode, repeatedly confronted with the grotesque ironies of combat or the grievous inequities of nature, I'd learned to do precisely that, to create some psychological workspace between the truth and how I felt about it.

But I found such detachment impossible during the latter days of July on the volcanic moonscape of northeastern Zaire, where corpses were accumulating faster than mass graves could be carved from the obdurate earth. In the wee hours of that first night, bone-tired but sleepless, I crawled from our tent and watched a huge moon leap straight up out from Rwanda, and saw in silhouette against its ivory light an endless line of refugees still trudging past, shambling along beyond the fence, headed north on the airport road. I listened for some time to the scrape of their bare feet against the macadam, to their coughing and their snuffling and the crying of the children cradled in their arms or swaddled on their backs, and for the first time ever on assignment, I wept.

No distance was possible. And no escape, either; no press room or office or filing center offering respite or retreat; no hotel bar dispensing anesthetic potions. For seven days human beings were constantly falling all around us. In many cases, we and the lenses of our cameras were the very last things they saw in the very last moments of their lives.

It was an excruciating dilemma: at last, a reality so wretched it demanded some degree of personal involvement; and yet a story whose wretchedness was of such epic proportions that any personal involvement was useless. The urge to *do something* was constantly answered by the grim realization that *nothing* would help. Along toward the end of my work there, in a conversation with Ted Koppel on *Nightline,* I suggested that should history produce such a moment again and our network ask me to cover it, I'd be inclined to refuse the assignment.

"I never thought I'd hear that from you," my wife said when I returned. "Not that I believe it."

But it's true. At least, I *believe* it to be true, and what follows here, drawn from notes scribbled in notebooks still black with the dirt of Zaire, is why.

> At dawn one day, at a cholera-infested camp, I walk with Yves, a young refugee working as a volunteer for Medecins Sans Frontieres, into a mass of several thousand sick Rwandans waiting for treatment. It is difficult to move through them without stepping on a hand or a leg. Yves stops and stoops and touches a pretty young woman, then lifts and carries her slight body over to a pile of at least 500 corpses and deposits her between a baby and an ancient old man. He bends down to smooth the young woman's dress, tucks it modestly beneath her legs, then stands and goes back to work. In less than an hour, Yves will find more than thirty others who did not make it through the night.
>
> Later, as we talk, with the camera rolling, I listen to his recollections of how he escaped from his homeland, of how his

brother had died here in this camp, and of how he does not think his aging parents will survive, but as he talks I cannot help but notice over his left shoulder, just a few feet behind him, a young man about his age lying on his side. Our eyes meet for a moment, then his slowly close. He coughs weakly and dies. Yves finishes his answer and I ask another question.

In decrepit little Goma, just inside Zaire's border with Rwanda, there are corpses at every corner, every intersection, in the narrow spaces that separate the derelict buildings, stacked against their crumbling walls, in between the empty gas pumps at an abandoned service station, under carts filled with rotting produce at the filthy market, lined up side by side in neat rows outside a convenience store, at the edge of the open ditches that serve as sewers, scattered across the central circle in the middle of the city. No matter where I glance, it is impossible *not* to see a body. I finally close my eyes and try to concentrate on something else, anything else: my wife's pleasant face, my favorite photograph of our family, the memory of one of my daughters standing next to a sizable fish she had pulled from the Atlantic. Yet when I open my eyes again the car is moving past a large sign advertising an infant formula, a colorful photograph of plumply beautiful African babies over a slogan, *Tout Va Bien,* All Is Well. At the foot of one of the poles supporting the sign lies a tiny bundle the size of a pillow.

Beyond the town is Lake Kivu, vast and cool, yet contaminated by the refugees' waste and garbage and thousands of bodies, the strange bitter fruit of Rwanda's maniacal spring—dark bodies bleached nearly white by the water and the equatorial sun, bodies dipping and bobbing and rolling face up or face down. A mile away, children frolic in the water, spitting mouthfuls at each other. From the road that runs above the lake the thousands of refugees gathered at its edges look like the Fourth of July crowd at the Jersey shore. Cattle wander through it and into the water, dipping their formidable horns, scattering the laughing children in all directions. Their parents and grandparents wash their tattered clothes and spread them on the rocks to dry. An elderly man unzips and urinates into the edge of the lake. A lovely young woman removes her filthy blouse and washes her breasts with handfuls of water from the lake as thousands of other refugees move down to the edge to fill their plastic jerry-cans and take them back to their families. They don't understand that they are carrying poison, that the water may kill them.

In the afternoon, a large dump truck moves slowly along the airport road as teams of Rwandan men follow behind, in surgical masks and latex gloves, lifting the bodies and heaving them into the back. Two of the men scale the sides and rearrange the bodies to make room for more. A kilometer on, the truck veers into a banana grove and backs up to a deep trench half the length of a football field and half filled with bodies, a terrifying tableau of arms tangled with legs interwoven with torsos bent at mad angles. A naked baby, missing its blanket, seems to be sleeping comfortably in the crook of an old man's arm. Nearby, a pregnant woman's hands are locked in rigor mortis atop her swollen stomach. The odor is overwhelming. With a hydraulic whine, the bed of the truck slowly rises and tilts and its cargo goes sliding into the crowded pit.

One evening, scanning my script for the evening broadcast, my producer finds the word *madness* four times. "It's a two-minute piece," he says. "Twice, I'll give you, but . . ."

I have no recollection of having used then reused the same stark term. But there it is: *madness . . . madness . . . madness . . . madness . . .*

It is straight-up noon. We come upon a group of young boys sprawled in the dirt near the airport. They're all orphans and all in bad shape. Two are clearly beyond help. They're both naked, both lying on their backs, one's head resting on the other's legs. They're so frail, so weak; just barely breathing. I watch Fletcher Johnson, an enormous African-American man, in whose hands a heavy television camera seems a mere toy, shooting this scene with his usual meticulous skill. He lifts his face from his viewfinder and our eyes meet. "This is fucking crazy," he says. From our van we retrieve what little water we have and along with the others in our crew we try to get some of it into the two dying children. I slip my hand beneath one small back and raise him. He is feather light. They both stir and open their mouths like baby birds. Fletcher uses a bottle cap as a glass. It is still too much. They cough and sputter but open their eyes wide and silently plead for more.

It doesn't help.

That night, screening the videotape, I notice that Fletch has erased all shots of the two little boys.

Past the camp where Yves is working, the airport road rises into the mountains. All along it, small children carry enormous bundles on their heads for miles. Women walk for hours carrying heavy water-cans. A teen-ager at the roadside in a Michael Jordan T-shirt raises his hand as we pass, then rubs his stomach. Nearby, a man's body lies halfway on the berm, halfway on the road. He has been run over several times.

In more than thirty years as a reporter, this is like nothing I've seen. Not like the famine in Somalia, not like the flight of the Iraqi

Kurds into the snowy mountains of Turkey and Iraq, not like the sieges of Beirut and Sarajevo. It is not *like* anything.

The last afternoon. It's nearly dark and we have schlepped our gear back across the tarmac into a twin-engine King Air chartered for Nairobi. Packed with supplies for our colleagues who are staying, it had arrived without seats. Sprawled on the floor, exhausted, we wait an hour for takeoff clearance. Finally, the plane lifts itself lightly from the runway and banks east toward Tanzania and Kenya, and for a long moment, as the little plane climbs away, we are all silent. There is nothing to say. In varying degrees, as we begin our journey home, each of us is taking along a piece of the madness below.

Chapter 9

THE INTERNET AND COMPUTER-ASSISTED REPORTING

The World Wide Web opens new avenues for reporting and for reaching readers. But with new technology comes new responsibility—and a new uncertainty.

In this chapter, four journalists examine the Internet's wide-ranging impact on the profession. Dan Okrent begins by declaring the imminent death of print media—then offers reassurance that the need for quality reporting and editing will survive. Jonathan Dube provides an array of tools for writing well for the online reader. Mark Bowden reveals the powerful and dramatic ways that online publication influenced his reporting and his relationship with readers. Michael J. Berens sounds a cautionary note about computer-assisted reporting: Nothing, he says, can take the place of human sources. All of these writers have journeyed into online territory by taking a traditional journalistic path through print media. Their insights are informed by experience in both worlds.

DAN OKRENT

The end of the print media world as we know it—newspapers and magazines and books—lies just around the corner. So says Dan Okrent, editor-at-large of *Time* and a man who has spent his entire professional career writing and editing in those media. The author of four books, Okrent worked in publishing as an editor at Alfred A. Knopf and the Viking Press, and he was editor-in-chief of general books at Harcourt Brace Jovanovich. He founded and edited *New England Monthly,* which twice received the National Magazine Award for general excellence. Despite his passion for print, Okrent predicted its demise in an address given at Columbia University in January 2000 and excerpted here. Newspapers and magazines and books, he said, are merely vessels by which information and entertainment are delivered. The need for reliable content and good writing will always survive; only the means of delivery will change.

The Death of Print?

Looking out at an audience of so many people who would forgo tonight's episode of *Dharma and Greg* or *Rivera Live* to come hear me talk, I feel highly responsible to provide you with entertainment or elucidation sufficient to justify your sacrifice. I also feel the burden to live up to the provocative title that the lecture's producers and I have cooked up to get you out of your apartments and into this hall: "The Death of Print?" has both a nice, millenarian finality to it, and a perfect op-ed page sort of cop-out attached to it, namely that temporizing question mark.

"The Death of Print?" also makes it pretty clear that I'm not going to be talking about the shrinking news staffs at the major networks, or the increasing tendency of local television news shows to devote their time to either highway mayhem or idiotic, grinning man-or-woman on the street interviews with people whose only qualification for demanding our attention is that they are, in fact, on the street.

If you sense a certain antipathy to television journalism in my tone, you're right. This is one way that I hope to establish my credentials with you as a paragon of print, an ink-stained wretch, someone with printer's ink coursing through his veins—pick your print media cliché, and it applies to me. Newspapers, magazines, books—all those other wonderful creatures made possible by Gutenberg five centuries ago—are, I'm sure you'll agree, the media that matter.

I've spent my entire career engaged by them—going back to working on a daily newspaper when I was in college, then nine years in the book business, several more as a writer of books, and finally, until 1996, 14 years as a magazine editor. Forgive me the three years I spent on the Web, navigating a turbulent sea of bits and bytes as Time Inc.'s editor of new media. I touched land several months ago, and now I'm writing and editing again. It's nice to be back.

Newspapers, magazines books: A newspaper gives you timeliness, a magazine perspective, a book lasting value. Each is a firm, palpable entity, a presence in our lives, a companion to our days.

I remember what it was like when I was a child, and my father brought home the newspaper after work. My mother would take what we called in those distant, benighted days the women's section—recipes, fashion news, the advice columns. My older brother, who was readying himself for a business career—he took the stock market pages. I reached for sports, the news of the athletic wonders committed daily by my heroes. My father had the general news section, and we'd each disappear into our own engagements with the wider world, regrouping in time for dinner and a shared conversation about what we had encountered in the daily paper.

What could possibly replace something so comfortable, so safe, so adaptable as a daily newspaper?

As for magazines—well, I work for the world's largest magazine company, so it shouldn't be hard for me to make a case for the magazine. There are nearly 10,000 different magazines available in the U.S. today. Great, giant, mass circulation magazines like those Time Inc. publishes—*Time, Life, People, Fortune,* and so on—and tiny, narrowly focused magazines to cater to the reader's most special interest.

I'm a scuba diver. I subscribe to two different scuba diving magazines, and if I wanted to I could subscribe to a dozen more. Magazines bring us together into real communities, coming into our house as regular, periodic welcome visitors, requiring us to do nothing more than make a once-a-year request to the publisher to keep them coming. What could be easier than that?

Books? Every one of us could write an anthem to the book. The feel of a fine binding, the smell of newly opened pages, the satisfying heft of a book in your hands—can anything top it?

As you can see, I can get sentimental about these things we call, by inference, the old media. They mean a lot to me, emotionally as well as economically.

I believe they are, after food, clothing and shelter, and after our family relations and our friendships, the most important things in our lives.

And I believe one more thing: I believe they, and all forms of print, are dead. Finished. Over. Perhaps not in my professional lifetime, but certainly in that of the youngest people in this room. Remove the question mark from the title of this talk. The Death of Print, full stop.

Twenty, thirty, at the outside forty years from now, we will look back on the print media the way we look back on travel by horse and carriage, or by wind-powered ship.

But first I would like to tell you why I am so convinced that those media to which I have devoted my thirty years of professional life are as relevant to our future as the carrier pigeon.

And please understand: I did not come to this conclusion as a zealot. Until I moved into my job as editor of new media for Time Inc., the Internet was merely a place for me to get late stock market news, or the baseball box scores. I didn't move into my new media job out of passion, or conviction, or technological facility, or even a particular interest in the subject. When I asked Don Logan, Time Inc.'s CEO, why he and Norman Pearlstine, our editor-in-chief, thought I was right for this job, Don said, "Because we need a little gray hair in that organization." In other words, I qualified because I was old.

So, to the point: Why is print dead? It's a two-part argument, the first part fairly simple but worth some elaboration, the second part as obvious as the morning sun.

Part one, in a phrase, is that we have, I believe, finally learned not to underestimate the march of technological progress. A little over 30 years ago, I saw my first electronic calculator. It was about the shape of a laptop computer, maybe three inches deep, it weighed eight or nine pounds, and it cost my father's law firm \$500—in 1967 dollars. Today, you can buy calculators the size and heft of a credit card in a convenience store for two dollars.

I purchased my first computer, an Apple IIe, in 1980. What a wonder it was! White type—capital letters only—dropped out of a black screen; it processed words at a speed less than 1 percent as fast as the three-pound laptop that has become the locus, the library and the lever of my entire professional life. Its built-in memory couldn't accommodate a long magazine article. And my friends and neighbors—sophisticated, educated people—would come over evenings to watch me move blocks of text from here to there on it. It was that new, that extraordinary.

I don't need to tell you what the average computer can do today, nor do I need to tell you similar stories about telephones, or audio equipment, or any other piece of technology. If we imagine it, they will build it.

So imagine this (and if you find it hard to imagine, trust me: I've seen it already, in the development office of a well-established Japanese computer electronics company): Imagine a tablet, maybe half an inch thick, shaped when held one way like an open book or magazine, when turned sideways much like a single page of a newspaper. It weighs six ounces. It's somewhat flexible, which makes it easy to transport. (The truly flexible one, which you'll be able to roll up and put in your pocket, is still a couple of years away, so this one will have to do.) Its screen, utterly glare-free, neither flickers nor fades nor grows dull.

To move beyond the first screen in whatever it is that you're reading, you run your finger across the top of the tablet—a physical metaphor for the turning of the page. You are sitting on a beach on a Saturday afternoon with this little wonder, and you're reading this week's *Time* magazine.

Then you decide you'd like something a little more, oh, entertaining. You press a series of buttons, and a cellular hookup to a satellite-connected database instantaneously delivers you—well, Evelyn Waugh's *Scoop*. And when you've had enough of that—click, click—you move on, to the football news, or the office memoranda you didn't finish reading on Friday afternoon, or whatever it is that you want.

Click, click again: each download, coming to you at dazzling speeds, and a central rights-clearance computer charges your account, much like a telephone account, for what you've read or listened to. The satellite operator keeps a small portion of the income, and the rest goes to the "publisher"—that is, to the agency that either created the material you are reading, or that represents the interests of those who created it.

Or imagine this: Another message comes to you, from—let's say Coca-Cola. It's an advertising message, and you have been paid to read it. You have been targeted by Coca-Cola, the marketers from that company have found you on the beach, and for the privilege of getting their message in front of you they have paid the satellite operator a carriage fee. The satellite operator, wanting to guarantee the advertising agency that the impression has been made, credits your master account a few cents. For reading the one-minute message from Coca-Cola, you get the first five minutes of tomorrow's electronic newspaper for free. Everyone's happy.

As I said, this technology already exists. It's far too expensive today, and the critical elements of payment systems and copyright protection and royalty accounting have not yet been created. But I guarantee you that such systems are either in development today or soon will be.

But, you say, who wants to read a good novel on a computer screen, no matter how clear and snappy and portable it is? Who wants to forgo the tactile engagement with a newspaper or magazine, or even more so the deeper, more gratifying physical connection with a book, and replace it with this potentially alienating form of modern technology?

Well, that brings me to part two of my argument, the part I promised was as obvious as the morning sun. And that is this: Last year, Time Inc. spent $1 billion dollars on paper and postage.

End of argument.

Or, if you'd like, let me put it this way: You may prefer to ride across town in horse-and-carriage, or across a lake in a wind-powered yacht, but no one makes that carriage or that yacht for you anymore, at least not at a reasonable price. So, too, with the book: In the future I am imagining, the book becomes an elite item for the very few, an *objet*, a collectible—valuable not for the words on the page, but for the vessel that contains those words.

Will it matter to book-loving litterateurs? Probably so, though I can't imagine why. Will it matter to the millions who buy a John Grisham paperback and toss it when it's done? Not a chance.

Nor should it. For we—we who work today by accident in paper and ink; who demand, however sheepishly, that vast forests be cut down to make our paper, for vast sums to be invested in hypermodern printing presses and bindery machines that consume megawatts of environment-befouling energy—we should be happy. For we know—we must know—that the words and pictures and ideas and images and notions and substance that we produce are what matter—and not the vessel that they arrive in.

I want to step back for a few moments here to elaborate on business models, consumer prejudices and what I hope is a somewhat sober-sided consideration of a few of the risks this new world will pose.

First, business models. We have seen very few media institutions find a way to charge for their digitally delivered content: *The Wall*

Street Journal, which is as close as one gets in American journalism to being both unique and essential, has been the leader to date.

I admire the *Journal* hugely, both in print and online, but I do want to share with you the real reason for its success, the thing that makes it essential. This was explained to me by my boss, Norm Pearlstine, several years ago when he was the *Journal*'s editor: The paper's indispensability, he said, is predicated on the mortal fear, shared by every middle manager in American business, that the boss will say to him or her, "Did you see the piece in the *Journal* this morning about X?"

Well, that works online, too, and several hundred thousand people are now paying Dow Jones for the online paper. But note that they are paying $59 for an annual subscription to the online edition, while the print edition costs $175. That's partly because the physical costs—the nearly one billion a year, in our case, that Time Inc. spends on manufacturing and distribution—have evaporated. In other words, savings have been passed on to the reader, and everybody wins. Except, of course, the paper manufacturers, the delivery services, and the U.S. Post Office—so all of you who have been planning careers at International Paper or with the Postal Service, forget it.

But the real power of the business model resides in the potential of digital advertising. Until the Internet came along no advertising medium existed, except for direct mail, in which the advertiser could be sure his message was received by his targeted audience. We go to the bathroom during commercials, we flip the pages past magazine and newspaper ads, radio and billboards are white noise. But with a truly interactive medium—with say, a question about the advertisement asked next to the button that gives you your 30-cent credit against the cost of reading your *Wall Street Journal*—the effectiveness of media advertising changes radically.

Second digression: consumer prejudices. Inevitably, whenever and wherever I talk about the Death of Print, someone jumps up and says, "But I hate reading on a computer." This is after I have already explained that the technology will change, that economic incentive will create consumer-friendly reading devices, that my father once paid as much for a four-function telephone book–sized calculator as he did for a low-end used car. Or that Oscar Dystel, the former chairman of Bantam Books and one of the founders of the American paperback book industry in the 1940s, once said, "In due course, the word *paperback* will lose its taint of unpleasantness." And he said that in 1984.

No, you won't be reading on a cathode-ray tube sitting on your desk. No, the screen won't flicker, and the type won't have visible ragged edges. It won't feel anything like a computer. It won't even feel like those early avatars of the form, the Rocket eBook and the SoftBook Reader, that are already showing up in Christmas catalogs and in consumer electronics stores—not any more than a Model T feels or looks or drives like a 1999 BMW Z3.

There's even a guy at MIT, an engineering genius named Jacobson, who's devised something called electronic ink, a palette of digitally changeable molecules that sit on a surface very much like a sheet of paper, and rearrange themselves sequentially into actual sentences and paragraphs.

Ah, but you say, who will be able to afford such wonderful devices? In fact, nearly everyone. Because we—the big media companies like Time Warner, the eight or ten major copyright oligarchs, as I like to call them, who control so much of the nation's supply of worthwhile content—we will give them away, for all practical purposes, on the cellphone model. Agree to subscribe to *Time* and *Sports Illustrated* for two years, as well as to listen to a certain amount of, say, Warner Bros. music, and we'll give you the device. We aren't interested in making money off of hardware; we make money off of what you read and watch and listen to.

Last digression: risk. Yes, there are risks. Disaggregated content has already been somewhat socially injurious, and it's only going to get worse, at least insofar as we like to imagine a citizenry that is not only informed, but informed across a range of subjects. The ability to be your own editor—to pick just what news on what topics you wish to read—destroys the potential for serendipity, and the ease with which we achieve balance. I don't know how we'll solve this one, but we must.

Similarly, there's a risk in the mutability of digital content. The good news is that if you libel someone at 9 A.M., you can correct it at 9:10 or at noon or whenever it is that you learn of your mistake; it's not like sending out a fleet of trucks with a million copies of the [*New York*] *Times* and then realizing what you did wrong. But by the same token, if the words are never written in stone, or at least in ink, what happens to the notion of historical record?

But, of course, that cat is already out of the bag. If great writers are producing their works on computer, as most now do, first drafts no longer exist for the study of future scholars—just as the hurried prose of a daily newspaper, "the first rough draft of history," as it has been called, may disappear to the corrections of lawyers.

Yet I think we can live with these things, largely because we must.

I will assert once again that The Death of Print is going to happen, far sooner than many of you may think. The word *Internet* was all but unknown in the U.S. six years ago, and Time Inc., which had not yet even imagined its potential impact, had no one working in the Internet arena. Today, the Internet is inescapable; through the advent of e-mail, it is ubiquitous. In the financial markets, it as essential as dollars. Throughout Time Warner, more than 1,000 people are developing copyrighted Internet product, or marketing it to consumers. Someday, we may even make money at it.

For now, though, all of this is destabilizing, particularly for those of us who are investing substantially in a future so tantalizingly clear in the ultimate goal, but the path to which is so tangled in thickets of doubt, uncertainty and confusion. Yet I, for one, take a strange kind of solace in this.

What I know to be true is that the human species is hungry for information. That the quality, timeliness and reliability of information is paramount. And that those of us who grew up in print, who look at the technological future through unconfident eyes, will be asked to do tomorrow exactly what we have done in the past, which is to reach people—intellectually, viscerally, any way we can—on matters they care about.

My colleagues and I did not grow up wanting to be in the ink and paper and staples business; we wanted to be in—we are in—the business of words and sentences and pictures and ideas. Don't worry about the future of newspapers or magazines or books any more than you would worry about corrugated boxes or shrink-wrap. They are containers; the substance resides elsewhere.

JONATHAN DUBE

Jonathan Dube is technology editor for MSNBC.com, the number one Internet news site. He is also the founder of CyberJournalist.net, a Web site offering "tips and talk for the wired world." He won the first national Online Journalism Award for breaking news for his coverage of the 1999 protests against the World Trade Organization in Seattle. Before joining MSNBC.com, Dube was a national producer for ABCNEWS.com. He has worked as a reporter for *The New York Times, New York Newsday,* and *The Charlotte Observer*. His weekly column for Poynter.org, the Web site of The Poynter Institute for Media Studies, offers advice on writing for online readers. The basics are the same as for any kind of journalism: The writing must be clear and lively, facts must be checked, ethical decisions made. But as Dube pointed out in this November 20, 2000, column for Poynter.org, the technology also affords writers new opportunities—and responsibilities.

Writing News Online

1. Know Your Audience

Write and edit with online readers' needs and habits in mind. Web usability studies show that readers tend to skim over sites rather than read them intently. They also tend to be more proactive than print readers or TV viewers, hunting for information rather than passively taking in what you present to them.

Think about your target audience. Because your readers are getting their news online, chances are they are more interested in Internet-related stories than TV viewers or newspaper readers, so it may make sense to put greater emphasis on such stories. Also, your site potentially has a global reach, so consider whether you want to make it understandable to a local, national or international audience, and write and edit with that in mind.

2. Think First—And Think Different

Before you start reporting and writing a story, think about what the best ways are to tell the story, whether through audio, video, clickable graphics, text, links, etc.—or some combination. Collaborate with audio, video and interactive producers. Develop a plan and let that guide you throughout the news gathering and production process, rather than just reporting a story and then adding various elements later as an afterthought. Also, look for stories that lend themselves to the Web—stories that you can tell differently from or better than in any other medium. . . .

3. Tailor Your News Gathering

Just as print and TV reporters interview differently because they are looking for different things, so must online journalists tailor their interviewing and information gathering specifically to their needs.

Print reporters tend to look for information. TV reporters look for emotion on camera, sound bites and pictures to go with words. Online journalists must constantly think in terms of different elements and how they complement and supplement each other: Look for words to go with images, audio and video to go with words, data that will lend itself to interactives, etc. . . .

Remember that photos look better online when shot or cropped narrowly, and streaming video is easier to watch when backgrounds are plain and zooming minimal. Tape interviews whenever possible in case someone says that would make a powerful clip. Look for personalities who could be interesting chat guests. And always keep an eye out for information that can be conveyed more effectively using interactive tools. . . .

4. Write Lively and Tight

Writing for the Web should be a cross between broadcast and print—tighter and punchier than print, but more literate and detailed than broadcast writing. Write actively, not passively.

Good broadcast writing uses primarily tight, simple declarative sentences and sticks to one idea per sentence. It avoids the long clauses and passive writing of print. Every expressed idea flows logically into the next. Using these concepts in online writing makes the writing easier to understand and better holds readers' attention.

Strive for lively prose, leaning on strong verbs and sharp nouns. Inject your writing with a distinctive voice to help differentiate it from the multitude of content on the Web. Use humor. Try writing in a breezy style or with attitude. Conversational styles work particularly well on the Web. Online audiences are more accepting of unconventional writing styles.

At the same time, don't forget that the traditional rules of writing apply online. Unfortunately, writing quality is inconsistent throughout most online news sites. Stories suffer from passive verbs, run-on sentences, mixed metaphors and clichés. This is a result of fast-paced news gathering, short staffing and inexperienced journalists. This is also a big mistake. Readers notice sloppy writing and they don't forgive. They'll stop reading a story and they won't come back for more. Unlike local newspaper readers, online readers have options.

5. Explain

Don't let yourself get caught up in the 24/7 wire-service mentality and think all that matters is that you have the latest news as fast as possible. Readers rarely notice, or care who was first. People want to know not just what happened, but why it matters. And with all the information sources out there now, in the end it will be the sites that explain the news the best that succeed. Write and edit all your stories with this in mind. . . .

6. Never Bury the Lead

You can't afford to bury the lead online because if you do, few readers will get to it. When writing online, it's essential to tell the reader quickly what the story is about and why they should keep reading—or else they won't.

One solution is to use a "Model T" story structure. In this model, a story's lead—the horizontal line of the T—summarizes the story and, ideally, tells why it matters. The lead doesn't need to give away the ending, just give someone a reason to read on. Then the rest of the story—the vertical line of the T—can take the form of just about any structure: the writer can tell the story narratively; provide an anecdote and then follow with the rest of the story; jump from one to another, in a "stack of blocks" form; or simply continue into an inverted pyramid.

This enables the writer to quickly telegraph the most important information—and a reason to keep reading—and yet still retain the freedom to write the story in the way he or she wants to. . . .

7. Don't Pile On

Another story structure that has evolved online, mostly by accident, is what I call The Pile-On.

A common problem with online writing occurs in breaking news stories. In an effort to seem as current as possible, sites will often put the latest development in a story at the top—no matter how incremental the development. Then, they'll pile the next development on the top, and the next—creating an ugly mish-mash of a story that makes sense only to someone who has been following the story closely all day. Unfortunately, the only people who are usually doing so are the journalists. Few readers visit a site more than once a day. Remember this when updating stories, and always keep the most important news in the lead. . . .

8. Short But Sweet

Most stories online are too long for a Web audience, and I imagine few readers finish them. Roy Peter Clark has written a wonderful essay arguing that any story can be told in 800 words—a good guideline for online writing. But let that be a guideline, not a rule. Readers will stick with longer stories online if there is a compelling reason for a story to be that long—and if it continues to captivate their attention.

Making readers scroll to get to the rest of a story is generally preferable to making them click. Online news users do scroll. If someone has clicked to get to a page, it's generally because they want to read the story, and thus chances are high that they will. The Poynter eyetrack study showed that about 75 percent of article text was read online—far more than in print, where 20 to 25 percent of an article's text gets read, on average. Print readers have less vested in any given story, because they haven't done anything proactive to get the article.

9. Break It Up

Larger blocks of text make reading on screens difficult, and you're more likely to lose readers. Using more subheads and bullets to separate text and ideas helps. Writing should be snappy and fast to read. Keep paragraphs and sentences short. Like this.

Try reading sentences out loud to see if they're too long. You should be able to read an entire sentence without pausing for a breath.

It also helps to extract information into charts, tables, bulleted lists and interactive graphics. Even a simple box with a definition or summary can help break up text and convey information in an easy-to-read format. . . .

10. Eliminate the Guesswork

People often don't know what they're going to get when they click on stuff. And people are not going to click on something unless they know what they're getting. When they click on something that's not worth it, they lose trust in you as a source and are less likely to come back and click on things in the future. So make sure you tell people what they are going to get.

Studies show online news users preferred straightforward headlines to funny or cute ones. Cute headlines didn't do as good a job of quickly explaining what a story is about and thus discouraged online users from clicking through. . . .

11. Do Not Fear the Link

Don't be afraid to link. Many sites have a paranoid fear that if they include links to other sites, readers will surf away and never return. Not true! People prefer to go to sites that do a good job of compiling click-worthy links—witness Yahoo!'s success. If people know they can trust your site, they will come back for more.

At the same time, journalists have a responsibility to apply news judgment and editorial standards to the links they choose. Avoid linking to sites with blatantly false information or offensive content. Select links that enhance the value of the story by helping readers get additional information from the people behind the news.

And of course, link to related stories on your site, past and present. This is truly one of the advantages of the Web. By linking to other stories to provide context and background, writers have more freedom to focus on the news of the day without bogging stories down with old information. . . .

12. Take Risks . . . But Remember the Basics

Online journalism is a new and evolving industry and we are writing the rules as we go along. Challenge yourself and your colleagues to question the way things are being done and to stretch the boundaries of what can be done. There are no rules, only ideas. Take risks. Try something different.

But don't forget the fundamentals of journalism. Facts still have to be double- and triple-checked; writing still needs to be sharp, lively and to the point; stories should include context; and ethical practices must be followed. Don't let the 24/7 speed trap and the new tools distract you from these basics.

With so many alternative news sources now at everyone's fingertips thanks to the Web, it is now more important than ever that we stick to the fundamentals of journalism to produce news people can trust, because in the end that's what will keep people coming back for more.

MARK BOWDEN

Mark Bowden has been a reporter for more than twenty years at *The Philadelphia Inquirer,* where his best-selling book *Black Hawk Down* first appeared in twenty-eight daily installments. It was a National Book Award nominee for nonfiction in 1999 and was made into an Academy Award–winning motion picture in 2001. Though Bowden writes a column for the paper, he mostly devotes himself to reporting and writing narrative stories that are published in the *Inquirer* before becoming books. In this essay for the Fall 2000 issue of *Nieman Reports,* a publication of the Nieman Foundation for Journalism at Harvard University, Bowden says *Black Hawk Down* was the first of his projects to get full-fledged treatment on the paper's Web site, Philly Online. The response from readers was phenomenal, but even more satisfying to Bowden than knowing people were reading the series were the unexpected benefits of the Web. He credits its interactive features with increasing his credibility with readers and putting him in touch with new sources for his reporting. He concludes that multimedia presentations offer reporters—and readers—opportunities no single medium can match.

Narrative Journalism Goes Multimedia

Three years ago I wrote an extended series of articles for *The Philadelphia Inquirer* entitled "Black Hawk Down," a detailed account of the tragic battle on October 3, 1993, between the elite American Rangers and the heavily armed citizenry of Mogadishu, Somalia.

While the battle had been a dramatic turning point in U.S. foreign policy, particularly military policy, the full story of what happened that day had never been told. Eighteen American soldiers were killed and 73 were wounded. Estimates of Somali casualties numbered over 1,000. No American reporters had been in Somalia to cover it, even though it was the most severe combat involving American soldiers since the Vietnam War. I set out to capture both the drama and the importance of the episode and thought the best way to do that would be to write a narrative account, to tell the story of the battle through the eyes of the men who fought it.

In the three years since, "Black Hawk Down" has become a best-selling book, and is on its way to becoming a feature film. Its success has far outstripped any of our expectations. But one of the most remarkable things about the project, and one of the big reasons for its ultimate impact, is the pioneering way it was presented on the Internet. Assembled by editor Jennifer Musser of Philly Online, the *Inquirer*'s official Web site, the daily unfolding of the series in cyberspace during 28 days in November and December of 1997 drew in hundreds of thousands of readers from all over the world. At its height, the electronic version of the story was getting 46,000 hits every day. The Web site's rendering of the story featured the full text of the series along with photographs, video and audiotape snippets of the battle itself and interviews with key participants, maps, graphics, documents. As the article moves forward, readers can click on a variety of these hyperlinks to consult a map or hear an interview from which I extracted a quote or read a document that I refer to in the text. Its interactive "Ask the Author" feature nearly wore me out. But the Philly Online display offered a powerful glimpse of this medium's potential for journalistic storytelling, both heightening the experience for readers and significantly enhancing the strength and credibility of my reporting.

I'd like to say that I planned it this way. I am an old-fashioned newspaper reporter, one who blanched 25 years ago when the editors first announced plans to replace our beloved typewriters, scissors, paste pots and Wite-Out with computers. Five years ago, when I first started working on "Black Hawk Down," I hardly knew what the Internet was, other than some vague technological tide that someday, we were told, would sweep away the practice of printing words on paper. By then I figured to be long retired, if not dead and gone. My only concern for "Black Hawk Down" was to report and write it in such a way that it would read like good fiction, but would be rigorously and demonstrably true. I envisioned it as a newspaper series for the benefit of readers in the Philadelphia area and then a book that might reach a broader audience. None of us at the *Inquirer* foresaw the story's ultimate reach.

When we began planning the series' publication at the *Inquirer* in the summer of 1997, I never even considered how the story would be presented on the Internet. Max King, then the newspaper's executive editor, and Bob Rosenthal, then his deputy, decided that if the newspaper was going to run a series during an entire month it ought to exploit the story in every way possible. King envisioned it as a multimedia event. He drew in the *Inquirer*'s film department, K-R Video, which primarily made short video clips for Philly Online, and producer

Chris Mills began creating a documentary film to be aired on the local PBS affiliate, WHYY, in conjunction with the series. Public Broadcasting had an impressive history of tying together documentary TV and book publishing, and I viewed working on a film companion to the series as an exciting and different opportunity.

In those early meetings I remember seeing Philly Online's editor, Jennifer Musser, at the table quietly taking notes, and assumed she had a simple job mounting the text of the series on the *Inquirer*'s Web site. To the extent I thought about it at all, I thought the Web site would give readers who picked up the series in midstream an opportunity to go back and catch up on the earlier installments, which would be particularly beneficial because the story was such a long, dramatic narrative.

To make the documentary, Mills sent cameramen to Somalia, which I had already visited to interview those who fought against American soldiers, and dispatched crews around the country to re-interview some of the scores of soldiers I had tracked down. He also obtained from the Pentagon snippets of videotape from the battle itself. We worked together to fashion a narration for the film, and Mills hired a professional voice to read it. I divided my time between working on the documentary and huddling with David Zucchino, my editor, to get the series in shape for the newspaper. We were pushing to get the series in the paper on time and had already decided to begin it without having the last few parts finished.

Sometime that fall, Musser stopped by my desk to ask if I had any resource material she could use.

"What do you want?" I asked.

"Audiotapes, documents, photos, maps — everything you've got," she said.

There were plenty of maps, documents and photos in my files. Soldiers had been sending me snapshots they had saved from their service in Somalia, and Peter Tobia, an *Inquirer* photographer, had traveled with me to that devastated country and brought back an amazing portfolio. I handed them over. As for audiotape, I had piles of it. When I began the project the year before, I had taped my interviews with the soldiers. I eventually stopped, because the sheer number of interviews made transcribing the tapes too time-consuming, but I still had shoeboxes filled with cassette tapes at home. I had even managed to collect bits of audiotape from the radio transmissions of soldiers during the battle, sounds that captured the frenzy and terror of the fight. So I swept all the tapes into a bag and dumped them on Musser's desk the next morning. I expected her to complain.

Instead, she was thrilled. She asked to see my handwritten transcriptions of the tapes and began painstakingly studying them, finding and highlighting some of the most dramatic passages, then locating them on the audiotapes. I still didn't have a clear idea of what she planned to do with all the material. Weeks before the series was set to run, as Zucchino and I still worked to finish it, Fred Mann, the director of Philly Online, asked me if I would mind answering questions from readers on the Internet as it unfolded.

"We'll probably get a dozen or so," he said.

I agreed.

The series debuted on Sunday, November 16th. The Friday before, I sat with King in his office discussing it. "I don't know how this is going to be received," said King, who had invested an unprecedented variety of resources in the series. "If nobody is interested, we're going to look pretty foolish with a series running day after day for a month. But you know what? If a story like this doesn't sell, then I'm not sure I want to be involved in journalism anymore."

He needn't have worried. Sales of the newspaper jumped by 20,000 during the month the series ran. Every day my desk was piled with letters and phone messages from excited readers. The head of the *Inquirer*'s circulation department paid a rare visit to the newsroom, asked to meet me and shook my hand.

But this turned out to be only the smaller part of it. Jennifer Musser's presentation of "Black Hawk Down" was exploding on the Internet. Prior to this series, the most heavily read story on the Web site had been an account of the death of Richie Ashburn, the Phillies baseball great and popular TV announcer, which had collected 9,000 hits in a day. "Black Hawk Down" debuted with numbers higher than that, and with each day it kept growing, to 15,000 hits a day, then 20,000 a day, then more. When the number of hits hit 40,000, the Web site's overworked server crashed, forcing them to go out and buy another to handle the demand. The online division tracked the sources of those hits to military bases, government offices, universities and headquarters for some of the largest corporations in the military-industrial complex. These were all places where workers, students, soldiers, sailors and cadets were computer literate and had access to high-powered, fast computer connections.

The outpouring was easy to understand. Whatever the drama and importance of the story itself, Musser and her team designer Ches Wajda, photo editor John Williams, and programmer Ranjit Bhatnagar had created an extraordinary way for readers to experience the story of "Black Hawk Down." The technology of the Internet, paired with the creativeness of the editing team, meant that far more could be offered online to the reader than by the series in the newspaper. On the Web site, the story became part illustrated book, part documentary film, part radio program. It was all these things and more, because it allowed readers (who at times became viewers) to explore the story and its source material in any way they chose.

Those who arrive at the Web site can read the story straight through and then go back and view the audio, video, photos, etc., or they can click on hyperlinks as they read and just explore at will. All of the source material, things usually simply noted in agate in a bibliography or endnotes, were on display. Unlike the maps in the newspaper, those on the Web site, designed by Matthew Ericson, were animated. Ericson created one that showed the whole plan for how the Ranger raid was supposed to have unfolded, with helicopters flying in over the target house, Rangers roping to the street, and trucks pulling up to load up prisoners and soldiers and drive them away. There was a copy of the stirring handwritten letter sent by the American commander, General William F. Garrison, the day after the fight.

Even more remarkable, when the series first launched, was the interactive aspect. Those "dozen" questions from readers? They flowed in by the hundreds daily, from men who had fought in the battle, from soldiers at military bases all over the world, from appreciative and critical readers. I sat for hours every morning while the series ran answering them one by one. The *Inquirer*'s then managing editor, Gene Foreman, concerned that the final parts of the series had not been finished, walked by my desk one morning and announced how pleased he was to see me writing away so furiously.

"Is that the last part?" he asked, hopefully (no doubt with visions of my being hit by a truck and the paper being left with its highly popular story unfinished).

"No Gene, I'm answering the e-mail. If I don't do this every morning I'll never keep up with it."

For the rest of the month I was completely swept up in this Internet phenomenon. The Web site vastly improved the story in several ways. It gave readers all over the world a chance to instantly comment and correct. Military experts are notably finicky about getting the details of weaponry and equipment exactly right, and I was given a great number of helpful corrections. And because the story was mounted in cyberspace, instead of merely running a correction and apology the next day on an inside page of the newspaper, we could immediately correct the story. Readers who pointed out errors returned the next day to find them corrected, with an e-mailed apology and thanks from me.

This greatly enhanced the account's credibility. Instead of dealing with the reporter as a distant "expert," and speculating on the reasons for mistakes or omissions, readers saw my own eagerness to simply get the story right, something which in my own experience is the primary motivation of most reporters. Those who sent e-mail messages offering more information on key points in the story were contacted immediately, by phone or e-mail. Interactivity helped to break down the normal wall of suspicion between soldiers and reporters, and I found myself suddenly offered whole new sources for the book version. It also made the process of running the story memorably fun. Instead of leaning back and wondering how the work was being received, I was in an arena with my readers, explaining, defending and correcting the story as it unfolded. I never had so much fun with a story.

Credibility was enhanced in another way. Stories written in a dramatic, narrative fashion, as I tried to write "Black Hawk Down," typically dispense with the wooden recitation of sources. If you write, "according to so-and-so" in every sentence, in the manner of old wire copy police stories, storytelling quickly loses its pace and clarity. Often writers who avoid this kind of belabored source-noting in the text are accused (and in some notable cases have been guilty) of embellishing the truth, filling in gaps of knowledge with flights of fancy, or rearranging time sequences and other details to smooth out the narrative. It's easy to see why. Without clear delineation of sources, even careful readers can't tell where the reporter has gotten the information, so they tend to be suspicious of it. Hyperlinks solved that problem. If a reader, for instance, wondered how I could possibly know exactly what was in Staff Sergeant Matt Eversmann's head as he slid down the rope into battle, then they could click on the hyperlink at Eversmann's name and listen to him explaining what was in his head. That was one of those audio clips Musser lifted from my interview tapes. In some cases, because of the work Mills and his documentary crew had done, there were video clips of interviews. Because readers could listen to some of the hundreds of interviews and view some of the broad documentation that was the foundation for this simple, fast-paced story, it gave the account weight it might not have had, had it run only in the newspaper. Along with the finished product, discerning readers could inspect the building blocks of the story, could see how it had been assembled. These audio-visual features not only added to the fun of reading the story, but grounded it more firmly in reality.

Philly Online's presentation of "Black Hawk Down" won the Editor & Publisher Award for the best journalistic series on the Internet in 1997. I have felt free to brag about it ever since because not only did I not create it, it didn't occur to me to do so, and if it had, I wouldn't have known how to do it. What Musser, Mann, Ericson, Williams, Wajda and Bhatnagar had done was groundbreaking, and suggested to this old typewriter hacker how amazing this new media soon will be. Because of limitations in the speed of computing and Internet connection, the most "Black Hawk Down" could offer were tiny windows of video and small samplings of audio. Imagine what such an experience will be like when full-screen color video and audio can be accessed instantly. Multimedia presentation of news stories, investigations, history, and sports will offer storytelling opportunities no solitary medium can match.

Imagine, just for fun, an Internet presentation of a Super Bowl. Within hours of the game's end, an enterprising journalist could combine written accounts of the game with video, so that as a reader goes back to look at a key play, he could click on a hyperlink and watch it on screen from a variety of angles. He then could click on another hyperlink to hear the players involved talk about that play in post-game interviews, or hear coaches and commentators break it down critically. Such a display could offer the complete seasonal history of every player in the game, breakdowns of every game played by each team, etc. A serious fan could spend days wandering happily through the site. Or imagine a work of history presented complete with all its source material, historical reading, background material, commentary and analysis available at the click of a mouse. Such a presentation would combine the authority of a book with the entertainment value of a film and give scholars not just advice on where to go for more detailed information, but the information itself. In the future, I suspect, nonfiction writers will routinely consider how to present their work with sounds, images and source material as well as their own well-chosen words. I know I will never again write a major work without doing so.

Still, the medium is in its infancy, and by any standard I'm a dinosaur. Whatever uses I can imagine for Internet journalism will seem narrow and dated to those who grow up using computers. By definition, creative minds will come up with ways of using this new medium, combining sound and image and text in ways that we cannot yet foresee.

MICHAEL J. BERENS

Michael Berens is a projects reporter for the *Chicago Tribune* who frequently uses computer databases to aid and guide his reporting. Computer-assisted research has formed the backbone of stories in which he detailed a secretive state plan to house young psychiatric patients in geriatric nursing homes; revealed the possibility of a serial killer trolling truck stops nationally; and exposed cops who owned crack houses. But Berens, who was a finalist for the Pulitzer Prize for beat reporting in 1995, notes that a reporter's human sources—not his databases—make for the most fascinating reading. In this essay from *When Nerds and Words Collide,* published by the Poynter Institute for Media Studies in 1999, Berens says computer-assisted reporting can identify a lead or lend authority to a story, but is not a substitute for old-fashioned legwork.

The Myth of the Machine

It was the darkest of nights in a windowless room when the source, perched on my desk, quietly delivered a stunning revelation: City police officers owned crack houses. Years later, the source imparted another gem: A serial killer was trolling truck stops in five states for female victims. Most recently, and still going strong after a facelift, my confidant divulged that Chicago nursing homes were secret dumping grounds for violent state psychiatric patients.

For the last decade, there has been no more exhilarating and exasperating a source as my computer, a modern-day Siren whose seductive call leads to journalistic ecstasy—or certain ruin for the unwary.

We call it computer-assisted reporting, CAR for short. There are impressive self-help books and manuals wrapped with sample disks, training classes touting chi squares to regression analysis, self-described gurus who've become data gods, and reporters who possess more electronic equipment than common sense. Obscured behind the technobabble is a simple truth: The best computer-assisted reporting is born from the heart, not the machine.

Critics often charge that CAR represents a barrier to good storytelling. There are no shortages of examples to confirm this fear. Of course, the telephone has been used for bad stories, too; skeptics are not shunning *that* journalism tool. The best computer-assisted reporting is invisible within the narrative, a hidden backbone that authoritatively supports the story. A random sample of this country's best journalism will, more often than not, reveal the role of computer-assisted research.

It helps to envision the computer as a person, someone with frailties and faults, a woefully naïve child who only repeats what it has been told, but possessing an innocence that can spot simple truths. Stories are unlocked by penetrating questions, not by the capacity of the Pentium chip. Vision, intuition, and imagination should combine bits and bytes into words that cause the reader to bolt into anger or shed a tear.

More than a decade ago, I owned nothing more than a boxy Macintosh Plus and a piece of accounting software, Microsoft Excel. The resulting stories still stand tall today. Vice squad officers who got drunk on duty, juvenile prisoners raped by state guards, police informants who framed innocent citizens—these stories resulted from filling in blanks of little Excel squares, resembling blank graph paper on the screen. It was a valuable lesson: Start simple.

All I had to do was fill in the blanks. This was something I could understand. And the computer could reorganize the information in ways that seemed, well, magical. I would stare at the information for hours. I looked for patterns and anomalies, sorting and re-sorting to my every whim. Later came the realization that I was interviewing the data just as I would any other source.

Do most nursing homes mix young psychiatric patients with elderly residents? Is it normal for police cruisers to crash in half of all high-speed pursuits? How many fugitives are secretly released because police don't want to pay for extradition?

Following analysis of a court database, I determined that 90 percent of domestic violence cases were eventually dismissed. Some might jump at this lead, trumpet the computer findings, snag a few prosecutor quotes, touch base with victim advocates, and mix it all into an instant story. This would be a CAR failure.

Why were there so many dismissals? Again, ask the computer for clues. Dismissals were typically granted during arraignment hearings, computer analysis showed. Arraignment hearings are held within 24 hours of the crime. What the heck was going on? A visit to the hearings provided the answers: Cases were automatically dismissed if victims could not make it to the hearing, even if they had no transportation or had been hospitalized just hours before. If victims did show, they were required to stand just feet away from their attacker, an intimidating requirement for some women who fled in tears. Some male judges unmercifully grilled female victims who asked for protection orders. Traditional reporting skills still create the outer covering, the contour, and the texture. The resulting human stories were a CAR success.

The myth of the machine hit home in the early 1990s when a Cable News Network crew visited the newsroom to film a segment on how I documented the existence of a possible serial killer. Using a spreadsheet program, I tracked the unsolved deaths of women whose bodies were found along highways. The computer was a significant tool, but breakthroughs occurred through interviews and leaked law enforcement documents.

"How did you do the story?" the producer asked. My answers stressed old-fashioned legwork coupled with the power of the computer. My answer was unsatisfactory. Surely I discovered some sort of technological alchemy; perhaps a complex mathematical formula was employed, no? The producer was sure that I was trying to be modest. "Come on," she said. "You can tell us how you really did it."

Later, the FBI invited me to Quantico, Va., to explain how my trusty Macintosh outmatched the bureau's mainframes, which were programmed to spot pattern crimes. It's not the size of the computer, but the human behind it that matters most, I told a crowd of homicide detectives. "Sounds like it was blind luck," one agent quipped.

Indeed, luck is part of the quotient. For example, I computerized search warrants on a spreadsheet to analyze the success of the crack war. One of the fields—reluctantly included following an editor's suggestion—designated the time and day of the raid. I was looking for corruption, not a feature story. But the computer findings surprised us: No raids were ever conducted on a weekend. My partner and I ran out to some crack neighborhoods. One dealer smiled as he told us, "Sure, we know about that. That's why we are open only on weekends."

To this day, I adhere to three basic philosophies:

- Begin small.
- Think simple.
- No detail is unimportant.

It's not necessary to learn how to write programming language. Learn what is necessary to accomplish the job. The computer should serve you. With each story comes more skill. Before you know it, you'll find yourself knee-high in magnetic tapes and relational database programs.

Some industry observers says that journalists have arrived at a technological crossroad. The advent of the Internet has dramatically altered how we accumulate information, and given rise to reader expectations. We already have multimedia newsrooms as print reporters double as television hosts, and assist in web page design. The birth of virtual reality will further transform the journalistic landscape.

Sadly, newsrooms have been slow to react. And the majority of reporters remain modern-day illiterates—unable to read a world of computerized information. Newsroom training remains one of the most inexcusable deficiencies. For most, the crossroads are still many miles away.

The secret is not to follow the machine. Instead, follow your passion for the story; use the computer to track your ideas and test those hunches. When that happens, you will have a lifetime source like no other.

Chapter 10

ETHICAL JOURNALISM

The ironclad rules of journalism are few, yet every so often a plague of serious violations becomes public: plagiarism, making up sources, labeling a work of fiction nonfiction. Each time an ethical boundary is breached, whether by accident or by calculation, the reputation of the profession suffers.

In this chapter, three writers examine issues of ethics. Roy Peter Clark looks at why plagiarism continues to crop up in newsrooms. Marjie Lundstrom points to a less recognized ethical dilemma: geographical stereotyping. Ben Bradlee describes one of journalism's darkest hours and the lessons his newspaper—and the profession—learned from it. Collectively, the insights of these authors provide a good place to start thinking about ethics in journalism.

ROY PETER CLARK

Roy Peter Clark, senior scholar at The Poynter Institute and founding director of the National Writers' Workshop, has coined an inspired phrase for describing plagiarism, the taking of someone's words and passing them off as your own: "unoriginal sin." Whether the product of sloppy work habits, lazy reporting, or intellectual dishonesty, plagiarism is one of journalism's most vexing problems, says Clark, who has worked as a writing coach and reporter at the *St. Petersburg Times*. He is also the author of *Free to Write: A Journalist Teaches Young Writers* and coauthor of *Coaching Writers: Editors and Reporters Working Together,* as well as numerous serial narratives for newspapers. His essay on plagiarism, which appeared in *Washington Journalism Review* in March 1983, is frequently cited in discussions about journalism ethics. In it, he says an informal survey revealed that the rules against plagiarism are ill-defined in most American newsrooms.

The Unoriginal Sin

Each day in American newspapers and magazines, journalists kidnap the words of other writers without attribution or shame.

The practice is called plagiarism, a name derived from the Latin word for kidnapper. In the academic world, it is the most serious of crimes. But in the world of journalism, a world without footnotes, the snatching of words and ideas is too often ignored, misunderstood or considered standard procedure.

Reporters plagiarize from novels, encyclopedias, textbooks, magazines, wire stories, syndicated columns, press releases, competing newspapers and the morgue.

Some who commit the unoriginal sin are charlatans. Others resort to it in moments of pressure or personal crisis. Others slide into it out of naivete or ignorance. They do not know how much borrowing is too much, because teachers and editors have failed to set limits and suggest guidelines.

Enough examples of blatant plagiarism have surfaced at good newspapers to make any conscientious editor wary.

- In 1975, a critic at *The Atlanta Constitution* borrowed most of a film review from *Newsweek*. Her editors chastised her. The woman claimed to have a photographic memory. She begged to be given another chance, and was. She did it again and lost her job. "It was the stupidest kind of plagiarism," remembers Ed Sears, [then] managing editor of *The Atlanta Journal and Constitution.* "She took the stuff verbatim from a recent edition of *Newsweek.*"

- In 1978, a columnist for the *Charlotte News* kidnapped an old Art Buchwald column and published it under his own name. He was new to column writing, was responsible for five columns a week, and on a dry day resorted to wholesale plagiarism. An alert reader discovered it. The columnist apologized to his readers. He was moved to the copy desk.
- In 1980, a columnist for the Louisville *Courier-Journal* wrote a column on the economy described by one of his editors as "brilliant." This surprised no one as the writer had proven time and again that he was capable of such work. The paper was later notified by a lawyer that passages from the column were lifted from his client's book. The columnist admitted that he had read a review copy of the book, that he had been influenced by it, and that he had used it without attribution. Managing editor David Hawpe apologized for his columnist in print and eventually moved him to the copy desk.
- In 1981, a Los Angeles reporter for the Associated Press resigned after it was learned that her story about high speed races on California highways was both a composite and an act of plagiarism. Without attribution, the writer used several anecdotes and passages taken verbatim from *New West* magazine. She tricked the reader into thinking that she had witnessed the race described in *New West.*
- In February of 1982, *The New York Times* discovered that a freelance writer had fabricated a story that appeared in *The New York Times Magazine.* Christopher Jones, 24, without leaving Spain, wrote an article that created the illusion he had visited remote regions of Cambodia and had caught a glimpse of Pol Pot. The hoax was uncovered when the *Village Voice* revealed that Jones' ending had been plagiarized from the André Malraux novel *The Royal Way.* Confronted by *Times* editors in Spain, Jones admitted that he had pilfered Malraux because "I needed a piece of color." . . .
- In 1972, shortly after becoming the editor of the *St. Petersburg Times,* Gene Patterson received a letter from the editor of *Better*

Homes and Gardens. It contained a copy of an elaborate color drawing that had appeared in the *Times*. Attached to it was an identical piece of art from the magazine. "It made me heartsick," said Patterson. "It was a beautifully imaginative, very complicated color drawing. Our artist had copied it exactly, in every detail." He was fired. Plagiarism, obviously, is not confined to words. The way artists borrow from each other deserves its own investigation.

Almost every newspaper I have consulted offers an anecdote about serious plagiarism. I have heard of editorials copied word for word from *The New York Times* and government handouts. I have heard, but have not been able to verify, stories about a managing editor at a small paper who routinely plagiarized stories from newsmagazines, stole a whole series from a larger newspaper and even stuck his name over the work of his own reporters. Such a man might have inspired Samuel Johnson's famous piece of sarcasm: "Your manuscript is both good and original; but the part that is good is not original, and the part that is original is not good."

Plagiarism in newspapers (ethical plagiarism, that is, not the violation of copyright, which is a legal question) is more common than imagined and in many cases escapes detection. Most cases are cloudier and less spectacular than the ones cited above. Like defensive pass interference in football, they may be blatant or accidental, but they always deserve the yellow flag.

On September 1, 1982, Jerry Bledsoe, a columnist for the *Greensboro Daily News and Record,* called me. He had just read *Best Newspaper Writing 1982,* an annual collection, which I edit, of the winning articles from the national writing competition sponsored by the American Society of Newspaper Editors (ASNE).

One of the stories, written by Tom Archdeacon of the *Miami News,* described Linda Vaughn, the buxom beauty queen of the racing car circuit. Bledsoe was attracted to the story because in 1975 he had written *The World's Number One, Flat-Out, All-Time Great Stock Car Racing Book,* which included a chapter on Linda Vaughn. When he read Archdeacon's story, Bledsoe was surprised to see some of his own words under Archdeacon's byline. He sent me a copy of his chapter, underlining 10 instances (about 100 words) in which Archdeacon had borrowed from him without attribution.

In 1975, Jerry Bledsoe had written: "To be a race queen is about the only way a woman can be involved in big time stock car racing."

In 1981, Archdeacon changed only the tense: "To be a race queen was about the only way a woman could be involved in big time stock car racing."

The most damning passage was one in which Archdeacon used Bledsoe's language to describe the reaction of grimy mechanics to this voluptuous woman. In Bledsoe's words, the sight of her made them "stand in awe, made them punch one another in the ribs and giggle like little boys. . . ." Archdeacon has them "stand in awe, bashful, punching each other in the ribs, giggling like school boys."

I wrote a report that was sent to ASNE seconding Bledsoe's cry of foul: "I believe that Tom Archdeacon is guilty of low-grade plagiarism and high-grade carelessness. There appears to be much original information in Archdeacon's story. . . . But the textual similarities speak for themselves. If Archdeacon were a student in my college English class, I'd give him a stern public lecture on the rules of plagiarism and make him write it again."

Bledsoe's phone call and my report set off a chain reaction. The ASNE contacted the *Miami News*. *Miami News* editors confronted Archdeacon. He later described the aftermath of that meeting in a report in the ASNE *Bulletin:* "It . . . had the effect of a baseball bat to the solar plexus. I spoke with them truthfully and quite frankly and then was excused from the room. I headed for my desk but never made it. I had to beeline for the bathroom, where I promptly threw up. And I haven't felt much better since."

Archdeacon told his editors that he admired Bledsoe's book, that he had used it for background on Linda Vaughn, and that under deadline he had confused Bledsoe's words with his own in more than 100 pages of sloppily taken notes. "I swear to God," Archdeacon wrote, "there was no deviousness intended."

Archdeacon flew to Greensboro to apologize to Bledsoe. They met for about 15 minutes in the newspaper coffee shop. "He was very contrite," says Bledsoe, "and I felt very sorry for him. It was a gray day and he was as downcast as the weather."

It was decided that Archdeacon would write a *mea culpa* for the November issue of the ASNE *Bulletin*. His publisher, David Kraslow, would declare that his writer had "made a serious error in judgment." And the ASNE board would chastise Archdeacon.

The board met in Washington, D.C., on October 21–22, and prepared a statement that read in part: "While what happened is a journalistic misdemeanor and not a felony—and appears to be a mistake rather than plagiarism—the board deplores that such gross carelessness and sloppiness could be part of the working procedure of such a talented writer." Archdeacon kept the award and his job.

In reviewing the case, it become clear to me that there is little agreement among journalists as to how the rules against plagiarism should affect the behavior of reporters. Most newspapers have no rules. Editors seem loath to define it, especially in marginal cases. Plagiarism is the skeleton in journalism's closet.

In preparing my report on Archdeacon, I found nothing—no guidelines, no warnings, not even the word *plagiarism* in indexes of the newspaper stylebooks and journalism textbooks on my shelf. I had to turn to English composition texts and handbooks for scholars for discussion on how much a writer can borrow.

Although most of the editors and senior staff members of the *Miami News* thought Archdeacon had blundered badly, the verdict was not unanimous. In a memo to ASNE, publisher Kraslow described the feeling of one dissenter, "that Tom did what most journalists do routinely with research material—weave it into the body of the story without attribution."

The ASNE board, according to three of its members, did not easily come to a consensus on whether Archdeacon had committed a mortal or venial sin or what his penance should be. Nevertheless, "There was no thought of rescinding the award," said Bob Stiff, editor of the St. Petersburg *Evening Independent*. Still, these 20 top newspaper editors were hazy on the definition of plagiarism. "Well, how much borrowing is too much?" Katherine Fanning, editor and publisher of the *Anchorage Daily News,* asked later. "Three words? Four words?"

The board accepted the notion that since the borrowing was unintentional, the act was not plagiarism. Jerry Bledsoe disagrees. "I think they need to examine their standards," he said. "I think that they've demeaned their awards."

Part of the problem is that all good reporters compile, borrow and assimilate. They do not read for fun. They read for work. They borrow juxtapositions, images, metaphors, rhythms, puns, emphases, structures, word orders, alliterations and startling facts. They store these in their memory banks and in their commonplace books. Months later these words emerge in a new context and with personal meaning, having become their own.

Journalists, like scholars, write within a climate of ideas, ideas that fly from newspaper to newspaper like migrating birds. The hard-working and curious reporter explores each new idea and collects everything on the landscape. But embedded in these good habits are dangers, for both the unprincipled and the undisciplined.

While a virtuous reporter can always avoid crude plagiarism, crude abuses may be nurtured by the ethically ambiguous practices that go on each day in newsrooms. Although I have probably practiced some of these myself, the following procedures now seem dangerous and unprofessional:

Robbing the Morgue

We file old newspaper stories in the morgue, a misnomer, because some of the stories live forever. It is a common and responsible newspaper practice to dig in those files for background, a sense of history and perspective. When we cover the trial of a murderer, we consult the clips on his arrest.

Most journalists recognize the dangers. Do we, under deadline, borrow paragraphs verbatim without verification or attribution? Do we recycle old quotations without letting readers know that a quote may be out of date or secondhand?

Ed Sears describes a case in Atlanta where "a reporter had lifted some paragraphs verbatim from the clips. We discovered it only because the facts he lifted turned out to be wrong, even though it had been written by a good reporter. I don't know how much of that goes on. As for our guidelines, there are none."

Some editors argue that a reporter may borrow an aptly worded paragraph, perhaps more, from an old story from his own newspaper.

A newspaper may have a good reason for permitting reporters to use information from the clips verbatim. Perhaps the paper has reduced a difficult concept (the Consumer Price Index) to a clear formula, or prefers to use the same paragraph of background for a running story.

In most cases, the writer should assimilate information from the clips and rewrite or let the narrative suggest that material derives from earlier accounts.

Such care becomes essential in an age when technology makes the mining of the clips easier—kidnapping by computer. *The New York Times,* for example, now has a split-screen capability on terminals, which can display a new story on the left and a story retrieved from the clips on the right. "Retrieved information," said a recent story in *Presstime,* "can be inserted electronically into the working story."

Abusing the Wires

Editors tell of wire stories that appear, almost word for word, under the bylines of local writers. The reverse can happen when reporters from the AP or UPI do not rephrase and summarize adequately the stories of local reporters.

Many newspaper stories combine original reporting with information compiled from news services. Such collaboration has a long history and is essential to daily journalism. But it can be done in unscrupulous ways.

Editors can help create a sense of source for the reader by clearly labeling when wire copy has been used in a staff story. This can be done with a tag line or in the text.

The AP bylaws give the wire service the right to use "spot" news stories from member newspapers as opposed to "enterprise" pieces. According to Louis D. Boccardi, AP vice president and executive editor, AP writers are expected to rewrite stories, although it is accepted that direct quotations will reappear word for word.

"I learned to rewrite everything," says Melvin Mencher, professor at the Columbia Graduate School of Journalism, and a former United Press staffer. "We were told to rewrite and I took that seriously. It had some moral compulsion. But we live in a different age, the age as media star. It's me, me, me the writer. Attribution comes awfully hard to that mindset."

Lifting from Other Newspapers and Magazines

Broadcast media—from local radio to network television magazine shows—steal from newspapers without attribution in order to preserve the myth of exclusivity.

But newspapers cannot complain. They feast on each other like sharks, a banquet that has gone on for years. Donald Murray, professor of English at the University of New Hampshire and newspaper writing coach, remembers his days as a rewrite man for the *Boston Herald* in the early 1950s. Every day he was tossed clips from all the competing newspapers in town. "It was nothing to turn out 50 quick run-throughs," he says. "Whatever scholarly ideas I had about plagiarism went by the board."

His experience on the police beat also tempered his idealism. "The copy desk would put into my story details from competing editions that I knew weren't true," Murray recalls. "One reporter in town would always find pink panties at a crime scene, even when the cops couldn't. The desk would always put the damn panties in my story."

Even today reporters loot and pillage other newspapers and magazines, using quotations and information without attribution or verification. "A badly trained reporter develops instincts and reactions that are immoral and dangerous for his career," says Mencher. "He's at a small paper somewhere. They're understaffed. He has to write about Sugar Ray Leonard. So he steals from *Sports Illustrated*."

Looting Press Releases

When I was film critic for the *St. Petersburg Times*, I received for each new film a press packet of canned feature stories with quotes from actors and directors. It was an open invitation to plagiarism.

Each day, newspapers receive dozens of releases. Responsible editors permit staff writers to work these over, to elaborate on them and check them for accuracy.

A different type of journalism was practiced last year at the *Trenton Times*, where a reporter was fired his first day on the job. "His offense," according to *The Wall Street Journal*, "was not writing up a news announcement exactly as a company had submitted it." The editors had ordered the press release run without a change to protect a big advertiser. The competing paper, the *Trentonian*, published the release without alteration.

"Apparently it's all right to plagiarize from press releases," says Don Murray. "You see university press releases published everywhere, word for word."

Perhaps newspapers should add a tag line to stories taken exclusively from press releases. It could read "released from . . . ." If an editor is ashamed to do that, he or she should make sure the story contains additional reporting, verification and rewording.

Hiding Collaboration in the Closet

When a number of writers collaborate on a project, care should be taken to preserve the integrity of the byline. Did the person named write most of the story? Are the contributions of others noted at the bottom?

Billie Bledsoe, food editor of the *San Antonio Express*, recently exposed a case of veiled collaboration involving the famous food critic James Beard, whose work is distributed by Universal Press Syndicate. Bledsoe wrote that Beard "has admitted falsifying a column about two meals he claimed to have eaten in San Antonio on September 20." The column fooled the reader into thinking that Beard had attended the events. Beard admitted to Bledsoe that he based his review on notes by an assistant.

Professor Murray says some of his college students get hired as stringers, perhaps to cover local basketball games. According to Murray, the work of his students sometimes appears under the bylines of staff writers.

Cribbing from the Books, Scholarship and Research of Others

Reporters have the same responsibility as scholars to attribute work derived from the research of others. The difference is that journalists have not inherited the attributive scaffolding that hangs, sometimes clumsily, on the work of scholars. Nor do they want readers distracted by *ibids* or lengthy parentheses.

Good advice comes from William Rivers and Shelley Smolkin in their book *Free-Lancers and Staff Writers:* "It is unnecessary, of course, for the writer to try to trace down the origins of every captivating phrase. . . . It is not at all absurd, however, to give credit for a sentence. One worth using should be clothed in quotation marks and attributed to its author. Not . . . with the footnoting that is common in scholarly journals—but with a smooth note in the text."

Design consultant and journalism professor Mario Garcia is the author of *Contemporary Newspaper Design.* He has seen his work used time and again without proper credit. "When editors do a graphics stylebook for in-house consumption," says Garcia, "they will take huge sections of my book without any mention of my name. That hurts."

The Archdeacon case falls in the category of unattributed research. He could have probably spared himself much grief by simply dropping Jerry Bledsoe's name into the text.

Recycling Your Old Stories

A low-grade ethical problem is the borrowing by a writer of his own work. Even Ann Landers has been caught and criticized for passing off old work as new. As writers move from newspaper to newspaper, they take files of their stories with them and are not above copying themselves when pressed. Such exhumation should be done with the permission of the newspaper in which the story first appeared and with a note of explanation to the reader.

These questions are not designed to put obstacles in the writer's path or to confuse minor abuses with major ones. But misdemeanors can lead to felonies, and an ethically loose atmosphere fosters sloppy work and journalistic malpractice.

While much confusion tangles the issue of plagiarism, some possible paths can be cut through the thicket.

Journalism textbooks and newspaper stylebooks should take up the issue and suggest guidelines for writers. Plagiarism, including the abuses of faculty members, such as ghostwriting of textbooks and kidnapping by professors of the work of graduate assistants, should be discussed in college classrooms. Students should be told—and in writing—what is expected of them.

If I were a city editor, I would call my staff together to talk about plagiarism in all its manifestations and to spell out these reasons for tightening standards:

1. Plagiarism is a form of deception.
2. Plagiarism is a violation of language. Linguists, like Noam Chomsky, emphasize the essential creativity of all language. Almost every sentence is unique. If you don't believe that, apply this test: Count all the sentences in all the stories in *The New York Times* for any given year. How many are identical? Plagiarism is a crime against the nature of language.
3. Plagiarism is a substitute for reporting. A reporter who assumes the accuracy of information in the clips or in wire stories or in textbooks is living in Cloud Cuckoo Land. Of course, reporters consider the source of information and are always fighting the clock. But to the extent that they depend upon the work and words of others, they distance themselves from events and people and create an environment for inaccuracy.

   Important mistakes, especially when they turn up in usually reliable sources of information, become fossilized in the clips. "What you get," says Mel Mencher, "is this installation of inaccuracy in the record."
4. Plagiarism is a substitute for thinking. "Writing is discovery," says Donald Fry, professor of English at the State University of New York, Stony Brook. "Plagiarism is secondhand thinking."
5. Plagiarism poisons the relationship between writer and reader. "What readers want to believe," says Fry, "is that they're listening to a real voice conveying his own thought."

Because plagiarism is hard to detect, some editors feel they must fire those who practice it. Gene Patterson fired his offending artist "to send a clear message to the staff."

Other editors have taken milder measures, hoping to rehabilitate the writer, permitting him to work his way back to respectability. This has happened, by all accounts, in Charlotte and Louisville.

There is no agreement on how journalism students should be punished. Some universities view expulsion as the only way to raise standards. Expulsion is what happened to a student at Columbia who "borrowed copiously" from *Newsweek* in his master's thesis.

Others favor less severe punishment. "Plagiarism can be an opportunity to teach," says Neale Copple, dean of journalism at the University of Nebraska. "You make sure the kid never does it again. You don't brand him for life. You just make it a learning experience for everybody."

Free-lance scoundrels can ply their trade through plagiarism. Newspaper and magazine editors who often do not know personally the free-lance writers they deal with should watch out for plagiarists. Free-lancers can more easily escape detection and punishment than staff writers. When a malefactor is exposed, his name should be circulated privately or through trade journals.

This was done in *Liaison* magazine, a journal for evangelical religious publishers. Last summer the journal printed a notice exposing a writer who was selling plagiarized articles, written under different names, to several religious publications. The notice in *Liaison* saved *Perspective* magazine from publishing a plagiarized article submitted by that writer. *Liaison* promised to "spread the word on the cheaters in the trade."

Tom Archdeacon admits that his plagiarism of Jerry Bledsoe was a failure of technique. He failed to distinguish in his notes between his own words and the words of another. If bad work habits lead the writer astray, he is as responsible for the result of his actions as the drunk driver.

Careful work habits help the writer walk a straight line. Don Murray suggests that the first draft be written without notes. "I teach my students not to be a secretary to their notes," he says. "Let it flow. Put all those notes aside. You can always go back to them."

Jacques Barzun and Henry F. Graff, in *The Modern Researcher,* suggest that all researchers rewrite material into their notes rather than copy them verbatim. This practice has three beneficial effects: "You have made an effort of thought which has imprinted the information on your mind; you have practiced the art of writing by making a paraphrase; and you have at the same time taken a step toward your first draft, for here and now these are *your* words, not a piece of plagiarism. . . ."

In the most serious cases, plagiarism is a human problem rather than a technical one. It is practiced by people under duress, people who act without grace under pressure. Editors need to be sensitive to those pressures.

Surely the saddest case was that of Emily Ann Fisher, a reporter/intern at *The Washington Post* who was a Phi Beta Kappa graduate of Harvard. In July of 1973, she inserted dialogue from *Catcher in the Rye* into a feature story she had written for the *Post*. She was fired. Friends say she was a brilliant, deeply troubled woman who had a photographic memory. No one is sure how intentional her act was or what emotional pressures led her to borrow from Salinger. But she later took her life.

Ultimately, it is the plagiarist who suffers most from plagiarism. This self-inflicted pain was well expressed by a veteran reporter from the *St. Petersburg Times,* who in July of 1979 kidnapped about one-third of a magazine article on credit cards from *Changing Times*. On the day of her resignation, she pinned a brave letter to the newsroom bulletin board: "Twelve years of dedicated journalism down the drain because of a stupid mistake," she wrote. "I am writing this public explanation for a selfish reason. It will be easier for me to live with myself knowing that the truth is known. But I hope my mistake will serve as a lesson to others. I have let the *Times* down. I have let myself down. But most of all, I have let the profession down. And for that I am truly sorry."

MARJIE LUNDSTROM

Marjie Lundstrom is a senior editor and columnist at *The Sacramento Bee,* a former investigative reporter, and a winner of the Pulitzer Prize for national reporting. But it is her identity as a Nebraska native that informs her view on the geographical stereotyping sometimes committed in "parachute journalism," in which reporters are dispatched to unfamiliar but suddenly newsworthy places. In this essay, written as a 2001 Ethics Fellow at The Poynter Institute, Lundstrom warns of this deadly combination: lack of time, an editor's unrealistic expectations, and a reporter's unexamined biases. The mix can result in a powerful misrepresentation of a place and its people.

Farm-Fresh Clichés

Media people, it seems, have this thing about farm animals.

Chickens, pigs, goats, cows—bulls and steers, too, assuming they know the difference—but they sure can't get out of Nebraska without traipsing through pastures.

I grew up in the Cornhusker state, but I don't always recognize the place nonnative journalists see on the rare occasions they visit.

To them, Nebraska is amusing, a simple and quaint spot where men sport seed caps 24-7 and women wear floral dresses and sensible shoes, their upper arms jiggling like blocks of Jell-O.

This, they pronounce solemnly, is the "heartland," though few who live there would ever call it that.

Visiting journalists tell folksy stories about the good settlers—solid, law-abiding, church-going stock, as though killer Charles Starkweather never existed, and the Nebraska state prisons sit empty on the plains.

News stories in the two largest cities are generally what bring them, but they are more likely to shoot a silo than the architecturally unique state capitol in Lincoln.

Then they pack up and leave until the next time around, when news happens to find the "heartland" again.

. . . [S]o it is in journalism today, where intense media competition and 'round-the-clock deadlines have made for some disturbingly predictable and often distorted accounts of places and the people who live there.

Politely, the practice is called "parachute journalism," the dispatching of globe-trotting reporters and camera crews to the likes of Sand Point, Idaho, and Kearney, Neb., and Union, S.C., to cover the latest breaking news.

There's nothing polite about some of the outcomes.

While news operations have focused mightily in the past decade on eliminating racial, ethnic and gender bias from their coverage, a less apparent but equally stubborn bias persists: geographic bias.

In the pressure-cooker climate to get in fast, get the story first—and, by the way, explain What It All Means (by 10 o'clock, please)—the assumptions, short-cuts and stereotyping can be rampant. Even without pressing deadlines, some journalists' biases about certain regions simply go unchecked.

Put it together and . . . presto! A new reality, one even the natives can scarcely recognize.

How can news people purport to be purveyors of truth—the guiding principle of ethical journalism—if personal bias and sloppy shortcuts keep getting in the way? If choppering into unknown locales is a recipe for sweeping conclusions, over-arching assumptions and silly stereotypes—not to mention factual errors?

No wonder the public is dubious.

As a journalist, I often find myself wondering: Why do we *do* this? Why do we wedge people's complex lives into neat little geographic boxes with nice little labels? Why is it that the less we know about a people or place, the more we tend to say? Does our very "outsider-ness" somehow give us license to be that much more authoritative, as though ignorance is synonymous with being "fresh"?

I am guilty, too.

When I was a national writer, I traveled to Florida—practically a foreign country to me—to cover the 1989 execution of serial killer Ted Bundy. The party and carnival-like atmosphere outside the Florida State Prison near Starke was so astonishing I felt compelled to write an op-ed piece.

Mercifully, it was never published.

"It was a community affair," I wrote, "a celebration of sorts for the people of Starke and the whole state of Florida, who gussied up and turned out en masse for the death of Ted Bundy. Young mothers brought their children and retired couples lugged lawn chairs and coolers and teenagers posed in homemade T-shirts for pocket Instamatics."

Why I decided to speak for the "whole state of Florida" in the top of the story remains a mystery to me, since the bottom of the piece was loaded with people who spoke just fine for themselves—and made the point I was trying to make. One young mother had taken her 6-year-old twin daughters out of school and, along with an infant, driven up from Orlando for what she called an educational "field trip." In the pre-dawn darkness, there were her adorable twins, dressed in matching lavender jackets, chanting "Fry Bundy, fry Bundy," before the television cameras.

In a complex world, it is often tempting to view people and places as one-dimensional, especially when their lives are so different from our own. In the Midwest, the journalistic declaration that "life is simpler here" is so predictable it is cliché, and each time I hear it or read it, I want to shout: "Simpler than *what?*"

Today I live in California, but roots run deep. A few years back, a *Sacramento Bee* sports writer wrote a feature about the die-hard Nebraska fans who had traveled to Berkeley for a football match-up between the Huskers and Cal.

"It wasn't the strangest thing the Nebraska faithful had ever seen," the lede began. "After all, earlier in the day they had stood with their jaws in vapor lock on Telegraph Avenue."

The message was unmistakable: Hicksville meets the City.

Yet in the same way not all Floridians celebrate the death penalty, it is also true that not all Nebraskans lead sheltered lives devoid of skylines, water and pretty bridges.

Nebraskans have these things, too. (And anyway, they do let us out sometimes.)

The challenge for journalists, day in and day out, is to set aside expectations and stereotypes and find the authentic story. Granted, that is especially tough for the traveling correspondent, whose job definition defies lingering too long in any one place.

Perhaps we as journalists—whatever our roots—should begin to think more in snapshots than in sweeping images. To talk about the three or four Husker fans who stood in awe on Telegraph Hill instead of the "Nebraska faithful." To describe in detail the mother of the 6-year-old twins, not the "whole state of Florida."

And when in doubt, consult a native.

Had anyone ever asked, I could have told them all about the back-roads of Nebraska—literally and figuratively. For starters, much of the state is neatly carved into perfect, one-square-mile road grids—a byproduct of the Northwest Ordinance of 1785, but a very handy state of affairs for every high school kid trying to find the secret weekend keg party.

And that's where the uniformity ends, as this is a state more textured and rich than many journalists would have it seem.

There are latte houses and salad bars with mixed baby-greens and arugula, happily co-existing with corner cafes and chuckwagon steakhouses.

The state is said to be the birthplace of the reuben sandwich and, for better or worse, it is definitely the home of Spam.

Nebraska is the only state in the nation with a unicameral, or single-house, legislature.

One-third of the state's entire population lives in just two large cities, meaning a lot of Nebraskans can't tell the difference between winter wheat and alfalfa.

Many successful, cutting-edge Americans call this place home, among them Omaha investor and Berkshire Hathaway Chairman Warren E. Buffett and the late great author, Willa Cather, who chronicled life on the plains.

Oh, yes, and the farm animals. I'm happy to say my hometown of Wayne is also home to the annual Chicken Show and "cluck-off" contest, as well as a respected state college.

It's all part of the "pasture," if only we journalists would look.

And, for once, watch where we step.

BEN BRADLEE

One of journalism's darkest hours—the revelation that a Pulitzer Prize–winning story was made up—came on Ben Bradlee's watch as executive editor of *The Washington Post*. He had guided the paper to greatness as it broke some of the most important stories in American journalism, including the publication of the Pentagon Papers and the Watergate investigation. But in 1981, the deceits of staff writer Janet Cooke began to unravel at the *Post* just hours after she received the prize for "Jimmy's World," her story on the life of an eight-year-old heroin addict.

How had a twenty-six-year-old reporter managed to circumvent the editorial defenses of one of America's greatest papers? What lessons would the *Post* learn? Bradlee, who retired as executive editor in 1991 and is now vice-president-at-large of the Washington Post Company, answers those questions in this chapter from his 1995 memoir, *A Good Life: Newspapering and Other Adventures*.

Janet Cooke

Janet Cooke is a beautiful black woman with dramatic flair and vitality, and an extraordinary talent for writing. She is also a cross that journalism, especially *The Washington Post*, and especially Benjamin C. Bradlee, will bear forever. At the age of twenty-six, she wrote a vivid, poignant story about an eight-year-old heroin addict who was regularly shot up by his mother's live-in lover. The story made page one, on Sunday, September 28, 1980, and held the city in thrall for weeks. The story earned Cooke the Pulitzer Prize for feature reporting on April 13, 1981.

In the earliest hours of the morning of April 15, 1981, Janet Cooke confessed that she had made it all up: there was no Jimmy, there was no live-in lover. From that moment on, the words "Janet Cooke" entered the vocabulary as a symbol for the worst in American journalism, just as the word "Watergate" went into the vocabulary as a symbol for the best in American journalism.

I had known about the story as it worked its way up the reporting and editing ladder. I had read it thoroughly the week before it ran on page one, and found it riveting. It was titled "Jimmy's World," and it started this way:

> Jimmy is 8 years old and a third generation heroin addict, a precocious little boy with sandy hair, velvety brown eyes and needle marks freckling the baby-smooth skin of his thin brown arms.
>
> He nestles in a large, beige reclining chair in the living room of his comfortably furnished home in Southeast Washington. There is an almost cherubic expression on his small, round face as he talks about life—clothes, money, the Baltimore Orioles, and heroin. He has been an addict since the age of 5.
>
> His hands are clasped behind his head, fancy running shoes adorn his feet, and a striped Izod T-shirt hangs over his thin frame. "Bad, ain't it," he boasts. "I got me six of these."

And it ended this way:

> [Ron] grabs Jimmy's left arm just above the elbow, his massive hand tightly encircling the child's small limb. The needle slides into the boy's soft skin like a straw pushed into the center of a freshly baked cake. Liquid ebbs out of the syringe, replaced by bright red blood. The blood is then reinjected into the child.
>
> Jimmy has closed his eyes during the whole procedure, but now he opens them, looking quickly around the room. He climbs into a rocking chair and sits, his head dipping and snapping upright again, in what addicts call "the nod."

In between, around a startling illustration of young Jimmy reaching his arm toward the reader, Janet Cooke promised authenticity with details such as these:

- *On Jimmy's mother:* She never knew her father. Like her son, Andrea spent her childhood with her mother and the man with whom she lived for 15 years. She recalls that her mother's boyfriend routinely forced her and her younger sister to have sex, and Jimmy is the product of one of those rapes. Depressed and discouraged after his birth ("I didn't even name him, you know? My sister liked the name Jimmy, and I said, 'OK, call him that . . . who gives a fuck. I guess we got to call him something' "), she quickly accepted the offer of heroin from a woman who used to shoot up with her mother.
- *On Jimmy's house:* Death has not yet been a visitor to the house where Jimmy lives. The kitchen and upstairs bedrooms are a human collage. People of all shapes and sizes drift into the dwelling and its various rooms, some jittery, uptight, and anxious for a fix, others calm and serene after they finally "get off."

. . . To me, the story reeked of the sights and sounds and smells that editors love to give their readers. The possibility that the story was not true never entered my head.

After the fact, some reporters, particularly Courtland Milloy, a streetwise black reporter, told me that they had questioned the story. Milloy had taken Cooke in his car to look for Jimmy's house. When she couldn't find it, he shared his doubts with Milton Coleman, the savvy city editor, en route to becoming a national reporter and then assistant managing editor for Metro. Coleman told others he thought Milloy was jealous, but he did pass on Milloy's opinion to Howard Simons. The story still had a long way to go, and Howard kept his feelings to himself.

The day Cooke won the Pulitzer Prize, April 13, 1981, the story—and my world with it—began to fall apart. The *Toledo Blade,* where Cooke had once worked, and the Associated Press started preparing biographical sketches about Cooke. The sketches were fatally contradictory. The AP sketch was based on a Pulitzer Committee handout, which in turn was based on biographical data submitted by Cooke herself, a few months earlier. The *Blade*'s sketch was based on its own Personnel Department records, and started when Cooke went to work there some years earlier.

The contradictions that emerged were devastating. One story said she had graduated *magna cum laude* from Vassar. Another said she had been to Vassar only for one year. One story said she had a master's degree from the University of Toledo, another said she had only an undergraduate degree. One story said she had attended the Sorbonne in Paris. The other said nothing about the Sorbonne. The Pulitzer bio said Janet Cooke spoke French, Spanish, Portuguese, and Italian. The old résumé claimed French and Italian.

The exact moment when I felt as if I had been punched in the stomach came in the early afternoon, when Dixie Sheridan from the admissions office of Vassar College called to say that she thought "we had a little problem." At the very same moment Simons was on the phone to Lou Boccardi, then the AP's vice president and executive editor, who was explaining the exact dimensions of "the little problem."

At this point in my life I didn't know much about confession. Not that I had never had to confess, starting with forging my father's distinctive signature on a bad report card from Miss Bean in the fifth grade of Dexter School. But I had spent rather more time witnessing confessions from others—and enjoying it much more. But thanks to

Watergate, I had learned a vitally important lesson: The truth is the best defense, and the whole truth is the very best defense.

Once we had identified the fraud, we set ourselves a simple goal: No one should ever learn anything more about the Janet Cooke case than *The Washington Post* itself revealed. The only question was how to achieve that goal. Twenty reporters on the *Post* asked me to name them as an investigative team to get the whole story, an invitation I declined quickly. This was no time for the inmates to take over the institution. I believed the investigation was tailormade for the resolutely autonomous Ombudsman.

The Ombudsman had a contract which allowed him to write on any subject he chose. He could not be edited; he could not be assigned; and he could not be fired. When "Jimmy's World" landed on us like a Kamikaze bomb, the Ombudsman was William Green. Bill had never been a career journalist. All told he had a couple of years on small papers in the South. He had been a public affairs officer in India for the United States Information Service, and he had worked as a special assistant to the former governor of North Carolina, Terry Sanford, while Sanford was president of Duke University. He taught a sophisticated course in journalism at Duke, and he was one wise and fair sumbitch, as the locals say, respected by the staff for his common sense and his respect for the individual.

In four days, working almost around the clock, Bill Green accomplished an incredibly difficult task: a no-holds-barred, meticulously reported account of what went wrong—18,000 words spread over the front page and four full pages inside.

How could any reporter, even someone I once described as a one-in-a-million liar, penetrate the editorial defenses of a newspaper whose commitment to truth was unequaled?

"Jimmy's World" got into the paper, Green concluded, because of the failure of the system that is called "quality control" in other industries and "editing" in newspapers. By publishing "Jimmy's World," *The Washington Post* was "humiliated," Green said in the lead of his front page story, on Sunday, April 19, because editors abandoned their vaunted professional skepticism.

Cooke had first come to my attention in a letter saying she thought she was ready for the big time, after more than two years at the *Toledo Blade*. An editor gets dozens of such letters every month. Hers stood out because she produced clips that showed she could write like a dream; she had top-drawer college credentials; and she was black. The answer to a modern editor's prayers. I passed her résumé on to

[Bob] Woodward, who was then assistant managing editor for Metro, with an expression of interest. Female Phi Beta Kappa graduates of Seven Sisters colleges who can write the King's English with style don't grow on trees, white or black, and we were a decade into our commitment to increase the number and quality of minorities and women on the staff. The *Post* hired Cooke six months later, after she impressed all the editors who interviewed her, myself included, except for Herb Denton, the black city editor who thought there was too much Vassar in her.

Her Vassar credentials were never checked. This was our first mistake, and it was fatal. If we had found out that she lied when she claimed she had an honors degree from Vassar, of course, that would have been the end of it. She wouldn't have had the chance to make any more mistakes.

How come we never checked? Simply put, Janet Cooke was too good to be true, and we wanted her too bad.

There is a joke in our business that every blue moon or so, a reporter runs into a story, or more likely a rumor, that is so fantastic that it's almost a shame to check it out. Check rumors like these, and you run the almost certain risk of finding quick, credible evidence that the story is just plain not true. We resist that impulse with stories, but we did not resist the same impulse in making this particular personnel decision. At a time when we were struggling to meet our commitment to increase the quantity and quality of minority and female journalists on the paper, Janet Cooke had "can't miss" written all over her. What the hell were we waiting for? Grab her before *The New York Times* does, or *Newsweek*, or television.

And she was hired.

Janet Cooke hit the ground running at the *Post,* with fifty-two bylines in her first eight months on the staff. . . .

. . . She told one friend she wanted a Pulitzer Prize in three years, and a job on the National staff in three to five years. She soon lost herself in an assignment to look into a new kind of heroin, circulating in the city, so strong it was said to ulcerate the skin.

She brought back 145 pages of handwritten notes taken during this assignment. Aplin-Brownlee thought they were good enough to show to Milton Coleman, and Coleman thought them good enough to bring Cooke in for a talk about how they should be "storified"—made into a story. It was during this conversation that she first mentioned reports of an eight-year-old addict. Coleman stopped her short: "That's the story. Go after it. It's a front page story."

Three weeks later Cooke told Coleman she had found the eight-year-old addict, had even talked to his mother. Coleman told Cooke she could promise the boy's mother confidentiality first, then anonymity. With that, Coleman felt no need to know the woman's name, at least not then.

"The jugular of journalism lay exposed," in Bill Green's great phrase, "the faith an editor has to place in a reporter."

Should Coleman have gotten the name of the "addict" and his mother? Probably. If not then, damn soon. Should he have gotten the address? In sober second thought, yes. An address is an anchor that can be checked by anyone, any time. Names of unknowns are ephemeral. But Cooke's first memo, which we all saw, was filled with such a rich supply of apparently convincing detail—eight-foot plastic sofas, blue and green Izod shirts, Panasonic stereo equipment, fake bamboo blinds, rubber trees, brown shag rugs, and much more—that doubts died before they matured. For the first time, the "addict" had a name, Tyrone, and we knew which elementary school he attended when he wasn't playing hooky. And so it moved—glacially, inevitably toward publication.

I knew nothing about Jimmy's World. There were virtually no circumstances in which I would come into contact with Jimmy's mother, or her live-in boyfriend, Ron, much less have a meaningful conversation with either of them. The same was true for Howard Simons. By the time the story was ready to publish, everyone concerned had so much at stake.

Almost 900,000 copies of the *Post* rolled off the presses early Sunday morning, September 28, 1980. The *L.A. Times–Washington Post* News Service took "Jimmy's World" to more than three hundred newspapers in the United States and around the world. Jimmy was an overnight sensation. The *Post*'s phones rang off the hook. The police chief launched a mammoth search for the boy and his mother. Police threatened to subpoena Cooke and her notes, but backed off in face of *Post* resistance. Mayor Marion Barry quickly announced that the city knew Jimmy's identity. There were also reports that Dr. Alyce Gullattee, director of Howard University's Institute for Substance Abuse, knew Jimmy and his family. . . .

By December, when newspapers nominate their best work for Pulitzer prizes, "Jimmy's World" was the *Post*'s sole entrant in the category of local news reporting.

And on April 13, 1981, the worst happened: "Jimmy's World" won a Pulitzer Prize.

In destroyers, under battle conditions, one of the most important jobs is damage control: How can the damage from a torpedo hit amidships, or a Kamikaze crash, or a boiler explosion be controlled so that the ship can limp back into port, and survive to fight another day? As an assistant damage-control officer of the U.S.S. *Philip* (DD498), I had learned that damage control is one of the most important jobs on any naval vessel. As the damage-control officer—read executive editor—of *The Washington Post*, I had learned that damage control is one of the most important jobs on a newspaper.

The first lesson of damage control is to get an accurate picture of the damage as soon as possible. At the *Post,* after "Jimmy's World" exploded in the city room, we began our exercise in damage control by examining Janet Cooke's Vassar credentials, figuring that if she lied there, it was likely that she lied elsewhere. I told Milton Coleman to take Miss Cooke "to the woodshed," an old political practice described to me by Jim Rowe, once a member of FDR's Kitchen Cabinet, and a longtime Washington powerbroker. Jim Rowe had taken Hubert Humphrey to the woodshed at the request of President Lyndon B. Johnson, before LBJ decided on Humphrey as his vice-presidential running mate. When you take someone to the woodshed, Rowe told me, you get him off in a room alone and grill him about his taxes, his health, his girlfriends, his finances, his war record, his debts, his addictions, his innermost secrets. Both parties in the woodshed have to do their jobs for the process to be useful.

Coleman took Cooke to the woodshed by walking her across L Street to the bar of the Capital Hilton Hotel. At first Cooke stuck to her guns, but when Coleman called Vassar right then and there, she began her retreat. She had run into emotional problems at Vassar, she said, and completed only one year. What about languages, Coleman asked. Cooke insisted she spoke four. What about the Sorbonne? Cooke insisted she had attended the Sorbonne.

"And the Jimmy story?" Coleman asked.

"It's true," she lied.

At this point Coleman called in and we suggested he bring Cooke back into the side entrance of the *Post,* and up to the corporate offices on the eighth floor. When Woodward and I arrived, Janet Cooke was sitting on the sofa crying, Bill Green remembers, and said, "You get caught at the stupidest thing."

But Janet Cooke was practicing her own brand of damage control—admitting to phonying her Vassar records but nothing else. I suddenly felt we had been pussyfooting around too long (because she was a woman and a black?), and what followed was not a pleasant conversation.

First, I asked her to say two words in Portuguese, any two. (I myself knew only two words of Portuguese, period: *O gis* . . . The chalk.) She said she couldn't. I asked her if she had any Italian. She said she did not. I have spoken French since I was six years old, and I started asking her questions in French. Her replies suggested nothing like an ability to speak French. I told her she was lying. She was trying to cover up the truth. Just like Richard Nixon, I said, and that pissed her off. She didn't like my questioning any more than I liked her answers. I finally told her she had twenty-four hours to prove that the Jimmy story was true, and walked out.

Woodward told her he didn't believe the Jimmy story and was going to prove that she was lying if it was the last thing he ever did, and left the room.

Next we sent Coleman out with Cooke to find Jimmy's house. Coleman called half an hour later, and said she couldn't find it. He was now convinced that Cooke had made the whole thing up. The only holdout was Cooke herself. Simons and I went home, leaving Cooke in the hot seat answering tough questions from Woodward, assistant managing editor Tom Wilkinson, Coleman, and David Maraniss, the Maryland editor. Cooke complained that the questioning was "getting too cruel."

"All I have is my story," she added.

Finally, she was left alone with Maraniss, and Bill Green's report described this conversation:

> *Cooke, crying:* "I was afraid I was going to be left alone with you. The first time I saw you today I thought, 'Oh boy! He knows and I'm going to have to tell him.' I couldn't lie to you. I couldn't tell them. I never would tell Woodward. The more he yelled the more stubborn I was. Wilkinson represents the corporation. It means so much to Milton [Coleman]. You guys are smart. Woodward for the mind, you for the heart. . . . Why are you smiling?"
>
> *Maraniss:* "Because I had a tremendous surge of empathy for you, refusing to submit to the institution in an absurd situation. You were strong not to give in. The institution will survive."

Maraniss and Cooke talked for more than an hour, about their childhoods, about what she had gone through after her story was nominated for a Pulitzer Prize.

"You don't have to say anything to the others," Maraniss told her. "I'll do it for you. What do I tell them?"

And suddenly the ordeal was over.

"There is no Jimmy, and no family," Cooke confessed. She said she felt she knew enough to get away with it. She knew that Jimmy could never be found because he didn't exist. She said she had prayed she wouldn't get the Pulitzer, surely a first in the annals of journalism.

It was after 2:00 A.M. when I was called with the news that I had known for hours was coming. Once we had her written resignation in hand—and I can't explain now why I let her resign rather than fire her on the spot for the grossest negligence—I woke Joe Pulitzer up in St. Louis to tell him we were returning the prize, with apologies.

Chapter 11

ISSUES IN JOURNALISM

As our world grows more complex, so does journalism. The rise of "infotainment," a hybrid of information and entertainment, is just one example of a blurring of lines that makes the journalist's job more complicated and more confusing. What is news? Is the primary purpose of a news organization to inform, to grab readers' attention, to entertain, to educate? Is it possible for a news organization to do all of these things, or are there certain lines that should not be crossed?

How we answer these questions helps shape the profession—and its credibility. Sandra Mims Rowe argues, in the first reading in this chapter, that the crucible of September 11 brought journalism back to its more serious purpose and provided an opportunity for rebuilding readers' trust. Ann Marie Lipinski takes on the question of the proper role for a journalist in the community he or she covers. Lowell Bergman describes his experience with corporate censorship, but warns that a far more subtle and pervasive self-censorship is just as damaging to the profession. Aly Colón makes the point that the call for diversity—both in newsrooms and in the communities we cover—may lead journalism to its next great frontier.

SANDRA MIMS ROWE

Sandra Mims Rowe is a newspaper editor and the daughter of a newspaper editor; so to say she has newspapering in her blood is less a cliché than it is the truth. She has not only devoted her career to journalism, but she has provided leadership in the industry by speaking candidly about its weaknesses and challenging its conventions. As editor of the Portland *Oregonian* since 1993, she has led the paper to three Pulitzer Prizes. She is chair of the Pulitzer Prize Board and a past president of the American Society of Newspaper Editors, the nation's largest and oldest organization of daily newspaper editors.

This selection is excerpted from remarks Rowe delivered at the University of North Carolina at Chapel Hill in November 2001. Just two months after the terrorist attacks on the World Trade Center and the Pentagon, she articulated her vision for the ways in which the craft can be shaped for the better by this historic event. Journalism, she says, has a chance to "recapture respect and reconnect with our readers."

Journalism Rediscovers Its Serious Purpose: Eight Ideas That Could Help It Last

The journalistic landscape is changed, and we are the better for it. We have turned from titillation and the trivial toward matters of consequence and substance. News that captured headlines and the public's attention in August is not even a blip in the public consciousness today.

What of Gary Condit's sex life? Bill Clinton's sex life? How about the length of President Bush's Texas summer vacation? Remember the sparring over the lockbox? Or Al Gore's beard? Oh, how irrelevant, even absurd, it all seems now.

On our good days, newspapers are mirrors reflecting back to the public an accurate, authentic picture of life in our times and informing them on matters of consequence.

In the September 11 tragedy, we have rediscovered our serious purpose, what historian Doris Kearns Goodwin calls "our larger public selves." In this deeply troubling time the press has an opportunity to recapture respect and reconnect with our readers.

We had better seize this historic moment. It may not come our way again.

The landscape has changed in ways we never could have imagined in the lazy days of late summer.

Who would have thought that getting the mail every day would cause deeply anxious moments for so many, that in hundreds of thousands of offices and homes, ordinary folks would wear rubber gloves and masks to open mail delivered by our own U.S. Postal Service?

Who would have thought that all airports in the country would be shuttered and retail activity would grind to a complete halt for the better part of a week?

Who would have thought a recording of the *Star Spangled Banner* would one week in October be the top selling CD in America, and that thousands of stores around the country would sell out of American flags?

None of us could have foreseen our new reality, our "new normal" as our leaders call it.

So, too, the press has a new reality. What was conventional wisdom just two months ago is no longer easily accepted. The old conventional wisdom is giving way to the new. And not a moment too soon.

1. Old Conventional Wisdom: Cynicism Comes With the Journalistic Territory. New Conventional Wisdom: Cynicism Is Dead.

Declaring the age of cynicism over is fairly typical of the grandiose statements and sweeping generalities the chattering class floated in the first few days after the attack. Dream on. But there is evidence that journalistic cynicism has been tamed and tempered by the acts of savage zealotry we witnessed September 11. It's a good thing. We had raised cynicism to an art form, to the detriment of our credibility.

Now in the aftermath of the most evil, murderous acts imaginable, the world looks as different to journalists as it does to real people. More frightening, certainly, but perhaps more importantly we are aware of the fundamental goodness and the potential for selfless acts of heroism from ordinary citizens and high officials alike. Journalists, too, are deeply affected by that.

Cynicism, long excused as skepticism on steroids, as intellectual toughness, has never been a legitimate journalistic tool. It has given rise to our own worst elitist tendencies. Cynicism is and has always been the enemy of both rigor and fairness, which are the touchstones of excellence.

Cynicism has caused the press to fail to see clearly that folks mostly strive to do right, that public officials are not fundamentally corrupt. Cynicism has encouraged us to assume motive where none can be proved; to see ineptness as malfeasance. Cynicism has kept us from acting on our obligation to celebrate struggle and success and humanity as vigorously as we point out flaws—and there is plenty of humanity to celebrate, it turns out.

What a difference one tragic day makes.

Before September 11, police in New York City were thought of by many as racist thugs with badges; the mayor of New York as a hard-hearted bully with a penchant for saying the wrong thing at the wrong time, a mayor David Letterman once vilified and now calls the personification of courage. We are as one with Letterman. The goats are now the heroes. Could they have changed that much that fast? Of course not. It is, in part, the prism through which we view them that has changed.

Cynicism, it turns out, cannot survive the warm embrace of kinship and shared emotions. And make no mistake about it: Journalists have felt, and shown, the same emotions as other citizens during the past 60 days. Imagine that. Just like "real people," as we are fond of referring to those outside of newsrooms.

2. Old Conventional Wisdom: These Are the Worst of Times for the Press. New Conventional Wisdom: The Press Rules.

As we closed out the 20th century, many of the best minds in journalism saw us as a profession in trouble, an institution vital to democracy and commerce and community with a growing fault line between its highest ideals, its day-to-day practices, and the public's view of its performance.

Because of consolidation of the industry, the relentless push for ever-increasing profits from Wall Street, and the supremacy of entertainment values in media, people saw business imperatives in conflict with our public purpose.

Most deeply troubling was our own frustration and disappointment with the profession. When a profession is itself disheartened, unsure of its standards or its worth, it is dangerous going indeed. Saddest of all wasn't that the public had low expectations of us, which we still sometimes failed to meet, but that we were not meeting our own expectations.

We have had a rough patch, no doubt. I think there is hope that the low opinion of us has bottomed out. Because of the tragic events of September 11, we have a chance to find our way, climb out of the muck, turn away from the celebration and elevation of the inconsequential, redirect our gaze away from celebrity chitchat and the scandal du jour to what really matters.

It is only by doing so that we can honor our hopes and faded ideals and fulfill our larger public purpose.

The high road is there if we will just take it. If newspaper journalism and journalists long for greater respect, then newspaper editors have only to play down—not play up—the trivial, the perverse, the bizarre.

The tragic events of September 11 have given us a chance to reclaim and reassert the best that journalism has to offer a wary public.

3. Old Conventional Wisdom: Objectivity Requires a Bloodless Detachment from News and People at the Core of It. New Conventional Wisdom: It's a Small World and We're All in It Together.

How sad that we have succeeded so well in setting ourselves apart from the rest of the country. We did this by approaching almost all stories—even stories overflowing with pathos and heartbreak—from the outside.

We had ramped up professional detachment to the point of callousness and mistaken bad manners for legitimate inquiry.

We wore our detachment as a badge. We acted as if we could maintain professional standards only by being detached—separated from other people and their concerns. We were wrong. Being members of an elitist class cost us dearly in trust and credibility.

Post September 11, an unnatural detachment from events is more jarring to normal folks than ever. Take the case of David Westin, ABC News president. Last week Westin was skewered by Matt Drudge, of all people, for saying he had no opinion when asked at a Columbia University forum whether the Pentagon was an appropriate military target. Actually he did worse than just saying he had no opinion. He lectured the audience on the importance to a free press of him not having an opinion.

C'mon. No opinion of whether the Pentagon was an appropriate target? Is the public really supposed to believe that and buy it? And, even if they did, doesn't that make the press so detached as to be without normal morals or emotions?

We can, and mostly are doing better than this knee-jerk, old conventional wisdom of expressing detachment, which is at odds with common sense.

4. Old Conventional Wisdom: People Stories Aren't Real News and, Besides, We Have Told Them All Already. New Conventional Wisdom: Never Underestimate the Power of the Personal Story.

Every editor in America knows that the best executed stories of humanity receive the strongest reaction. Yet I know of no editor who believes she pays enough attention to that in her newsroom or does them well enough. They are kissed off, dismissed as news lite, and too often ghettoized in feature sections. Worse, the same rigor that is brought to the most ambitious work is not often applied to these stories of humanity.

We have consistently underestimated readers' longing for the real and the human.

Last year the *Oregonian* won the Pulitzer Prize for feature writing with a four-part series on a 14-year-old boy with a severe facial deformity who risked life-threatening surgery to appear more normal. The story reminded us that we all need to be accepted and painted a powerful portrait of what we will do to gain that acceptance. More than 3,500 readers wrote or called the newspaper to thank us for the story. More than a year later, readers still stop the reporter on the street to ask how Sam, the boy, is doing.

Similarly, *The New York Times*'s mini-profiles of the victims of September 11 have struck a stronger chord with readers than any other coverage they have done. They have been running a full page—each one containing stories of about 15 victims—every day. These stories, no more than four or five paragraphs each, tell you—not the facts—but the lives of the individuals. You start to know who dreamed of going back to school, who spent weekends at their children's soccer games, who had just celebrated an anniversary or volunteered in soup kitchens, or simply excelled in being a friend. Real life, in other words. In all its glory.

Readers devour them. This page is the one *New York Times* editors say they see people reading on subways.

The great and glorious *New York Times* respected these 3,000 ordinary folks enough to present an honest snapshot of their lives. That's a powerful statement. No wonder readers responded. Read these nuggets and we see ourselves, we see our own dreams and lives. The *Times* has decided to keep publishing these until they are done, 15 or so a day, a full page, every day for what will likely be almost a year.

Make no mistake about it. These simple stories are as important to journalism as they are to loved ones left behind. The fact that *The New York Times,* the gold standard in our business, is devoting several dozen reporters and a full page of space a day to do this speaks volumes. It has changed the relationship of *The New York Times* with some of its readers and I predict will be discussed in journalism schools long after all the victims have been profiled.

Why? Because we are not used to *The New York Times* showing so much humanity. And by doing so, and doing so in such a visible, sustained way, it influences the rest of the craft.

Regarding that, no one understood better the role of humanity in demonstrating journalism's relevance to the public or raised craft to a higher level than your alumnus, Charles Kuralt.

Kuralt wanted to know about people and what they did; his love was language and his art—storytelling. He celebrated a world of joy, loss, trial, and achievement. He traveled the country honoring lives of all sort.

In a speech almost 20 years ago, Kuralt pleaded with us to turn at least part of our attention away from pursuit of the entertainer, the politician, and the criminal and toward "the decent and honest and sometimes noble lives of our fellow citizens."

We could do worse.

5. Old Conventional Wisdom: What Is Relevant Is Close-to-Home Information We Can Act On.
New Conventional Wisdom: Relevance Is Relative—and May be Farther Away Than the Next County.

In a search for relevance as the key to readership, too many editors acted as if relevance demanded a myopic focus on the mundane, the minutae that occupies much of daily life. So, if a newspaper gave you information you could apply directly to decisions you made in preparing that night's dinner, provided you helpful hints on shopping for pillows, or told you how to lose 20 pounds before the end of the week, it was seen as relevant.

Before, not many of us—editors or readers—saw as equally relevant the arcane activities of a fanatical sect based in Afghanistan. Not many editors, this one included, saw Osama bin Laden as relevant enough to publish even a fraction of the hundreds of thousands of words we have published since September 11.

But if something happened within twenty miles of the newspaper office (the closer the better), we saw its relevance as being off the charts. And Afghanistan, my lord, that was so far away it was our metaphor for total irrelevance to our readers' lives.

We allowed our focus and our strength—our localness—to limit our ambitions. Suddenly we have found we can be defined by local without being limited by it. What is local is not necessarily geographically limiting any more than it is journalistically limiting.

Relevance is relative, and it is on today's relevance that we have a chance to reconstruct our image and rehabilitate relations with our readers.

6. Old Conventional Wisdom: Foreign News Is Boring and Difficult. New Conventional Wisdom: Never Underestimate Readers' Willingness to Devour Difficult Subjects.

The long decline of foreign news coverage is well established in all media, reflecting—or possibly contributing to—a decreased appetite for foreign news among the public. The evidence abounds.

Well, we're back in the world. And now we're seeing that foreign news isn't just headlines; it's really a cultural story. Previously, we've presented the Middle East as individual countries locked in a death struggle, as requiring occasional reporting on a never-ending conflict. What we should have been doing and what we are now, belatedly, attempting is to cover the Middle East not just as conflict, but as culture, as a place with a difficult history and different values. In other words, to give it context.

We covered conflict because we know how to cover conflict. That is how we have defined news. What we should have been covering better all along is the more complex cultural story. That's what provides insight and understanding beyond the breaking news headlines. The covering of culture is, and will remain, central to the new, expanded definition of foreign news.

7. Old Conventional Wisdom: General Knowledge is OK for Journalists. You Don't Really Have to Know Much; Just be Curious and Ask Good Questions. New Conventional Wisdom: The Public Expects—and Deserves—a Press that Knows More than How to Use a Rolodex.

We're surface folks and generalists. We know how to dig; we have the best research in the world available to us. But we have too often tried to pass off fact-gathering as understanding, or worse yet, as knowledge.

Journalists must be knowledgable in order to be able to report on complex subjects with authority, authenticity, and insight.

The role of the press, second only to that of the academy, is to educate. Because we have underestimated the need for historical, literary, sociological, and political context and for exploring stories of great complexity, we were ourselves ill-prepared.

The problem has never been that we don't have all the answers. The real danger is if we are not smart enough to ask the right questions.

But one thing journalists do well is react to the moment at hand. And react we have. Very well, extraordinarily well for the most part. In our newspapers we have had dozens of pages of background on Islam and the Taliban and germ warfare and anthrax. We have published graphics and timelines and maps and have resurrected the too-often-ignored Q & A. Readers have rewarded our scramble for news and knowledge by devouring it. They have demonstrated they have a reason and a desire to learn and look to newspapers as crucial to that understanding.

8. Old Conventional Wisdom: Sexy Headlines Sell.
New Conventional Wisdom: Do Not Sensationalize,
Do Not Sensationalize, Do Not Sensationalize.

We have not brought honor to ourselves with the coarseness of the media and the drift into celebrity and sleaze. It's not just bad taste but destructive and irresponsible. It is an abuse of gifts from the ages and the founding fathers.

Citizens want and deserve better than the trashy entertainment popular culture has served up. The notion that readers have created this demand for muck is false. You've heard of blaming the messenger. Sisela Bok, philosopher and ethicist, calls this flimsy excuse of ours "shooting the recipient."

Sensationalizing now has a particularly high cost. If cable news sensationalizes questions about Gary Condit and Chandra Levy—which they shamelessly did all summer [of 2001]—it really is of no consequence except to their own reputation. The same is not true when they sensationalize and play to people's worst fears about anthrax, reporting in an endless loop old news and the most minute incremental developments with breathless urgency.

In the raucous, rowdy media world of the go-go '90s, newspapers, too, have pandered and been pulled down to the level of other media. We are not television. Newspapers never should have succumbed to the entertainment and sensationalistic values of television news, which grossly underestimates people's intelligence and attention.

In the days since September 11, millions of Americans have bought newspapers, devoured them, put them away in family trunks for future generations. They have done this because they recognize the historical nature of events. They also have done this because they recognize newspapers as authentic recorders of that history.

It is reminiscent of the assassination of JFK. I was then a fifteen-year-old, the daughter of a small-town newspaper editor. I was not allowed to have a regular paper route because girls didn't do that back then. But on the afternoon of November 22, 1963, I was drafted, along with everyone else in the larger newspaper family, to hawk Extras. I was sent to the local college campus, where normally uninterested college students nearly grabbed them out of our hands.

Newspapers were that day, as they have been throughout the history of this great country, the town criers. Today, despite the speed of the Internet, despite the video razzle-dazzle and hypnotic effect of television, despite the drumbeat of talk radio, newspapers continue to hold their place as a respected community voice.

At our best, praise God, newspapers are still recognized as offering depth and understanding and insight when it most matters. At our best, we can tackle "why" and "how." At our best, we can calmly and authoritatively explain the seemingly inexplicable.

James Carey, journalistic scholar and professor at Columbia University, tells us that when matters of fundamental importance surface in news, they cannot be treated as secular mysteries and left unexplained. They must be accounted for, must be rendered sensible. "The economy and the political system form the sacred center of modern society," Carey says. "We insist [they] be explicable."

Don't hold your breath waiting for commercial TV to deconstruct complexity. It is up to newspapers and individual newspaper editors to see that this happens.

So the old conventional wisdom is giving way to the new. But now, two months into this "new normal," newspapers must determine whether they will continue to appeal to our larger public selves rather than revert to the trivial.

• *We will be challenged in keeping to the high road by our own limited attention span.* The press—and the public—gone soft from a period of unparalleled affluence and lack of threat, displays the attention span and the need for immediate gratification of the average four-year-old. Our focus, like the public's, has been defined by our ability to reduce the significant to the sound bite, by the brief moment between TV commercials, by the dizzying speed of our own lives.

Even at our best, media have episodic tendencies. You can see it already in the shift in emphasis from rescue, to airport security, to war, to all anthrax all the time. We must have sustained coverage on all these matters to be truly informed.

These are suddenly serious times, with the nature and extent of our freedom hanging in the balance. We can ill afford a press that lives moment to moment and illuminates not at all.

• *We will be challenged in keeping to the high road by owners and shareholders who place more value on short-term results than on creation of enduring value.* Our success ultimately must be tied to the public trust more than to next quarter's profits. And make no mistake about it: It is expensive and difficult. Many doubt whether media conglomerates, even today, will make the investment necessary for true public-service journalism. Our survival may depend on it. Certainly our reputation does.

• *We will be challenged in keeping to the high road by people who do not want to hear voices of dissent.* People today want our government and its leaders to succeed. We want this on a gut, emotional level, whether or not we agree with their politics. Therefore, voices of dissent feel particularly discordant.

I live on what we fondly (and you derisively) call the Left Coast, which has a proud history of dissent. *The Oregonian*'s readers remind us every day of the importance of dissent. We have been averaging more than 500 letters to the editor a week since September 11, by far the vast majority opposing the war or taking issue with some aspect of its conduct.

I remember the early days of protest against the Vietnam War. I was a student at East Carolina, not exactly a hotbed of anti-war protests, so at first we treated protesters as a breed apart. Fringe thinkers, to be sure, Communists maybe. We were sure they were wrong. But things were not what they seemed.

The seeds sown in those protests grew into an anti-war movement that destroyed Lyndon Johnson's presidency and contributed to the ending of the war. Then, thirty years later, one of the principal architects of that war, Robert McNamara, apologized for lying to the American people. That was powerful confirmation that things are not always what they seem. Let the voices of dissent ring loud as a bell of freedom.

• *We will be challenged in keeping to the high road by a government that in times of threat hunkers down and keeps information hidden even more than normal.* There are many people who believe it is inappropriate for the press to ask too many questions when we are at war. Indeed, even the president's press secretary, using the sympathetic public as his shield, said, "The press is asking a lot of questions that I suspect the American people would prefer not be asked. Report the news to the American people," Ari Fleischer said, "but if you report it in its entirety, that could raise concerns," to which the president of Sigma Delta Chi said, "Let the White House run the war and let us report the news." To which we all should say, amen. No one in the media or among citizen-consumers of news wants information that could compromise national security. But information from the military is always filtered. Government has a need, even an obligation, to keep some things secret. But the press has an obligation to ask questions and to be skeptical of pat answers, evasiveness, or inconsistencies. When information is more difficult to obtain and verify is when a vigorous, rigorous press is most needed. Information is not dangerous, perilous to our health.

The Pentagon, we have learned to our nation's great sorrow, is capable of willful deception about its own policies. But this is not Vietnam; nor is it the Gulf War, the let's-have-a-glass-of-wine-turn-on-the-TV-and-watch kind of war. This war is, even in its earliest stages, a ground war with a shadowy enemy in a country with almost no access for journalists. We are more dependent on the quality of our questions than on observable events and verifiable facts. We had better ask the right questions.

• *We will be challenged in keeping to the high road by those who are fearful.* When terrorists attack our symbols of trade, of prosperity, and of military might, when they threaten our freedom of movement and our communications, it is natural that we are afraid. But facts themselves do not add fear; rather they steady the nerves of sensible people. If you don't believe it, look at the steadying effect of Rudy Giuliani's straight-talking manner in the chaotic early days. Information, no matter how unsettling, is not the threat. It is more nearly the safeguard of our freedom.

The news media cannot be cowed by those who wish to tell us only what they think is good for us. The press must not soft-pedal the difficult questions. We must not forget our duty to shine light in dark corners. Democracy demands that we serve this function, in good times and in bad.

The high road is, as it has been, there for us.

We can provide true public service as citizens struggle to learn what they need to know to go about daily life, what they need to know to ensure the public safety, what they need to know to help preserve our freedoms.

The country's strength and, as we have learned, its vulnerability come from our best qualities—our incredible freedom of movement, our relatively open borders, our pluralism and increasing diversity.

If our openness and our strength as a free society make us vulnerable and are at stake here, then the press could not possibly have a more important role at this moment in our history. And if purpose is what the press has needed to reengage with its own values, then purpose we have and reengage we must.

It is today, as it always has been, a great privilege to be a journalist. Journalism matters more than it has in decades. Despite our shortcomings, we have never been more able to meet the challenge than we are today.

The attackers, we are told, thought they would undermine democracy. Instead, we have an opportunity to shore up the foundations of democracy by vigorously defending freedom of the press and honoring the ideals on which it stands.

It is a worthy goal.

ANN MARIE LIPINSKI

Former *Time* magazine foreign correspondent Charles Eisendrath, head of a prestigious journalism fellowship program at the University of Michigan, has said, "Every generation has two or three newspaper editors whose names have marquee value. Gene Roberts, John Seigenthaler, Ben Bradlee. I think Ann Marie will be in that crowd."

The brand name in the making is Ann Marie Lipinski. She began her career at the *Chicago Tribune* as a summer intern in 1978, and twenty-two years later became its editor-in-chief. She is the first woman to hold that title in the newspaper's 154-year history.

She was one of three *Tribune* reporters who won a Pulitzer Prize in 1988 for an investigation of the Chicago city council. She directed the coverage of the paper's award-winning "Killing Our Children" series, in which the newspaper chronicled the murders of children in the Chicago area. And in 2001, her decision to deploy twenty-six reporters to document a day in the life of the nation's chaotic air traffic system resulted in a Pulitzer Prize for explanatory journalism.

In October 2000, Lipinski was among three media leaders who spoke on the future of journalism at a symposium in New York held by the Pew Center for Civic Journalism. Among the values Lipinski articulated in her address, which follows, was her vision of the newspaper as a leading civic voice in a community.

The Number One Citizen

From the time my daughter, now 6, could speak she would play newspaper. She invented a newspaper called *Bostona*—for reasons neither her father nor I have ever been able to determine—where she pretended to work as a reporter.

One day when she was about 3½, I came home to find that she had been promoted to managing editor, until recently my title at the *Tribune*. "Well, congratulations," I said. "And what does the managing editor of *Bostona* do?"

"Oh," she said in her most world-weary voice, "I talk to people about their problems."

I think of that answer often and find it as worthy a description of my job, and perhaps that of my fellow panelists, as any I have ever heard. Dwindling circulation, rising newsprint costs, increased competition for staff, declining ad revenue. And that's not even talking about the journalistic challenges.

But with all that, I remain an editor who is bullish and enthusiastic about the future of newspapers. It turns out I'm at the right company, one that spent over $6 billion to buy a group of newspapers, including *Newsday* and the *Los Angeles Times,* betting the future on a medium seemingly more aligned with Gutenberg than Gates. But a year into the dot-com decline, ink-on-paper is still looking pretty good.

I'd like to highlight a few things that will help keep newspapers looking pretty good. So five of those, if I may.

The first: One of my favorite photographs in the *Tribune* archives is a shot of Clarence Darrow making his closing argument at the Scopes monkey trial. In the frame is a lone radio microphone with the call letters WGN. That stood for "World's Greatest Newspaper," the late Colonel Robert McCormick's brazen claim for his beloved *Chicago Tribune.*

McCormick would probably regard a woman as editor of the *Tribune* about as highly as I regarded his use of a printing press to advance a suspect political agenda, but I'll give him this: For a conservative Midwestern newspaper publisher, he was a great technological visionary.

While his fellow publishers were banding together to lobby against the upstart medium called radio, McCormick created a radio station. And when television—an even greater threat—came along, McCormick went and got himself one of those stations, too, branding it with the same call letters.

I recount this to explain the bemusement with which I and my *Tribune* colleagues regard questions about new technology overtaking print. As focused as we are on growing and nurturing the newspaper, we also understand that each medium has a role to play in both our corporate and our journalistic successes.

If you visit me in Chicago, your trip from O'Hare Airport to my Michigan Avenue office will take you past the WGN television studios on the northwest side of the city, the *Chicago Tribune* printing plant on the near west side of the city, the WGN radio studio on the first floor of Tribune Tower, the *Tribune* Internet offices down the hall from me, and the *Tribune's* own Chicagoland Television Cable cameras right outside my door.

This week, a *Tribune* investigative series on mob influence in the Chicago police department that was a year in the making by one of our finest investigative reporters found a home in most of those *Tribune* venues, significantly expanding the audience for a brilliant story beyond our newspaper subscribers.

My bosses and the gurus on Wall Street can and have made the business case for what is glibly known as "synergy," but let me make the journalist's case. Finding things out and telling people what we know is the essence of what we do. McCormick understood this and, like him, newsrooms need to seek new ways to tell their stories, both within their news pages and beyond, in ways that deepen and do not compromise our social purpose.

Secondly, a couple of months ago an editor from a well-known daily newspaper, which may or may not publish in our nation's capital, came to Chicago and took me to lunch. He was researching a book about the newspaper industry and wanted to talk to me about the *Tribune*. He asked about staff levels and why they weren't exactly the same as at his newspaper. He asked about the A-section and why the space configurations were different from his newspaper. And there was a similar line of questioning about the newspaper's Internet operations and editorial ratios.

By the end of it, all I could think of was that great musical question posed by Professor Henry Higgins, "Tell me why can't a woman be more like a man?"

The Washington Post, The Boston Globe, the *Los Angeles Times* are all great and wonderful newspapers, none of which is ideal for the readers of Chicago. Just as the *Tribune* would be presumably ill-matched to the needs of those markets.

There is such a sameness across the land in the ways in which newspapers are both good and bad—the monotony of syndicated columnists, no matter how talented; the gray and pat coverage from Washington or the campaign; the predictability of the portfolios divided into world, nation, metro, business, and sports.

Great newspapers will thrive not by imitating other great newspapers but by speaking in a cadence unique to their readers and unique to their markets.

There are certain core values that all great journalistic enterprises must embrace—honesty, fairness, accuracy. And those are not geographically bound. But there are many ways to achieve journalistic excellence and few of them have anything to do with parroting the other guy.

The third point is a short one and let me try this out on you. I'm kind of grappling with the language myself, but it's something I've been thinking about. I attended an interminable two-day—it felt like two weeks—conference on journalistic excellence. There was a half a sentence up on the board which stated: "The next great newspaper will . . ."

And all these answers were flying up. There was one that struck me and that I've thought about and it may be the only thing I wrote down over the two days. One person finished the sentence this way: "The next great newspaper will need to personify itself as the number-one citizen in the community, the one who beats up the bully, who cries at the tragedies, who provides the big ideas to create economic development, who is the school teacher/tutor for children when their schools fail them."

I'm not a big fan of what has come to be called public journalism. There's some redundancy in that to me. I'm not sure I even understand what it means. But I do like this notion of the newspaper as the leading civic voice of a community.

In 1993, the *Chicago Tribune* undertook a yearlong series of stories called "Killing Our Children," which set out to chronicle the homicide of every child under the age of 14 in our six-county metropolitan area. We published more than 200 stories before the end of the year, the work of 150 reporters and photographers.

What you felt over the course of that year was a sense of a steamship turning course, of an entire city becoming engaged around a single important subject.

The *Tribune* did the same thing with a series of stories on the death penalty in Illinois that resulted in a pro–death-penalty governor calling a moratorium on the death penalty in our state.

Looking forward, I look back to those and know that the next great newspaper, and our newspaper if it will continue to be great, needs to find more of those occasions, more of those moments where it can stand up and either gather up all the lone, lonely voices out there speaking independently on a subject or put an end to something that nobody else is talking about. In that sense, it does become the leading citizen of a community, no matter how small or how large the community.

The fourth thing, and many people in this room know him, comes from Bill Kovach. Ten years ago, when I was crossing to the dark side from reporting to editing, becoming metro editor of the *Tribune,* I got a long and wonderful letter which I keep in my top desk drawer from Bill Kovach, who was a great newspaper man and at the time was curator of the Nieman Foundation at Harvard.

He gave me many, many wonderful pieces of advice. One I want to talk about today, because I think it's more prescient now than it was at the time. He wrote:

> You are now a manager, and under the rules of the game as it's played today, you are expected to be a businessperson as well as a journalist. You can't escape that but you can avoid thinking like a businessperson.
>
> You can, in fact, turn it to your advantage and the advantage of the news department and your readers. You can do this by listening to the business people, their problems and their plans. More importantly, learn more about their problems than they know. Usually they *react* more than they *think*. Use every tool at your command to learn about circulation in your area and about advertising. Be informed so you can't be misled or bulldogged into doing something you know is wrong.

Underlying all of this is the fact that, in the modern world of journalism, there are many voices promoting, protecting, defending, and expanding the commercial interests of the newspaper. Only one voice represents our First Amendment rights.

There are many times I have longed for the simplicity of my predecessors' lives—editorships free of business realities. They thought it was tough to compete with six different newspapers in town, all of which were being read by millions of people reading three and four newspapers a day. I'd take that on any day.

As Bill noted 10 years ago, that's an unrealistic notion any longer, and most editors I know have become, if not quite the experts in circulation and advertising exigencies that Kovach envisioned, smart enough on the subjects to hold their own.

What so many of us have failed at is the cross-training, the education that goes the other way. The cross-training that might have prevented, say, the Staples Center incident at the *Los Angeles Times*. At the *Tribune,* we have recently begun something called *news disciplines*—two- and three-day training sessions on journalistic values that are mandatory for every company executive, from the chairman on down.

Every day a good editor walks through the doors prepared to teach and lead. And that leadership, in the coming five years and beyond, will be just as relevant outside the newsroom as it is inside. An editor's ability and interest in articulating the journalistic mission to non-journalists may be the most important business contribution and journalistic contribution we can make in the coming years.

The fifth one, and this is an old-fashioned one, but it's the everything-old-is-new-again and is, maybe, the most important thing from a day-to-day editing perspective. When a reporter goes home at the end of the day and her husband asks what she did, she may well respond that she wrote a story. But in most cases, that would be a lie.

We write lots and lots of reports and lots and lots of accounts, but we rarely write newspaper stories, things that we would define from our earliest reading experience as having beginnings, middles and ends, characters, plots and other tools of engagement. We all recognize those when we hear them. We read them to our kids every day, but we very rarely read them in our own newspapers.

Last year on a Monday in mid-August, nearly 20,000 more people than usual bought a copy of the *Chicago Tribune* in Chicago. There was no pressing news that day. God knows, our city's sorry baseball teams had done nothing to draw readers to the newsstands.

The reason for the circulation spike was part two of a four-part series that recounted a year-old story of the shooting death of a rookie Chicago police officer and the toll that his death had taken on his partner and the police force.

Although it was a shooting that was well-reported at the time, the series, "Partners in Peril," offered a brilliantly told reconstruction of the drama playing out beneath the surface of the news headlines—a gripping tale of a naive cop's fantasy of police work set against the reality of urban crime.

It was a newspaper story with a beginning, a middle and an end and a cast of characters as riveting as those found in fiction. A human drama so engaging for readers that even Sunday-only subscribers from the *Chicago Tribune* felt compelled to buy the paper throughout the week to read the resolution.

One reader sent us a letter describing a scene he witnessed that Monday morning. He wrote:

> I sat in stunned silence at a restaurant on West Randolph Street. I had bought the *Tribune* to catch the second part of your story and was reading intently when I looked up and saw different customers reading the same article. I tried to follow their eyes and then it dawned on me that there was this total hush in the room. This was usually a very noisy place at 6:30 in the morning.
>
> I saw the owner of the restaurant sitting at his usual table. He looked up at me and asked if it weren't the saddest story about this policeman.
>
> I replied, "Yes, it is the saddest story I ever read."

Not everything we report can or should deserve such treatment, but we need to get much better in the coming five years—and the five years beyond that and the five beyond that—at recognizing the right opportunity. Reporting and story telling, the oldest, most old-fashioned tools in our tool belt, can silence a downtown diner on a busy Monday morning.

LOWELL BERGMAN

Lowell Bergman was a producer for the CBS program *60 Minutes* for sixteen years and now works as a producer and correspondent for PBS's *Frontline*. He is also a frequent contributor to *The New York Times* and a visiting professor at the Graduate School of Journalism at the University of California, Berkeley. His relationship with CBS ended when his investigation of the tobacco industry—including his exclusive interview with whistle-blower Jeffrey Wigand—was held up from broadcast by CBS. That incident later became the subject of the Hollywood movie *The Insider,* in which Bergman was played by Al Pacino. This selection, adapted from a talk Bergman gave at New York University in February 2000, explores the issues of corporate and self-censorship, and their implications.

Network Television News: With Fear and Favor

I spent twenty-one years in network television mostly as a producer for television newsmagazines, first at ABC and for sixteen years at CBS.

Now I am out. A gradual process, hastened by the movie *The Insider,* has led me to begin thinking about what the realities are behind the camera and the stories you see on network television news. The movie does something that you cannot do on network television news: It raises the issue of corporate censorship and, more importantly, self-censorship, and it explores both its implications and the choices it forces on those involved. Its subject, of course, is CBS's decision in 1995 to not air a *60 Minutes* report on Jeffrey Wigand, the former vice president of Brown & Williamson who charged that the company had hid the truth about tobacco's addictive and harmful properties from the American public.

Executives of the network news divisions say that they will report any story of public interest and import without fear or favor, without considering its potential commercial consequences. They say that, but do not believe it.

The menu of what stories will be initiated, what enterprise reporting will and will not be done, is formed by the networks' commercial interest. The idea of committing resources to do stories that in and of themselves are clearly in the public interest is dead. The exceptions prove the rule.

Now, it has always been difficult no matter where you worked in the media to propose a story that might affect a major advertiser, the publisher-owner, or his business partners.

The problem today especially in television news is that any obligation to report stories about unaccountable power, about individuals or institutions that are as powerful as you are, as your broadcast company is, has been lost. It was an ideal that television news strived for in the wake of Watergate and the Vietnam war. But it is an ideal that has died in the wake of deregulation and the unfettered growth of corporate power.

This censorship is rarely a result of external pressure. More often it is self-censorship that appears inside the company and is presented as common sense. That is what happened in the tobacco story. Brown & Williamson lawyers did not threaten to sue. They did not have to. That is what has changed.

I would venture that no assignment editor at the evening news broadcasts or executive producer at a so-called newsmagazine program would hesitate to pursue, or spend money pursuing, enterprise stories about the Monica Lewinsky scandal, O. J. Simpson, the Princess Di car crash, or the death of JFK Jr. Unfortunately, that commitment is not matched when it comes to stories about who wields unaccountable power over our lives; or who is behind the corporate mergers that now dominate the media.

That was what happened in the Brown & Williamson case in 1995. CBS's general counsel, Ellen Kaden, opposed airing the Brown & Williamson story. At a meeting I attended to discuss the situation, neither Don Hewitt or Mike Wallace exhibited any of their well-known ability to argue, cajole, and intimidate.

At a later meeting, Kaden reported outside counsel had supported her position. I knew the story was dead but argued with Hewitt and Wallace that we should not take orders from lawyers. What do CBS executives have to say?

They dismissed me for splitting hairs. As Hewitt put it: "You can't do the story!" But, I persisted. So on the morning of October 3, 1995, just to be absolutely clear that I knew what I was dealing with, I called Eric Ober, who was then the president of CBS News.

I said, "You sat in the meeting yesterday, Eric." (He had been very quiet, saying little.) "These are lawyers giving advice. What is the position of CBS News on this matter?" And without missing a beat, he replied, "The corporation will not risk its assets on the story." Period. [CBS eventually ran the story after canceling the original airing.]

Let me make it clear that I came out of print in the 1970s, and it was no surprise to me, based on stories I had done back then with various publishers ranging from *Rolling Stone* to *Penthouse* to the Hearst Corporation, that corporate interest obviously has an editorial influence over what publications will do and not do. It's a given.

So you know what the limits are. But a way of gauging a publication or broadcast is to find out how close they will let you get to that limit.

For example, I discovered at ABC News that you could not do an enterprise story about a supplier or a major advertiser. You could try to do it, but you were taking a lot of risks getting close to the limit. In one case we did manage to get a story on about the president of ABC, Inc. and his financial relationship to a supplier—Aaron Spelling. It slipped in during the summertime and led to all kinds of fallout, including a speculative financial magazine piece alleging that somehow the president of ABC News, Roone Arledge, might be using the story to get his boss's job. Arledge did not even know about the story when it ran.

This was such an exception that it prompted unwarranted speculation that there must be some corporate conspiracy going, jockeying for power. The exception proves the rule.

Conflict of interest was true then and is true today. The best example: If you are the owner of an NFL team, you have a virtual free pass, in terms of network television news. The network will not initiate a critical story about your business practices and history. No in-depth story will be commissioned. I was told that, at ABC News in 1981 in a meeting with an executive producer. At CBS News in 1997 the prohibition was repeated by a senior executive and a major on-camera personality.

I knew at the time that one of the NFL owners, Eddie DeBartolo Jr., was under grand jury investigation in New Orleans for bribery related to his gambling license. The whole issue of professional sports and the vast cash business around gambling has always fascinated me. Given the fact CBS did not have football, I figured there was a chance that we could do the story. I was wrong.

That fall I taught a seminar at the University of California's Graduate School of Journalism at Berkeley. Anticipating that the story would break in time, I got four of the students to work on it. I knew that whether or not CBS wanted to do it, now there would at least be follow-up coverage. Once a story becomes public—someone else does it in print, for example—then you can put pictures in it for a television version. Sure enough it all broke with an indictment in December 1997.

Remember, CBS did not have football. I had been told by the executive and on-air talent six months earlier that the one thing CBS's new CEO, Mel Karmazin, really wanted, was to get football back. So there was no way we could do any enterprise reporting about the NFL's owners even if they might be caught up in criminal activity.

But now the event had happened. DeBartolo had been indicted. CBS still did not have football. Due to my post-tobacco renegotiation I was no longer a staffer at *60 Minutes,* but I worked for all of CBS News. But I soon learned that due to the headlines there was *60 Minutes* interest in an in-depth piece. I thought, "Great." I've got these files. I've got the students who had already explored Eddie DeBartolo Jr.'s other legal problems. And his family history. I was in contact with the 49er organization and its then chief operating officer Carmen Policy.

Everything was set up. I got together with a *60 Minutes* producer, associate producer, and correspondent and it was agreed that we would do the story. I would coproduce and be the field person since I live in the San Francisco Bay area. Four weeks later, CBS signed up NFL football. Two weeks after that, I received a phone call saying that *60 Minutes* was no longer interested in doing the piece because "the 49ers didn't get in the Super Bowl." Bemused, I said well fine, but I've got Carmen Policy and all these people in the 49er organization interested and ready to let us shoot spring practice and the postseason. Why not do it, as we often did at *60 Minutes,* for the fall?

No, came the response. Not interested. End of story.

All of this is anecdotal information. A number of my colleagues have said to me that "Gee, this has never happened to me. No one has ever told me I could not do a story because of its content!" And in most cases I would agree. It is rare to have a story killed, an interview pulled. Usually the circumstances are much more subtle, the reasons are usually something like: "Who will go on camera?" "It's boring"; or "No one cares and no one will watch."

As a result, the reality of the world of news and information has regressed, especially in broadcasting. "News" no longer means what it once did. The very forms used by the broadcast news organizations emphasizing the "star" correspondent over the substance of the story has undermined their credibility. It is no surprise then that the commitment of media organizations to reporting without fear or favor has waned. And so today, it is more difficult than ever to do what so many of us had hoped we could do.

A prediction: There once was a fire wall between the commercial-entertainment side and the public service "news" side of broadcasting. That fire wall has been breached. It is the specter haunting the broadcast "news" business today. Soon an organization in the broadcast, cable, or more likely dot.com convergence world will understand that, and launch a new "news" outlet that will deserve the name and have in place a new fire wall that we can trust.

ALY COLÓN

Aly Colón is the former diversity reporter of *The Seattle Times* and a member of the Ethics Faculty at The Poynter Institute for Media Studies. He has worked at the *Herald* in Everett, Washington; at the *Oakland Press* in Pontiac, Michigan; and for Fairchild News Service in Seattle. He is the recipient of numerous fellowships, including a 1981 National Endowment for the Humanities in ethics. In this essay from *Quill,* a magazine published by the Society of Professional Journalists, Colón talks about the journalistic principles involved in covering diverse groups of people. In fact, he makes the case that it is in under-covered communities that a journalist will find the freshest and most compelling stories.

Making Connections with Diverse Communities

Sometimes learning about an under-covered community can be as simple as a conversation with a stranger.

When I arrive in a new city, I like to walk its downtown. It offers me an opportunity to see and hear things at the street level, where people interact more spontaneously and naturally.

I did this in one Midwestern city and I noticed a man who, to me at least, didn't fit my stereotype of a Midwesterner. He had thick, black hair combed straight back. The skin enveloping his tall frame sported a dark, copper color. His penetrating eyes resembled shiny, black marbles. His appearance made me curious about where he might be from. But I felt a little uncomfortable approaching him. After all, I was just out for a walk. He seemed busy looking at a monument that towered above us.

But then, I thought, how can I not ask? This is what I teach. Making connections with diverse communities. If I can't overcome my own discomfort about approaching strangers, how can I ask other journalists to do so?

So I squelched the feeling that, as a stranger, it might seem impolite to ask him questions and went up to the young man.

"Hello," I said, "are you a native to this city?"

"No," he responded, "I'm from India."

"Are you from New Delhi?" I asked, adding that I had a friend in that city.

"No. I'm from Bombay."

"Are you on vacation, visiting the United States?" I continued.

"I live here," he said.

"How did you happen to be living here?"

"I work for a computer company that's based in this city."

"Is it hard living so far away from your homeland?" I asked.

"Not really, there are a lot of other Indians here as well. There are a couple of hundred families that live in the city. We all work for this company."

"Well, you must miss the Indian food?" I said, noting that I like Indian food and wish I could find some in the city.

"I can recommend some," he said. "We have two or three of them here."

"No kidding," I replied.

I explained to him that I was a journalist who wrote about different cultures and appreciated his taking the time to talk to me. Then I pulled out a notebook and asked him if he'd mind writing down his name, phone number and some restaurants I might try. He kindly obliged.

The entire exchange took about five minutes.

The next day I asked the journalists in that city where I was conducting a seminar if they could tell me how many Indians lived in their city. Not one of them indicated they even knew any Indians did so.

I'd venture that had I been at some newsrooms in other parts of our country, I might have gotten the same blank stares I got in that Midwestern city. It's not that journalists aren't interested in ethnic and racial minorities who live in their cities. It's just that too often they don't take the time to find out if they even exist.

Let's face it. Despite our nose for news, we tend to be no different than anyone else: We have a natural tendency to stick with what we know. Unfortunately, for many of us, what we know tends to be limiting.

We drive through the same neighborhoods on our way to and from work. We eat at the same restaurants, usually with the same people, who often tend to be our colleagues. We usually visit and spend time with people we know well, who most likely look and think just like us. That leads to input and perspectives that limit the type and scope of story ideas that strike us as interesting and important.

A journalist who strives to do excellent work must go beyond such limitations. In fact, in my view, being an excellent journalist also requires you to be ethical.

You should not only have some knowledge of all kinds of people (with differences due to race, ethnicity, gender, abilities, religion, etc.) who live in your community, you also should strive to include their viewpoints in your everyday news coverage.

Now, I don't mean that every story must include every type of person in your community. I understand, but don't encourage, the approach some news organizations take toward creating lists of people who must be included in every reporting assignment.

That quota-like requirement turns most journalists off. We fancy ourselves independent investigators of the truth. We go where the news is, no matter where it leads, or whom it includes—or excludes.

But that's the point, isn't it? Our tendency is to go where we know everybody's name. That's why some news organizations believe they need to force us to contact different racial, ethnic and gender groups.

The editors and news directors of such news organizations know we often won't go to unfamiliar places or people for our stories. But this requirement obscures the true problem many journalists face. What many of them believe is that they are being required to do something that's not part of their job description. They feel coerced into carrying this additional burden.

"Just let us do journalism," they cry out. And I agree with them.

The only problem is they're not practicing journalism. At least not excellent journalism. Or comprehensive journalism. Or thorough journalism. Or complete journalism. Or accurate journalism. Or truthful journalism. Or fair journalism.

What they practice involves a very narrow, incomplete, inaccurate form of journalism that offers less than meets the reader's eye. They resemble a person with a patch over one eye—and there's nothing wrong with the eye beneath the patch. It's just covered up.

If you want to practice journalism, the very best type of journalism, then you need to make connections with all kinds of people. Here's a list of things you can do:

- Make it a point to go out into the many different communities in your city.
- Stroll their streets.
- Shop in their stores.
- Eat in their restaurants.

- Study their history.
- Learn their culture.
- Show them your face.
- Have a conversation with them.
- Listen. Listen. Listen.

Do all of this off-deadline, when you don't have to do a story. You need time, away from the pressure of production, to observe, absorb and reflect on information that may be new to you. And it allows the people in that community to get to know you as well.

Too often, we come into communities with notebooks flipped open, pens, microphones and cameras at the ready. We take, but we don't give.

We need to share ourselves with people we meet and interview: tell them who we are and where we're coming from. It helps them to understand what we do and why we do it. And it makes our relationship with them more complete, fair and honest.

For example, my short conversation with the man from India could have been longer. I could have indicated my interest in learning more about what brought him to the United States. I could have shared with him why I think it's important for us to be more knowledgeable about him. I could have offered him some understanding of where I come from—culturally as well as geographically.

Journalistically, my conversation with him offered an opportunity for interesting stories: How many more Indians live in the city, where do they live, what impact has their migration here had, what companies do they work for, how does that fit in with the labor market, what do they take back to their country from that city.

So go forth into those communities. What you see and what you hear may surprise you. The result will be journalism that can lead to stories that readers, viewers, listeners and online users will find refreshing, informative and compelling.

Acknowledgments

Jim Bellows, excerpt from *The Last Editor: How I Saved the New York Times, The Washington Post, and the Los Angeles Times from Dullness and Complacency* by Jim Bellows. Copyright © 2002 by Jim Bellows. Reprinted by permission of Andrews McMeel Publishing. All rights reserved.

Michael Berens, "The Myth of the Machine" from *When Nerds and Words Collide*, published by The Poynter Institute and edited by Nora Paul. Copyright © 1999 by Michael Berens. Reprinted by permission of the author and The Poynter Insitute.

Lowell Bergman, "Network Television News: With Fear and Favor." Adapted from a lecture at New York University. Copyright © by Lowell Bergman. Reprinted by permission of the author.

Carl Bernstein & Bob Woodward, excerpt from *All the President's Men* by Carl Bernstein and Bob Woodward. Copyright © 1974 by Carl Bernstein & Bob Woodward. Reprinted with the permission of Simon & Schuster Adult Publishing Group.

Mark Bowden, "Narrative Journalism Goes Multimedia" from *Nieman Reports*, Fall 2000. Copyright © 2000 by the President and Fellows of Harvard College. Reprinted by permission of the author and the Nieman Foundation.

Ben Bradlee, excerpt from *A Good Life* by Ben Bradlee. Copyright © 1995 by Benjamin C. Bradlee. Reprinted with the permission of Simon & Schuster.

Rick Bragg, excerpt from "Chicken Killers and True Heartbreak" from *All Over But the Shoutin'* by Rick Bragg. Copyright © 1997 by Rick Bragg. Used by permission of Pantheon Books, a division of Random House, Inc.

Edna Buchanan, "Fire!" from *Never Let Them See You Cry* by Edna Buchanan. Copyright © 1992 by Edna Buchanan. Reprinted by permission of Don Congdon Associates, Inc.

Roy Peter Clark, "The Unoriginal Sin" from WASHINGTON JOURNALISM REVIEW, March 1983. Copyright © 1983 by Roy Peter Clark. Reprinted by permission of Roy Peter Clark, The Poynter Institute, and the American Journalism Review.

Aly Colon, "Making Connections with Diverse Communities" from *Quill*, July 2000. Copyright © by Aly Colon. Reprinted by permission of the author.

Leonard Downie, Jr., excerpt from *The New Muckrakers* by Leonard Downie, Jr. Copyright © 1978 by Leonard Downie, Jr. Reprinted by permission of the author.

Claudia Dreifus, introduction from *Interview* by Claudia Dreifus. Copyright © 1997 by Seven Stories Press. Reprinted by permission of Seven Stories Press.

Jonathan Dube, "Writing News Online" from Cyberjournalist.net, November 2000. Copyright © 2000–2002 by Jonathan Dube. Reprinted by permission of the author.

Ken Fuson, "What Would Yogi Do?" from a lecture at The Poynter Institute for Media Studies, 2002. Reprinted by permission of the author, Ken Fuson of the Des Moines Register.

Florence Graves, "What We Investigate Is Linked to Who We Are" from *Columbia Journalism Review*, May/June 2001. Copyright © 2001 by Columbia Journalism Review. Reprinted by permission of the author and the Columbia Journalism Reivew.

Jeff Greenfield, excerpt from *Oh Waiter! One Order of Crow!* by Jeff Greenfield. Copyright © 2001 by Jeff Greenfield. Used by permission of G.P. Putnam's Sons, a division of Penguin Putnam Inc.

Jack Hart, "The Art of the Interview" from *The Oregonian* in-house newsletter. Copyright © 1993 by Jack Hart. Reprinted by permission of the author.

John Hersey, essay from *The Yale Review*, Autumn 1980. Copyright © 1980. Reprinted by permission of Blackwell Publishing Ltd.

Tracy Kidder, "Faith, Truth, and the Facts." Copyright © 2001 by John Tracy Kidder. First appeared in *Washington Post Book World*. Reprinted by permission of the author.

Jeff Klinkenberg, "Reporting the Fifth W: Where" from the *St. Petersburg Times* in-house newsletter, 1995. Copyright © 1995 by Jeff Klinkenberg. Reprinted with permission of the author.

Robert Kurlwich, "Sticky Storytelling" from *Nieman Reports*, V. 54 No. 3, Fall 2000. Copyright © 2000 by the President and Fellows of Harvard College. Reprinted by permission of the Nieman Foundation.

Paula LaRocque, "Hooking the Reader" from *Quill*, July 1995. Copyright © 1995 by Paula LaRocque. Reprinted by permission of the author.

Joseph Lelyveld, "A Life Not Infrequently Thrilling." Excerpt from Columbia University commencement speech, May 2001. Copyright © 2001 by Joseph Lelyveld. Reprinted by permission of the author.

Steve Lovelady, "25 Words or Less (and Other Secrets of Investigative Editing)" from *Columbia Journalism Review*, May/June 2001. Copyright © 2001 by Steve Lovelady. Reprinted by permission of the author.

Marjie Lundstrom, "Farm-Fresh Cliches." Copyright © 2001 by Marjie Lundstrom. Reprinted by permission of the author.

Jay Mathews, "Just Checking" from *The New Republic*, May 18, 1992. Copyright © 1992 by Jay Mathews. Reprinted by permission of the author.

Craig McCoy, "How We Got That Story: The Buried Rapes" from *Columbia Journalism Review*, January/February 2000. Copyright © 2000 by Craig McCoy. Reprinted by permission of Craig McCoy, staff writer for the Philadelphia Inquirer.

Donald Murray, "What I Need From My Editors." Copyright © by Donald Murray. Originally published in the *Cape Cod Times*. Reprinted by permission of the author.

Daniel Okrent, "The Death of Print?" excerpt from Hearst New Media Lecture, Columbia University Graduate School of Journalism, December 1999. Copyright © 1999 by Daniel Okrent. Reprinted by permission of Daniel Okrent and Darhansoff, Verrill, Feldman Literary Agents.

Geneva Overholser, "What We've Got Here is a Failure to be Skeptical" from *The Washington Post*. Copyright © 2001 by the Washington Post Writers Group. Reprinted with permission.

Suzi Parker, "When Death Was My Muse" from *The Washington Post*, May 3, 1998. Copyright © 1998 by Suzi Parker. Reprinted by permission of the author.

Bill Plaschke, "Trying Not to Look Like a Vulture" from *Columbia Journalism Review*, January/February 2000. Copyright © 2000 by the Columbia Journalism Review. Reprinted by permission of the author and the Columbia Journalism Review.

Anna Quindlen, "Hers" from *The New York Times*, April 10, 1986. Copyright © 1986 by The New York Times Co. Reprinted by permission.

Sandra Mims Rowe, "Journalism Rediscovers Its Serious Purpose: Eight Ideas That Could Help It Last" from a lecture at the University of North Carolina at Chapel Hill, November 2001. Copyright © 2001 by Sandra Mims Rowe. Reprinted by permission of the author.

Christopher Scanlan, "Storytelling on Deadline" from *Best Newspaper Writing 1994*, edited by Christopher Scanlan. Copyright © 1994 by Christopher Scanlan. Reprinted by permission of the author.

Diana K. Sugg, "Turn the Beat Around." Copyright © 2001 by Diana K. Sugg. Originally appeared on Poynter.org, 2001. Reprinted by permission of the author.

John Tierney, "Finding the 'Take'" from *Speaking of Journalism* by William Zinsser. Copyright © 1995 by John Tierney. Reprinted by permission of John Tierney.

Garrick Utley, excerpt from *You Should Have Been Here Yesterday* by Garrick Utley. Copyright © 2000 by Garrick Utley. Reprinted by permission of Public Affairs, a member of Perseus Books, L.L.C.

Steve Woodward, "Power Tools" from *The Oregonian* in-house newsletter. Copyright © Steve Woodward. Reprinted by permission of the author.

Jim Wooten, "Parachuting Into Madness" from *Columbia Journalism Review*, November/December 1994. Copyright © 1994 by the Columbia Journalism Review. Reprinted by permission of the Columbia Journalism Review and Jim Wooten, Senior Correspondent, ABC News.